SOCIAL THEORY

SOCIAL THEORY

A READER

Edited by
Jonathan Joseph

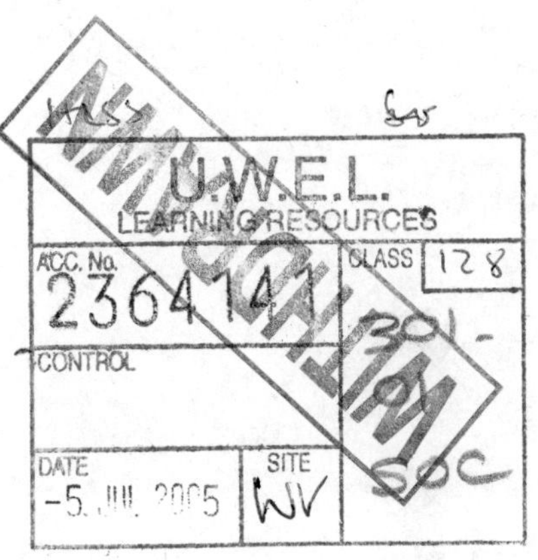

EDINBURGH UNIVERSITY PRESS

Edinburgh University Press Ltd
22 George Square, Edinburgh

Typeset in Sabon and Gill Sans
by TechBooks, New Delhi, India, and
printed and bound in Great Britain by
MPG Books Ltd, Bodmin, Cornwall

A CIP record for this book is available from the British Library

ISBN 0 7486 1948 8 (hardback)
ISBN 0 7486 1949 6 (paperback)

CONTENTS

INTRODUCTION

I. Theoretical Focus

This reader in social theory aims to introduce a wide range of social and political theory. However, since it would take a huge selection of readings to cover each theorist fully, the main focus of this reader will be on the issues of conflict, cohesion and consent. This book may therefore helpfully be read alongside my *Social Theory: Conflict, Cohesion and Consent*. The focus is on the issue of how society is constituted and how its different elements relate. The readings provided here will cover such things as the functioning of the economic system, the relationship between economy and the state, the role of culture, the role of ideology, the establishment of legitimacy and the achievement of consensus.

It is possible, as some of the class-based theorists such as Marx have argued, that social cohesion and consent rest on the suppression of fundamental social conflicts – or indeed that the politics of cohesion and consent are the ways in which that conflict is played out. Conflict may be taken to refer to struggle and contestation. And if conflict refers to the breakdown of consensus, then we may follow Gramsci in contrasting consent with coercion and the use of force to resolve such struggles. The different theorists covered here offer different accounts of what the fundamental social conflicts are and how they may be resolved (if indeed they may).

In Marx, for example, conflict is essentially class based and ultimately derives from economic interests (although he gives an account of political conflict in his *Eighteenth Brumaire*). However, even within Marxism there are debates as to whether conflict should be seen in terms of the relationship of one class to another (the bourgeoisie and working class) or whether the focus should be on more abstract things like the relationship of capital to labour or the conflict between forces and relations of production. Weber's approach is to focus on the relations between social groups, but his move is to suggest that such relations are not so strongly based on class or economic interest and that it is necessary to take account of such things as social status. Foucault's position is that in discussing conflict, we should move away from the focus on social groups altogether, or at least, we should begin by looking at power relations that cannot be reduced to any one group or any one source. His view is that power is everywhere and that wherever there is power there is resistance – although social theorists have struggled to find a way of developing this argument to bring back agency.

Gramsci's theory of hegemony clearly relies on active human agency in that it rests on the idea of consent or consensus. As a Marxist, Gramsci recognises the conflictual basis of society but argues that social groups attempt to overcome this by means of political projects that involve the agreement, legitimation, compliance and assent of the wider population. This is not necessarily a positive thing since hegemony implies a balance of consent and coercion and even consent may be obtained through manipulative or ideological means, presenting the interests of the hegemonic group and those of the wider population. Weber also follows a pessimistic route in suggesting that forms of legitimate authority are equally forms of domination and the means by which a particular form of political leadership establishes and justifies itself. The early critical theorists extend this pessimism to the cultural sphere to examine how cultural and material mass production produce an unthinking form of comfortable satisfaction. This pessimism is challenged by the later critical theorist Habermas, who reintroduces the idea of consensus as the basis of what he calls the lifeworld.

Consensus implies some sort of conscious agreement or process of legitimation or acceptance. Cohesion on the other hand relates more to how a social body holds together and functions. This cohesion may relate to a social group or to a political bloc or to an institution like the state or else to the whole social system. In Gramsci, cohesion complements consent as the main achievement of hegemony. In the functionalist sociology of Parsons and Durkheim cohesion relates to social norms and values that help reproduce the social system. Whereas some Marxists emphasise the role of agency, structural Marxists such as Poulantzas look at cohesion in relation to bodies like the state or processes like hegemony that unify the social formation. While structuralists look at cohesion in relation to material structures, poststructuralists such as Foucault relate cohesion to microstructres of power that are connected to disciplinary practices and forms of social regulation. The main problem, as has previously been mentioned, is whether this represents social cohesion without consensus or human agency.

Both cohesion and consensus imply that society is not something self-given and that social orders always require certain interventions – whether these be agential or structural – in order to maintain themselves or develop. Both in a sense imply at least potential conflicts arising from differences or divisions within society. In other words, the theorists covered here accept in different ways that social cohesion and consent does not come automatically. Differences and divisions have to be overcome in various ways. This reader will examine how different theorists have attempted to deal with this issue.

II. A Note on the Selections

This introduction is brief because each part has its own lengthy introduction. This is unusual for a reader, but hopefully it will provide the reader with the necessary general information. Since it is impossible to cover everything in the selections, the part introductions will provide additional information, use quotes from other works and link the selections together. The general format is to offer a comprehensive introduction followed by three or four selections from the original theory, then a modern interpretation or application of the ideas.

Part I

MARX AND ENGELS: CONFLICT AND DISSENT

rather take this for granted, assuming that radicalism immediately follows. The presumption that the development of capitalism will lead to the homogenisation of the workers into one large and active group underestimates divisions that exist within classes. The development of capitalism may well lead to a growth in the size of the working class and to a polarisation between the proletariat and bourgeoisie, but later writers such as Gramsci and Weber will note the stratification *within* these classes.

IV. The State

It is difficult to find a single overriding conception of the state in Marx and Engels so three positions will be outlined here – the abstract nature of the state and its relation to civil society, the idea of the state as a class instrument and the notion of the state as a factor of social cohesion. These issues are taken up in a contemporary extract by the state theorist Bob Jessop, who also looks at the debate between Poulantzas and Miliband.

In his early writings Marx criticises Hegel's view that the state acts to guarantee the universal interest. Rather, the state is run by a bureaucracy that develops its own interests: 'The bureaucracy must therefore protect the *imaginary* universality of particular interests, i.e. the corporation mind, in order to protect the *imaginary* particularity of the universal interest' (Marx 1975b: 107). The state is seen as an abstract system of political domination that denies the social nature of people and alienates them from genuine involvement in public life. Although Marx is not yet a communist, he is clearly moving towards a class position.

In *The Communist Manifesto*, Marx and Engels view the state as a class instrument that directly represents the economically dominant class. It acts in a coercive way to reinforce the exploitation of labour by capital. The problem with this view is that by stressing coercion it leaves little room for a sophisticated account of how consent is achieved through more subtle means. A theory of consent would also recognise that a diverse range of interests need to be appealed to, whereas the instrumentalist view tends to assume that the two main classes are fairly cohesive and that they act on clear interests.

Marx's later work *Civil War in France* concludes from the bloody suppression of the Paris Commune that 'the working class cannot simply lay hold of the ready-made state machinery, and wield it for its own purposes' (Marx 1974: 206). This goes somewhat against the instrumentalist view in that it recognises that the state is not the instrument of just any group and certainly the working class cannot use the existing state for its own purposes. Rather, it must smash the existing state and establish a new one. This moves us towards a third position where the character of the state is determined, not by who is in control, but by its intrinsic relationship to the capitalist system. This view of the state has a functional rather than an instrumental emphasis based on its relation to the mode of production.

INTRODUCTION

I. Economic Production

Marx and Engels start from the assumption that society has a material basis and that this is driven by the dominant mode of production. Based on historical materialism, Marxism examines our relationship to nature and the way in which through production, people are able to satisfy their wants and needs – food, clothing and shelter as well as more developed tastes. The focus on mode of production means examining how different societies have reproduced the material conditions necessary to sustain their existence.

The most basic idea in Marx's work is therefore that society is organised around the dominant mode of production and that this shapes the general character of social life. History has seen the development of various modes of production including the communal system of primitive society, the slave system of ancient society, the serfdom of feudalism and the wage-labour economy of capitalism. The latter is based on generalised commodity production and wage-labour. The purpose of Marx's *Capital* is to explain the economic laws of the capitalist mode of production as well as outlining the origins of capitalism and the contradictions that will lead to its future decline.

The first extract – Marx's 1859 'Preface' – is perhaps the most schematic but also the best known of his general outlines of social development. The model has influenced generations of Marxists due to its clarity, but has also given rise to criticisms of economic determinism. It argues that the mode of production determines the rest of social, political and cultural life and that society has an economic base upon which arises a political and legal superstructure and forms of social consciousness. In addition to this base – superstructure model, the Preface sets out Marx's distinction between the productive forces (means of production and labour-power) and the relations of production (classes and ownership). It gives primacy to the productive forces as the motor of history – leading to accusations of technological or productive forces determinism. These forces drive history forward, but then, at a certain stage of development, they come into conflict with the existing social relations of production, thus beginning a period of social revolution (Marx 1975a).

This raises the question of what role conscious human agency has in transforming society. The Preface argues that if society does change, this is only ever when the productive forces have fully developed. This immediately raises the question of the Russian Revolution, where social change took place before capitalism had fully matured. However, later extracts will show that Marx and Engels have a much richer conception of history and politics than this and that they do allow for human agency to play a full role in shaping social and historical development.

II. Capital and Commodities

Marx's *Capital* is a difficult book to read, but its first chapter is widely read as an example of Marx's method and focus. He begins his study of capitalism with an analysis of the commodity, an object which may be able to satisfy human needs, but which is produced in order to be exchanged. When an object assumes the form of a commodity it thereby acquires an exchange value based on its relation to other commodities. However, Marx's method in this chapter consists in starting with appearances, then moving to look at underlying reality. He therefore goes from the appearance of commodities in their exchange relations to underlying social conditions such as the social relation between capital and labour and the production of fetishised social forms.

The capitalist system claims legitimacy on the basis that the sale of labour-power by the worker to the capitalist is voluntary. This is of course not really the case since workers are economically compelled (by virtue of non-ownership of the means of production) to sell their labour-power. Nevertheless, the ideologues of the ruling class are able to claim that each individual is free to do as they wish and make the best of their particular abilities. Further, the exploitation involved in wage-labour is concealed by the wage-form which hides the real level of exploitation and presents the wage as a fair return for the work provided. It can be argued, therefore, that not only does the capitalist system have a built-in form of exploitation, but that it also has a built-in consensual (mystificatory) element that leads to workers accepting the exploitation of their labour-power.

This is a form of fetishism, where the worker's labour-power itself becomes a commodity to be bought and sold. The relation between people

therefore assumes the form of relations between thi[illegible] labour likewise become invested with magical proper[illegible] power of their own, independent of the human labour [illegible] The finished form of commodities and money conceals [illegible] of private labour by making these relations appear as if [illegible] between independent objects.

This could be described as a form of alienation where[illegible] estranged from each other and from the products of their [illegible] potentially creative and satisfying aspect of human labour is [illegible] arbitrary, alien and objective force. Humans are compelled [illegible] themselves to a production process that divides them up an[illegible] as little more than appendages of the machine. The division [illegible] therefore much more than a technical issue. It is bound up with [illegible] of the capitalist system, the private ownership of the means of [illegible] and the constant need to create more capital.

III. Classes and Class Conflict

In Marx's economic analysis conflict, cohesion and consent wou[illegible] to be the product of the system itself. People seem to consent to [illegible] of capital on the basis of a mystification generated by the system. [illegible] are defined objectively in relation to the process of production. An [illegible] ished chapter of *Capital* defines the working class as those who are [illegible] labourers or the owners of mere labour-power. The capitalist class is def[illegible] by ownership of the means of production with income derived from pr[illegible] (Marx 1981: 1025). This is an important definition, but it does not tell [illegible] whole story.

Marx's and Engels' political writings define class and class struggle i[illegible] much more active terms. These works are responding to political developments and are written as polemics. In *The Communist Manifesto* (1973) Marx and Engels note that classes have existed throughout history but that capitalism has created new classes, new conditions of oppression and new forms of struggle. Capitalist production has also played a progressive role, bringing together the means of production, collectivising the population and advancing political centralisation and modernisation. And because capitalism is a dynamic system (based on competition and the drive for profit), the bourgeoisie cannot afford to stand still but must continually revolutionise the relations of production. But this also leads to conditions of greater exploitation. The *Manifesto* argues that the distinctive feature of capitalism is that it has simplified class relations with society splitting up into two great hostile camps – bourgeoisie and proletariat.

The collectivisation and urbanisation of the working class at the same time gives it its potential power and makes it more aware of its common experiences and interests. In class terms, therefore, social cohesion is undermined by the historical process. The problem is that Marx and Engels

INTRODUCTION

I. Economic Production

Marx and Engels start from the assumption that society has a material basis and that this is driven by the dominant mode of production. Based on historical materialism, Marxism examines our relationship to nature and the way in which through production, people are able to satisfy their wants and needs – food, clothing and shelter as well as more developed tastes. The focus on mode of production means examining how different societies have reproduced the material conditions necessary to sustain their existence.

The most basic idea in Marx's work is therefore that society is organised around the dominant mode of production and that this shapes the general character of social life. History has seen the development of various modes of production including the communal system of primitive society, the slave system of ancient society, the serfdom of feudalism and the wage-labour economy of capitalism. The latter is based on generalised commodity production and wage-labour. The purpose of Marx's *Capital* is to explain the economic laws of the capitalist mode of production as well as outlining the origins of capitalism and the contradictions that will lead to its future decline.

The first extract – Marx's 1859 'Preface' – is perhaps the most schematic but also the best known of his general outlines of social development. The model has influenced generations of Marxists due to its clarity, but has also given rise to criticisms of economic determinism. It argues that the mode of production determines the rest of social, political and cultural life and that society has an economic base upon which arises a political and legal superstructure and forms of social consciousness. In addition to this base – superstructure model, the Preface sets out Marx's distinction between the productive forces (means of production and labour-power) and the relations of production (classes and ownership). It gives primacy to the productive forces as the motor of history – leading to accusations of technological or productive forces determinism. These forces drive history forward, but then, at a certain stage of development, they come into conflict with the existing social relations of production, thus beginning a period of social revolution (Marx 1975a).

This raises the question of what role conscious human agency has in transforming society. The Preface argues that if society does change, this is only ever when the productive forces have fully developed. This immediately raises the question of the Russian Revolution, where social change took place before capitalism had fully matured. However, later extracts will show that Marx and Engels have a much richer conception of history and politics than this and that they do allow for human agency to play a full role in shaping social and historical development.

II. CAPITAL AND COMMODITIES

Marx's *Capital* is a difficult book to read, but its first chapter is widely read as an example of Marx's method and focus. He begins his study of capitalism with an analysis of the commodity, an object which may be able to satisfy human needs, but which is produced in order to be exchanged. When an object assumes the form of a commodity it thereby acquires an exchange value based on its relation to other commodities. However, Marx's method in this chapter consists in starting with appearances, then moving to look at underlying reality. He therefore goes from the appearance of commodities in their exchange relations to underlying social conditions such as the social relation between capital and labour and the production of fetishised social forms.

The capitalist system claims legitimacy on the basis that the sale of labour-power by the worker to the capitalist is voluntary. This is of course not really the case since workers are economically compelled (by virtue of non-ownership of the means of production) to sell their labour-power. Nevertheless, the ideologues of the ruling class are able to claim that each individual is free to do as they wish and make the best of their particular abilities. Further, the exploitation involved in wage-labour is concealed by the wage-form which hides the real level of exploitation and presents the wage as a fair return for the work provided. It can be argued, therefore, that not only does the capitalist system have a built-in form of exploitation, but that it also has a built-in consensual (mystificatory) element that leads to workers accepting the exploitation of their labour-power.

This is a form of fetishism, where the worker's labour-power itself becomes a commodity to be bought and sold. The relation between people therefore assumes the form of relations between things. The products of labour likewise become invested with magical properties as if they have a power of their own, independent of the human labour that goes into them. The finished form of commodities and money conceals the social character of private labour by making these relations appear as if they were relations between independent objects.

This could be described as a form of alienation where people become estranged from each other and from the products of their own labour. The potentially creative and satisfying aspect of human labour is turned into an arbitrary, alien and objective force. Humans are compelled to subordinate themselves to a production process that divides them up and treats them as little more than appendages of the machine. The division of labour is therefore much more than a technical issue. It is bound up with the demands of the capitalist system, the private ownership of the means of production and the constant need to create more capital.

III. Classes and Class Conflict

In Marx's economic analysis conflict, cohesion and consent would seem to be the product of the system itself. People seem to consent to the rule of capital on the basis of a mystification generated by the system. Classes are defined objectively in relation to the process of production. An unfinished chapter of *Capital* defines the working class as those who are wage-labourers or the owners of mere labour-power. The capitalist class is defined by ownership of the means of production with income derived from profit (Marx 1981: 1025). This is an important definition, but it does not tell the whole story.

Marx's and Engels' political writings define class and class struggle in much more active terms. These works are responding to political developments and are written as polemics. In *The Communist Manifesto* (1973) Marx and Engels note that classes have existed throughout history but that capitalism has created new classes, new conditions of oppression and new forms of struggle. Capitalist production has also played a progressive role, bringing together the means of production, collectivising the population and advancing political centralisation and modernisation. And because capitalism is a dynamic system (based on competition and the drive for profit), the bourgeoisie cannot afford to stand still but must continually revolutionise the relations of production. But this also leads to conditions of greater exploitation. The *Manifesto* argues that the distinctive feature of capitalism is that it has simplified class relations with society splitting up into two great hostile camps – bourgeoisie and proletariat.

The collectivisation and urbanisation of the working class at the same time gives it its potential power and makes it more aware of its common experiences and interests. In class terms, therefore, social cohesion is undermined by the historical process. The problem is that Marx and Engels rather take this for granted, assuming that radicalism immediately follows. The presumption that the development of capitalism will lead to the homogenisation of the workers into one large and active group underestimates divisions that exist within classes. The development of capitalism may well lead to a growth in the size of the working class and to a polarisation between the proletariat and bourgeoisie, but later writers such as Gramsci and Weber will note the stratification *within* these classes.

IV. THE STATE

It is difficult to find a single overriding conception of the state in Marx and Engels so three positions will be outlined here – the abstract nature of the state and its relation to civil society, the idea of the state as a class instrument and the notion of the state as a factor of social cohesion. These issues are taken up in a contemporary extract by the state theorist Bob Jessop, who also looks at the debate between Poulantzas and Miliband.

In his early writings Marx criticises Hegel's view that the state acts to guarantee the universal interest. Rather, the state is run by a bureaucracy that develops its own interests: 'The bureaucracy must therefore protect the *imaginary* universality of particular interests, i.e. the corporation mind, in order to protect the *imaginary* particularity of the universal interest' (Marx 1975b: 107). The state is seen as an abstract system of political domination that denies the social nature of people and alienates them from genuine involvement in public life. Although Marx is not yet a communist, he is clearly moving towards a class position.

In *The Communist Manifesto*, Marx and Engels view the state as a class instrument that directly represents the economically dominant class. It acts in a coercive way to reinforce the exploitation of labour by capital. The problem with this view is that by stressing coercion it leaves little room for a sophisticated account of how consent is achieved through more subtle means. A theory of consent would also recognise that a diverse range of interests need to be appealed to, whereas the instrumentalist view tends to assume that the two main classes are fairly cohesive and that they act on clear interests.

Marx's later work *Civil War in France* concludes from the bloody suppression of the Paris Commune that 'the working class cannot simply lay hold of the ready-made state machinery, and wield it for its own purposes' (Marx 1974: 206). This goes somewhat against the instrumentalist view in that it recognises that the state is not the instrument of just any group and certainly the working class cannot use the existing state for its own purposes. Rather, it must smash the existing state and establish a new one. This moves us towards a third position where the character of the state is determined, not by who is in control, but by its intrinsic relationship to the capitalist system. This view of the state has a functional rather than an instrumental emphasis based on its relation to the mode of production.

This third position sees the state as a guarantor of social cohesion between economic and political spheres. This can be seen in Marx's *Eighteenth Brumaire of Louis Bonaparte* (1973a). France at this time was divided between different class fractions. Under these conditions the state seemed to become autonomous. Marx accepts that Bonaparte also represents a social class, but this is the class of small peasants, not the ruling class. This clearly goes against the view that the state is simply the instrument of the economically dominant class. In fact Marx argues that the ruling class had lost its vocation to rule. The Bonapartist state arose in order to hold things together when class and fractional conflicts could not be resolved. Power fell into the hands of the state executive. Although the case of Louis Bonaparte is an exceptional one, this view of the state as a factor of social cohesion can be applied more generally to describe the process whereby the state seeks to resolve or contain the conflicts between different groups and interests in order to protect the general needs of the economic system.

While on the issue of the state, a mention should be made of Engels's *The Origin of the Family, Private Property and the State*. This work looks at the rise of the state by linking it historically to the growth of class society and (importantly for a feminist approach) to the development of the family. Engels argues that there have been early societies that did without state power. However, 'at a certain stage of economic development, which necessarily involved the split of society into classes, the state became a necessity because of this split' (Engels 1978: 210). This occurs once human labour is able to produce more than is necessary for the maintenance of the producers, so the state is linked to the production, protection and distribution of this surplus. Most generally, the state is an organisation of the possessing class for its protection against the non-possessing class. Engels links the rise of the state to the development of the family, arguing that the emergence of private property requires a monogamous nuclear family capable of organising the inheritance of private property by producing children of undisputed parentage and guaranteeing the supremacy of the male line. With this comes the increased exploitation of women since household management now becomes a private affair and the wife becomes the chief servant of the household. While the man becomes the main wage-labourer, the woman of the family is confined to domestic slavery (Engels 1978: 85). Thus Engels shows how the division of labour within society is more than just a class issue but is also linked to a system of patriarchal relations.

V. Alienation and Ideology

We have already discussed how Marx's *Capital* discusses the ideology of commodity fetishism, whereby the products of labour come to life as independent things while actual human relations become alienated. Marx is here giving a precise cause for human alienation rooted in the process of commodity production. However, his concern with alienation goes back to his earliest work, where alienation concerns how human beings become separated from their true essence or species-being. In the early writings where his view of alienation or estrangement is not yet tied to a full economic analysis, it takes a more humanist form. Writing on James Mill, Marx says private property acts as an alien mediator through which

> man gazes at his will, his activity, his relation to others as at a power independent of them and of himself ... Hence this *mediator* is the lost, estranged *essence* of private property, private property *alienated* and external to itself; it is the *alienated mediation* of human production with human production the *alienated* species-activity of man. (Marx 1975c: 260–1)

The idea of estrangement from our true human essence plays a much stronger role than in the later writings, but these are anticipated by the focus on the role of private property. In extracts from the *Economic and Philosophical Manuscripts* (1975d), Marx looks at how economic production and alienation are bound together. Through estrangement workers find themselves confronted with the objectified powers of their own essence in the form alien objects. This in turn has an ideological or mystificatory effect as it creates a loss of reality in our heads.

To find ourselves again, Marx argues that we tend to shift consciousness away from the problems of daily life towards higher things while also making a virtue out of misery and suffering. Religion fills the gap caused by alienated social relations while deadening any pain in that

> *religious* suffering is at one and the same time the *expression* of real suffering and a protest against real suffering. Religion is the sigh of the oppressed creature, the heart of a heartless world and the soul of soulless conditions. It is the *opium* of the people. (Marx 1975e: 244)

If religious belief is regarded as a form of ideology, then in *The German Ideology* Marx and Engels discuss how this relates to material life. Such things as religion and morality, although they have the semblance of independence, are really the product of (imperfect) material intercourse. Marx and Engels write that the phantoms formed in the human brain are sublimates of our material life processes (Marx and Engels 1965: 37–8). They also go on to state:

> The ideas of the ruling class are in every epoch the ruling ideas: i.e. the class which is the ruling *material* force of society, is at the same time its ruling *intellectual* force. The class which has the means of material production at its disposal, has control at the same time over the means of mental production ... the ruling ideas are nothing more than the ideal expression of the dominant material relationships. (Marx and Engels 1965: 61)

So Marx and Engels see the causes of alienation and ideology in material conditions. Consequently, their advice for ridding ourselves of these ideas is to radically change our material conditions of existence.

How to change the system is more of a problem. Marx and Engels try to show how human action is possible. However, this is usually set within certain conditions. Marx's economic analysis therefore tries to look at structural conditions. If these start to break down, then social cohesion and consent also start to fail and a period of social revolution can begin. One of the most basic structural contradictions identified by Marx is the tendency of rate of profit to fall. He also talks of crises of overproduction where output exceeds demand. Our first extract shows how Marx conceives crisis more generally by connecting changes in production to changes in social relations.

Marx and Engels hold a dialectical view of social change whereby fundamental contradictions produce conflicts leading to revolutionary change. This process is said to end with the victory of the proletariat, the abolition of social conflict. With the end of conflict, the coercive nature of the state withers away as it is no longer required, and society, for perhaps the first time, becomes truly consensual.

PREFACE TO *A CONTRIBUTION TO THE CRITIQUE OF POLITICAL ECONOMY*

Karl Marx

I examine the system of bourgeois economy in the following order: *capital, landed property, wage-labour*; *the State, foreign trade, world market*. The economic conditions of existence of the three great classes into which modern bourgeois society is divided are analysed under the first three headings; the interconnection of the other three headings is self-evident. The first part of the first book, dealing with Capital, comprises the following chapters: 1. The commodity; 2. Money or simple circulation; 3. Capital in general. The present part consists of the first two chapters. The entire material lies before me in the form of monographs, which were written not for publication but for self-clarification at widely separated periods; their remoulding into an integrated whole according to the plan I have indicated will depend upon circumstances.

A general introduction,[1] which I had drafted, is omitted, since on further consideration it seems to me confusing to anticipate results which still have to be substantiated, and the reader who really wishes to follow me will have to decide to advance from the particular to the general. A few brief remarks regarding the course of my study of political economy may, however, be appropriate here.

Although I studied jurisprudence, I pursued it as a subject subordinated to philosophy and history. In the year 1842–3, as editor of the *Rheinische Zeitung*, I first found myself in the embarrassing position of having to

Karl Marx (1975), 'Preface (to *A Contribution to the Critique of Political Economy*)', in *Early Writings*, tr. Rodney Livingstone and Gregor Benton, Harmondsworth: Pelican.

discuss what is known as material interests. The deliberations of the Rhenish Landtag on forest thefts and the division of landed property; the official polemic started by Herr von Schaper, then Oberpräsident of the Rhine Province, against the *Rheinische Zeitung* about the condition of the Moselle peasantry, and finally the debates on free trade and protective tariffs caused me in the first instance to turn my attention to economic questions. On the other hand, at that time when good intentions 'to push forward' often took the place of factual knowledge, an echo of French socialism and communism, slightly tinged by philosophy, was noticeable in the *Rheinische Zeitung*. I objected to this dilettantism, but at the same time frankly admitted in a controversy with the *Allgemeine Augsburger Zeitung* that my previous studies did not allow me to express any opinion on the content of the French theories. When the publishers of the *Rheinische Zeitung* conceived the illusion that by a more compliant policy on the part of the paper it might be possible to secure the abrogation of the death sentence passed upon it, I eagerly grasped the opportunity to withdraw from the public stage to my study.

The first work which I undertook to dispel the doubts assailing me was a critical re-examination of the Hegelian philosophy of law; the introduction to this work being published in the *Deutsch–Französische Jahrbücher* issued in Paris in 1844. My inquiry led me to the conclusion that neither legal relations nor political forms could be comprehended whether by themselves or on the basis of a so-called general development of the human mind, but that on the contrary they originate in the material conditions of life, the totality of which Hegel, following the example of English and French thinkers of the eighteenth century, embraces within the term 'civil society'; that the anatomy of this civil society, however, has to be sought in political economy. The study of this, which I began in Paris, I continued in Brussels, where I moved owing to an expulsion order issued by M. Guizot. The general conclusion at which I arrived and which, once reached, became the guiding principle of my studies can be summarized as follows. In the social production of their existence, men inevitably enter into definite relations, which are independent of their will, namely relations of production appropriate to a given stage in the development of their material forces of production. The totality of these relations of production constitutes the economic structure of society, the real foundation, on which arises a legal and political superstructure and to which correspond definite forms of social consciousness. The mode of production of material life conditions the general process of social, political and intellectual life. It is not the consciousness of men that determines their existence, but their social existence that determines their consciousness. At a certain stage of development, the material productive forces of society come into conflict with the existing relations of production or – this merely expresses the same thing in legal terms – with the property relations within the framework of which they have operated hitherto. From forms of development of the productive forces these relations turn into their fetters. Then begins an era of social revolution. The changes in the economic foundation lead sooner or later to the transformation of the whole immense superstructure. In studying such transformations it is always necessary to distinguish between the material transformation of the economic conditions of production, which can be determined with the precision of natural science, and the legal, political, religious, artistic or philosophic – in short, ideological forms in which men become conscious of this conflict and fight it out. Just as one does not judge an individual by what he thinks about himself, so one cannot judge such a period of transformation by its consciousness, but, on the contrary, this consciousness must be explained from the contradictions of material life, from the conflict existing between the social forces of production and the relations of production. No social order is ever destroyed before all the productive forces for which it is sufficient have been developed, and new superior relations of production never replace older ones before the material conditions for their existence have matured within the framework of the old society. Mankind thus inevitably sets itself only such tasks as it is able to solve, since closer examination will always show that the problem itself arises only when the material conditions for its solution are already present or at least in the course of formation. In broad outline, the Asiatic, ancient, feudal and modern bourgeois modes of production may be designated as epochs marking progress in the economic development of society. The bourgeois mode of production is the last antagonistic form of the social process of production – antagonistic not in the sense of individual antagonism but of an antagonism that emanates from the individuals' social conditions of existence – but the productive forces developing within bourgeois society create also the material conditions for a solution of this antagonism. The prehistory of human society accordingly closes with this social formation.

Frederick Engels, with whom I maintained a constant exchange of ideas by correspondence since the publication of his brilliant essay on the critique of economic categories[2] (printed in the *Deutsch-Französische Jahrbücher*), arrived by another road (compare his *Lage der arbeitenden Klasse in England*[3]) at the same results as I, and when in the spring of 1845 he too came to live in Brussels, we decided to set forth together our conception as opposed to the ideological one of German philosophy, in fact to settle accounts with our former philosophical conscience. The intention was carried out in the form of a critique of post-Hegelian philosophy.[4] The manuscript, two large octavo volumes, had long ago reached the publishers in Westphalia when we were informed that owing to changed circumstances it could not be printed. We abandoned the manuscript to the gnawing criticism of the mice all the more willingly since we had achieved our main purpose – self-clarification. Of the scattered works in which at that time we presented one or another aspect of our views to the public, I shall mention only the *Manifesto of the Communist Party*, jointly written by Engels and myself, and a *Discours sur le libre échange*, which I myself published. The salient points of our conception were first outlined in an academic, although polemical, form in my *Misère de la philosophie*...[5] this book which was aimed at Proudhon appeared in 1847. The publication of an essay on *Wage-Labour*[6] written in German in which I combined the lectures I had held on this subject at the German Workers' Association in Brussels, was interrupted by the February Revolution and my forcible removal from Belgium in consequence.

The publication of the *Neue Rheinische Zeitung* in 1848 and 1849 and subsequent events cut short my economic studies, which I could only resume in London in 1850. The enormous amount of material relating to the history of political economy assembled in the British Museum, the fact that London is a convenient vantage-point for the observation of bourgeois society, and finally the new stage of development which this society seemed to have entered with the discovery of gold in California and Australia, induced me to start again from the very beginning and to work carefully through the new material. These studies led partly of their own accord to apparently quite remote subjects on which I had to spend a certain amount of time. But it was in particular the imperative necessity of earning my living which reduced the time at my disposal. My collaboration, continued now for eight years, with the *New York Tribune*, the leading Anglo-American newspaper, necessitated an excessive fragmentation of my studies, for I wrote only exceptionally newspaper correspondence in the strict sense. Since a considerable part of my contributions consisted of articles dealing with important economic events in Britain and on the Continent, I was compelled to become conversant with practical details which, strictly speaking, lie outside the sphere of political economy.

This sketch of the course of my studies in the domain of political economy is intended merely to show that my views – no matter how they may be judged and how little they conform to the interested prejudices of the ruling classes – are the outcome of conscientious research carried on over many years. At the entrance to science, as at the entrance to hell, the demand must be made:

> *Qui si convien lasciare ogni sospetto*
> *Ogni viltà convien che qui sia morta.*[7]

NOTES

1. Marx, 1857 Introduction', in *Grundrisse*, The Pelical Marx Library, 1973, pp. 81–111.
2. Engels, 'Outlines of a Critique of Political Economy', in *Selected Writings*, Harmondsworth, 1967.
3. Engels, *The Condition of the Working Class in England*, Oxford, 1958.
4. Marx and Engels, *The German Ideology*, London, 1964.

5. Marx, *The Poverty of Philosophy*, London, 1956.
6. Marx, 'Wage-Labour and Captial', in Marx and Engels, *Selected Works in Three Volumes*, Moscow, 1969.
7. Dante, Divina Commedia, Canto III, lines 14–15. (' Here all distrust must be abandoned; here all cowardice must die.')

FROM 'THE FETISHISM OF THE COMMODITY AND ITS SECRET'

Karl Marx

A commodity appears at first sight an extremely obvious, trivial thing. But its analysis brings out that it is a very strange thing, abounding in metaphysical subtleties and theological niceties. So far as it is a use-value, there is nothing mysterious about it, whether we consider it from the point of view that by its properties it satisfies human needs, or that it first takes on these properties as the product of human labour. It is absolutely clear that, by his activity, man changes the forms of the materials of nature in such a way as to make them useful to him. The form of wood, for instance, is altered if a table is made out of it. Nevertheless the table continues to be wood, an ordinary, sensuous thing. But as soon as it emerges as a commodity, it changes into a thing which transcends sensuousness. It not only stands with its feet on the ground, but, in relation to all other commodities, it stands on its head, and evolves out of its wooden brain grotesque ideas, far more wonderful than if it were to begin dancing of its own free will.[1]

The mystical character of the commodity does not therefore arise from its use-value. Just as little does it proceed from the nature of the determinants of value. For in the first place, however varied the useful kinds of labour, or productive activities, it is a physiological fact that they are functions of the human organism, and that each such function, whatever may be its nature or its form, is essentially the expenditure of human brain, nerves, muscles and sense organs. Secondly, with regard to the foundation of the quantitative

Karl Marx (1976), 'The fetishism of the commodity and its secret', in *Capital, vol. 1*, tr. Ben Fowkes, Hormondsworth: Pelican.

determination of value, namely the duration of that expenditure or the quantity of labour, this is quite palpably different from its quality. In all situations, the labour-time it costs to produce the means of subsistence must necessarily concern mankind, although not to the same degree at different stages of development.[2] And finally, as soon as men start to work for each other in any way, their labour also assumes a social form.

Whence, then, arises the enigmatic character of the product of labour, as soon as it assumes the form of a commodity? Clearly, it arises from this form itself. The equality of the kinds of human labour takes on a physical form in the equal objectivity of the products of labour as values; the measure of the expenditure of human labour-power by its duration takes on the form of the magnitude of the value of the products of labour; and finally the relationships between the producers, within which the social characteristics of their labours are manifested, take on the form of a social relation between the products of labour.

The mysterious character of the commodity-form consists therefore simply in the fact that the commodity reflects the social characteristics of men's own labour as objective characteristics of the products of labour themselves, as the socio-natural properties of these things. Hence it also reflects the social relation of the producers to the sum total of labour as a social relation between objects, a relation which exists apart from and outside the producers. Through this substitution, the products of labour become commodities, sensuous things which are at the same time supra-sensible or social. In the same way, the impression made by a thing on the optic nerve is perceived not as a subjective excitation of that nerve but as the objective form of a thing outside the eye. In the act of seeing, of course, light is really transmitted from one thing, the external object, to another thing, the eye. It is a physical relation between physical things. As against this, the commodity-form, and the value-relation of the products of labour within which it appears, have absolutely no connection with the physical nature of the commodity and the material [*dinglich*] relations arising out of this. It is nothing but the definite social relation between men themselves which assumes here, for them, the fantastic form of a relation between things. In order, therefore, to find an analogy we must take flight into the misty realm of religion. There the products of the human brain appear as autonomous figures endowed with a life of their own, which enter into relations both with each other and with the human race. So it is in the world of commodities with the products of men's hands. I call this the fetishism which attaches itself to the products of labour as soon as they are produced as commodities, and is therefore inseparable from the production of commodities.

As the foregoing analysis has already demonstrated, this fetishism of the world of commodities arises from the peculiar social character of the labour which produces them.

Objects of utility become commodities only because they are the products of the labour of private individuals who work independently of each other. The sum total of the labour of all these private individuals forms the aggregate labour of society. Since the producers do not come into social contact until they exchange the products of their labour, the specific social characteristics of their private labours appear only within this exchange. In other words, the labour of the private individual manifests itself as an element of the total labour of society only through the relations which the act of exchange establishes between the products, and, through their mediation, between the producers. To the producers, therefore, the social relations between their private labours appear as what they are, i.e. they do not appear as direct social relations between persons in their work, but rather as material [*dinglich*] relations between persons and social relations between things.

It is only by being exchanged that the products of labour acquire a socially uniform objectivity as values, which is distinct from their sensuously varied objectivity as articles of utility. This division of the product of labour into a useful thing and a thing possessing value appears in practice only when exchange has already acquired a sufficient extension and importance to allow useful things to be produced for the purpose of being exchanged, so that their character as values has already to be taken into consideration during production. From this moment on, the labour of the individual producer acquires a twofold social character. On the one hand, it must, as a definite useful kind of labour, satisfy a definite social need, and thus maintain its position as an element of the total labour, as a branch of the social division of labour, which originally sprang up spontaneously. On the other hand, it can satisfy the manifold needs of the individual producer himself only in so far as every particular kind of useful private labour can be exchanged with, i.e. counts as the equal of, every other kind of useful private labour. Equality in the full sense between different kinds of labour can be arrived at only if we abstract from their real inequality, if we reduce them to the characteristic they have in common, that of being the expenditure of human labour-power, of human labour in the abstract. The private producer's brain reflects this twofold social character of his labour only in the forms which appear in practical intercourse, in the exchange of products. Hence the socially useful character of his private labour is reflected in the form that the product of labour has to be useful to others, and the social character of the equality of the various kinds of labour is reflected in the form of the common character, as values, possessed by these materially different things, the products of labour.

Men do not therefore bring the products of their labour into relation with each other as values because they see these objects merely as the material integuments of homogeneous human labour. The reverse is true: by equating their different products to each other in exchange as values, they equate their different kinds of labour as human labour. They do this without being aware of it.[3] Value, therefore, does not have its description branded on its forehead; it rather transforms every product of labour into a social hieroglyphic. Later on, men try to decipher the hieroglyphic, to get behind the secret of their own social product: for the characteristic which objects of utility have of being values is as much men's social product as is their language. The belated scientific discovery that the products of labour, in so far as they are values, are merely the material expressions of the human labour expended to produce them, marks an epoch in the history of mankind's development, but by no means banishes the semblance of objectivity possessed by the social characteristics of labour. Something which is only valid for this particular form of production, the production of commodities, namely the fact that the specific social character of private labours carried on independently of each other consists in their equality as human labour, and, in the product, assumes the form of the existence of value, appears to those caught up in the relations of commodity production (and this is true both before and after the above-mentioned scientific discovery) to be just as ultimately valid as the fact that the scientific dissection of the air into its component parts left the atmosphere itself unaltered in its physical configuration.

What initially concerns producers in practice when they make an exchange is how much of some other product they get for their own; in what proportions can the products be exchanged? As soon as these proportions have attained a certain customary stability, they appear to result from the nature of the products, so that, for instance, one ton of iron and two ounces of gold appear to be equal in value, in the same way as a pound of gold and a pound of iron are equal in weight, despite their different physical and chemical properties. The value character of the products of labour becomes firmly established only when they act as magnitudes of value. These magnitudes vary continually, independently of the will, foreknowledge and actions of the exchangers. Their own movement within society has for them the form of a movement made by things, and these things, far from being under their control, in fact control them. The production of commodities must be fully developed before the scientific conviction emerges, from experience itself, that all the different kinds of private labour (which are carried on independently of each other, and yet, as spontaneously developed branches of the social division of labour, are in a situation of all-round dependence on each other) are continually being reduced to the quantitative proportions in which society requires them. The reason for this reduction is that in the midst of the accidental and ever-fluctuating exchange relations between the products, the labour-time socially necessary to produce them asserts itself as a regulative law of nature. In the same way, the law of gravity asserts itself when a person's house collapses on top of him.[4] The determination of the magnitude of value by labour-time is therefore a secret hidden under the apparent movements in the relative values of commodities. Its discovery destroys the semblance of the merely accidental determination of the magnitude of the value of the products of labour, but by no means abolishes that determination's material form.

Reflection on the forms of human life, hence also scientific analysis of those forms, takes a course directly opposite to their real development. Reflection begins *post festum*,* and therefore with the results of the process of development ready to hand. The forms which stamp products as commodities and which are therefore the preliminary requirements for the circulation of commodities, already possess the fixed quality of natural forms of social life before man seeks to give an account, not of their historical character, for in his eyes they are immutable, but of their content and meaning. Consequently, it was solely the analysis of the prices of commodities which led to the determination of the magnitude of value, and solely the common expression of all commodities in money which led to the establishment of their character as values. It is however precisely this finished form of the world of commodities – the money form – which conceals the social character of private labour and the social relations between the individual workers, by making those relations appear as relations between material objects, instead of revealing them plainly. If I state that coats and boots stand in a relation to linen because the latter is the universal incarnation of abstract human labour, the absurdity of the statement is self-evident. Nevertheless, when the producers of coats and boots bring these commodities into a relation with linen, or with gold or silver (and this makes no difference here), as the universal equivalent, the relation between their own private labour and the collective labour of society appears to them in exactly this absurd form.

The categories of bourgeois economics consist precisely of forms of this kind. They are forms of thought which are socially valid, and therefore objective, for the relations of production belonging to this historically determined mode of social production, i.e. commodity production. The whole mystery of commodities, all the magic and necromancy that surrounds the products of labour on the basis of commodity production, vanishes therefore as soon as we come to other forms of production.

NOTES

1. One may recall that China and the tables began to dance when the rest of the world appeared to be standing still – *pour encourager les autres*.[†]
2. Among the ancient Germans the size of a piece of land was measured according to the labour of a day; hence the acre was called *Tagwerk*, *Tagwanne* (*jurnale*, or *terra jurnalis*, or *diornalis*), *Mannwerk*, *Mannskraft*, *Mannsmaad*, *Mannshauet*, etc. See Georg Ludwig von Maurer, *Einleitung zur Geschichte der Mark-, Hof-, usw. Verfassung*, Munich, 1854, p. 129 ff.
3. Therefore, when Galiani said: Value is a relation between persons ('*La Ricchezza è una ragione tra due persone*') he ought to have added: a relation concealed beneath a

* 'After the feast', i.e. after the events reflected on have taken place.

material shell. (Galiani, *Della Moneta*, p. 221, Vol. 3 of Custodi's collection entitled *Scrittori classici italiani di economia politica, Parte moderna*, Milan, 1803.)

4. 'What are we to think of a law which can only assert itself through periodic crises? It is just a natural law which depends on the lack of awareness of the people who undergo it' (Friedrich Engels, Umrisse zu einer Kritik der Nationalökonomie, in the Deutsch-Französische Jahrbücher, edited by Arnold Ruge and Karl Marx, Paris, 1844) [English translation in Marx/Engels' Collected Works, Vol. 3, London, 1975, p. 433].

† 'To encourage the others'. A reference to the simultaneous emergence in the 1850s of the Taiping revolt in China and the craze for spiritualism which swept over upper-class German society. The rest of the world was 'standing still' in the period of reaction immediately after the defeat of the 1848 Revolutions.

FROM 'THE COMMUNIST MANIFESTO'

Karl Marx and Friedrich Engels

A spectre is haunting Europe – the spectre of Communism. All the powers of old Europe have entered into a holy alliance to exorcize this spectre: Pope and Tsar, Metternich[1] and Guizot,[2] French radicals and German police spies.

Where is the party in opposition that has not been decried as communistic by its opponents in power? Where the opposition that has not hurled back the branding reproach of Communism, against the more advanced opposition parties, as well as against its reactionary adversaries?

Two things result from this fact.

1. Communism is already acknowledged by all European powers to be itself a power.
2. It is high time that Communists should openly, in the face of the whole world, publish their views, their aims, their tendencies, and meet this nursery tale of the Spectre of Communism with a manifesto of the party itself.

To this end, Communists of various nationalities have assembled in London, and sketched the following manifesto, to be published in the English, French, German, Italian, Flemish and Danish languages.

Karl Marx and Friedrich Engels (1973), 'Manifesto of the Communist Party', in Karl Marx, *Political Writings, vol. 1: The Revolutions of 1848*, Harmondsworth: Penguin.

I. BOURGEOIS AND PROLETARIANS[3]

The history of all hitherto existing society[4] is the history of class struggles.

Freeman and slave, patrician and plebeian, lord and serf, guild-master[5] and journeyman, in a word, oppressor and oppressed, stood in constant opposition to one another, carried on an uninterrupted, now hidden, now open fight, a fight that each time ended, either in a revolutionary reconstitution of society at large, or in the common ruin of the contending classes.

In the earlier epochs of history, we find almost everywhere a complicated arrangement of society into various orders, a manifold gradation of social rank. In ancient Rome we have patricians, knights, plebeians, slaves; in the Middle Ages, feudal lords, vassals, guild-masters, journeymen, apprentices, serfs; in almost all of these classes, again, subordinate gradations.

The modern bourgeois society that has sprouted from the ruins of feudal society has not done away with class antagonisms. It has but established new classes, new conditions of oppression, new forms of struggle in place of the old ones.

Our epoch, the epoch of the bourgeoisie, possesses, however, this distinctive feature: it has simplified the class antagonisms. Society as a whole is more and more splitting up into two great hostile camps, into two great classes directly facing each other: bourgeoisie and proletariat.

From the serfs of the Middle Ages sprang the chartered burghers of the earliest towns. From these burgesses the first elements of the bourgeoisie were developed.

The discovery of America, the rounding of the Cape, opened up fresh ground for the rising bourgeoisie. The East Indian and Chinese markets, the colonization of America, trade with the colonies, the increase in the means of exchange and in commodities generally, gave to commerce, to navigation, to industry, an impulse never before known, and thereby, to the revolutionary element in the tottering feudal society, a rapid development.

The feudal system of industry, under which industrial production was monopolized by closed guilds, now no longer sufficed for the growing wants of the new markets. The manufacturing system took its place. The guild-masters were pushed on one side by the manufacturing middle class; division of labour between the different corporate guilds vanished in the face of division of labour in each single workshop.

Meantime the markets kept ever growing, the demand ever rising. Even manufacture no longer sufficed. Thereupon, steam and machinery revolutionized industrial production. The place of manufacture was taken by the giant, modern industry, the place of the industrial middle class, by industrial millionaires, the leaders of whole industrial armies, the modern bourgeois.

Modern industry has established the world market, for which the discovery of America paved the way. This market has given an immense development to commerce, to navigation, to communication by land. This development has, in its turn, reacted on the extension of industry; and in proportion as industry, commerce, navigation, railways extended, in the same proportion the bourgeoisie developed, increased its capital, and pushed into the background every class handed down from the Middle Ages.

We see, therefore, how the modern bourgeoisie is itself the product of a long course of development, of a series of revolutions in the modes of production and of exchange.

Each step in the development of the bourgeoisie was accompanied by a corresponding political advance of that class. An oppressed class under the sway of the feudal nobility, an armed and self-governing association in the medieval commune;[6] here independent urban republic (as in Italy and Germany), there taxable 'third estate' of the monarchy (as in France), afterwards, in the period of manufacture proper, serving either the semi-feudal or the absolute monarchy as a counterpoise against the nobility, and, in fact, corner-stone of the great monarchies in general, the bourgeoisie has at last, since the establishment of modern industry and of the world market, conquered for itself, in the modern representative state, exclusive political sway. The executive of the modern state is but a committee for managing the common affairs of the whole bourgeoisie.

The bourgeoisie, historically, has played a most revolutionary part.

The bourgeoisie, wherever it has got the upper hand, has put an end to all feudal, patriarchal, idyllic relations. It has pitilessly torn asunder the motley feudal ties that bound man to his 'natural superiors', and has left remaining no other nexus between man and man than naked self-interest, than callous 'cash payment'. It has drowned the most heavenly ecstasies of religious fervour, of chivalrous enthusiasm, of philistine sentimentalism, in the icy water of egotistical calculation. It has resolved personal worth into exchange value, and in place of the numberless indefeasible chartered freedoms, has set up that single, unconscionable freedom – free trade. In one word, for exploitation, veiled by religious and political illusions, it has substituted naked, shameless, direct, brutal exploitation.

The bourgeoisie has stripped of its halo every occupation hitherto honoured and looked up to with reverent awe. It has converted the physician, the lawyer, the priest, the poet, the man of science, into its paid wage labourers.

The bourgeoisie has torn away from the family its sentimental veil, and has reduced the family relation to a mere money relation.

The bourgeoisie has disclosed how it came to pass that the brutal display of vigour in the Middle Ages, which reactionists so much admire, found its fitting complement in the most slothful indolence. It has been the first to show what man's activity can bring about. It has accomplished wonders far surpassing Egyptian pyramids, Roman aqueducts, and Gothic cathedrals;

it has conducted expeditions that put in the shade all former exoduses of nations and crusades.

The bourgeoisie cannot exist without constantly revolutionizing the instruments of production, and thereby the relations of production, and with them the whole relations of society. Conservation of the old modes of production in unaltered form, was, on the contrary, the first condition of existence for all earlier industrial classes. Constant revolutionizing of production, uninterrupted disturbance of all social conditions, everlasting uncertainty and agitation distinguish the bourgeois epoch from all earlier ones. All fixed, fast-frozen relations, with their train of ancient and venerable prejudices and opinions, are swept away, all new-formed ones become antiquated before they can ossify. All that is solid melts into air, all that is holy is profaned, and man is at last compelled to face with sober senses, his real conditions of life, and his relations with his kind.

The need of a constantly expanding market for its products chases the bourgeoisie over the whole surface of the globe. It must nestle everywhere, settle everywhere, establish connections everywhere.

The bourgeoisie has through its exploitation of the world market given a cosmopolitan character to production and consumption in every country. To the great chagrin of reactionists, it has drawn from under the feet of industry the national ground on which it stood. All old-established national industries have been destroyed or are daily being destroyed. They are dislodged by new industries, whose introduction becomes a life and death question for all civilized nations, by industries that no longer work up indigenous raw material, but raw material drawn from the remotest zones; industries whose products are consumed, not only at home, but in every quarter of the globe. In place of the old wants, satisfied by the productions of the country, we find new wants, requiring for their satisfaction the products of distant lands and climes. In place of the old local and national seclusion and self-sufficiency, we have intercourse in every direction, universal interdependence of nations. And as in material, so also in intellectual production. The intellectual creations of individual nations become common property. National one-sidedness and narrow-mindedness become more and more impossible, and from the numerous national and local literatures, there arises a world literature.

The bourgeoisie, by the rapid improvement of all instruments of production, by the immensely facilitated means of communication, draws all, even the most barbarian, nations into civilization. The cheap prices of its commodities are the heavy artillery with which it batters down all Chinese walls, with which it forces the barbarians' intensely obstinate hatred of foreigners to capitulate. It compels all nations, on pain of extinction, to adopt the bourgeois mode of production; it compels them to introduce what it calls civilization into their midst, i.e., to become bourgeois themselves. In one word, it creates a world after its own image.

The bourgeoisie has subjected the country to the rule of the towns. It has created enormous cities, has greatly increased the urban population as compared with the rural, and has thus rescued a considerable part of the population from the idiocy of rural life. Just as it has made the country dependent on the towns, so it has made barbarian and semi-barbarian countries dependent on the civilized ones, nations of peasants on nations of bourgeois, the East on the West.

The bourgeoisie keeps more and more doing away with the scattered state of the population, of the means of production, and of property. It has agglomerated population, centralized means of production, and has concentrated property in a few hands. The necessary consequence of this was political centralization. Independent, or but loosely connected provinces, with separate interests, laws, governments and systems of taxation, became lumped together into one nation, with one government, one code of laws, one national class interest, one frontier and one customs tariff.

The bourgeoisie, during its rule of scarce one hundred years, has created more massive and more colossal productive forces than have all preceding generations together. Subjection of nature's forces to man, machinery, application of chemistry to industry and agriculture, steam navigation, railways, electric telegraphs, clearing of whole continents for cultivation, canalization of rivers, whole populations conjured out of the ground – what earlier century had even a presentiment that such productive forces slumbered in the lap of social labour?

We see then: the means of production and of exchange, on whose foundation the bourgeoisie built itself up, were generated in feudal society. At a certain stage in the development of these means of production and of exchange, the conditions under which feudal society produced and exchanged, the feudal organization of agriculture and manufacturing industry, in one word, the feudal relations of property became no longer compatible with the already developed productive forces; they became so many fetters. They had to be burst asunder; they were burst asunder.

Into their place stepped free competition, accompanied by a social and political constitution adapted to it, and by the economical and political sway of the bourgeois class.

A similar movement is going on before our own eyes. Modern bourgeois society with its relations of production, of exchange and of property, a society that has conjured up such gigantic means of production and of exchange, is like the sorcerer, who is no longer able to control the powers of the nether world whom he has called up by his spells. For many a decade past, the history of industry and commerce is but the history of the revolt of modern productive forces against modern conditions of production, against the property relations that are the conditions for the existence of the bourgeoisie and of its rule. It is enough to mention the commercial crises that by their periodical return put on trial, each time more threateningly, the existence of the entire bourgeois society. In these crises a great part not only of the existing products, but also of the previously created productive forces, are periodically destroyed. In these crises there breaks out an epidemic that, in all earlier epochs, would have seemed an absurdity – the epidemic of overproduction. Society suddenly finds itself put back into a state of momentary barbarism; it appears as if a famine, a universal war of devastation had cut off the supply of every means of subsistence; industry and commerce seem to be destroyed; and why? Because there is too much civilization, too much means of subsistence, too much industry, too much commerce. The productive forces at the disposal of society no longer tend to further the development of the conditions of bourgeois property; on the contrary, they have become too powerful for these conditions, by which they are fettered, and so soon as they overcome these fetters, they bring disorder into the whole of bourgeois society, endanger the existence of bourgeois property. The conditions of bourgeois society are too narrow to comprise the wealth created by them. And how does the bourgeoisie get over these crises? On the one hand by enforced destruction of a mass of productive forces; on the other, by the conquest of new markets, and by the more thorough exploitation of the old ones. That is to say, by paving the way for more extensive and more destructive crises, and by diminishing the means whereby crises are prevented.

The weapons with which the bourgeoisie felled feudalism to the ground are now turned against the bourgeoisie itself.

But not only has the bourgeoisie forged the weapons that bring death to itself; it has also called into existence the men who are to wield those weapons – the modern working class – the proletarians.

In proportion as the bourgeoisie, i.e., capital, is developed, in the same proportion is the proletariat, the modern working class, developed – a class of labourers, who live only so long as they find work, and who find work only so long as their labour increases capital. These labourers, who must sell themselves piecemeal, are a commodity, like every other article of commerce, and are consequently exposed to all the vicissitudes of competition, to all the fluctuations of the market.

Owing to the extensive use of machinery and to division of labour, the work of the proletarians has lost all individual character, and, consequently, all charm for the workman. He becomes an appendage of the machine, and it is only the most simple, most monotonous, and most easily acquired knack, that is required of him. Hence, the cost of production of a workman is restricted, almost entirely, to the means of subsistence that he requires for his maintenance, and for the propagation of his race. But the price of a commodity, and therefore also of labour,[7] is equal to its cost of production. In proportion, therefore, as the repulsiveness of the work increases, the wage decreases. Nay more, in proportion as the use of machinery and division of labour increases, in the same proportion the burden of toil also increases, whether by prolongation of the working hours, by increase of the work exacted in a given time or by increased speed of the machinery, etc.

Modern industry has converted the little workshop of the patriarchal master into the great factory of the industrial capitalist. Masses of labourers, crowded into the factory, are organized like soldiers. As privates of the industrial army they are placed under the command of a perfect hierarchy of officers and sergeants. Not only are they slaves of the bourgeois class, and of the bourgeois state; they are daily and hourly enslaved by the machine, by the overseer, and, above all, by the individual bourgeois manufacturer himself. The more openly this despotism proclaims gain to be its end and aim, the more petty, the more hateful and the more embittering it is.

The less the skill and exertion of strength implied in manual labour, in other words, the more modern industry becomes developed, the more is the labour of men superseded by that of women. Differences of age and sex have no longer any distinctive social validity for the working class. All are instruments of labour, more or less expensive to use, according to their age and sex.

No sooner is the exploitation of the labourer by the manufacturer so far at an end that he receives his wages in cash, than he is set upon by the other portions of the bourgeoisie, the landlord, the shopkeeper, the pawnbroker, etc.

The lower strata of the middle class – the small tradespeople, shopkeepers, and *rentiers*, the handicraftsmen and peasants – all these sink gradually into the proletariat, partly because their diminutive capital does not suffice for the scale on which modern industry is carried on, and is swamped in the competition with the large capitalists, partly because their specialized skill is rendered worthless by new methods of production. Thus the proletariat is recruited from all classes of the population.

The proletariat goes through various stages of development. With its birth begins its struggle with the bourgeoisie. At first the contest is carried on by individual labourers, then by the work-people of a factory, then by the operatives of one trade, in one locality, against the individual bourgeois who directly exploits them. They direct their attacks not against the bourgeois conditions of production, but against the instruments of production themselves; they destroy imported wares that compete with their labour, they smash to pieces machinery, they set factories ablaze, they seek to restore by force the vanished status of the workman of the Middle Ages.

At this stage the labourers still form an incoherent mass scattered over the whole country, and broken up by their mutual competition. If anywhere they unite to form more compact bodies, this is not yet the consequence of their own active union, but of the union of the bourgeoisie, which class, in order to attain its own political ends, is compelled to set the whole proletariat in motion, and is moreover yet, for a time, able to do so. At this stage, therefore, the proletarians do not fight their enemies, but the enemies of their enemies, the remnants of absolute monarchy, the landowners, the non-industrial bourgeois, the petty bourgeoisie. Thus the whole historical movement is concentrated in the hands of the bourgeoisie; every victory so obtained is a victory for the bourgeoisie.

But with the development of industry the proletariat not only increases in number; it becomes concentrated in greater masses, its strength grows, and it feels that strength more. The various interests and conditions of life within the ranks of the proletariat are more and more equalized, in proportion as machinery obliterates all distinctions of labour, and nearly everywhere reduces wages to the same low level. The growing competition among the bourgeois, and the resulting commercial crises, make the wages of the workers ever more fluctuating. The unceasing improvement of machinery, ever more rapidly developing, makes their livelihood more and more precarious; the collisions between individual workmen and individual bourgeois take more and more the character of collisions between two classes. Thereupon the workers begin to form combinations (trade unions) against the bourgeois; they club together in order to keep up the rate of wages; they found permanent associations in order to make provision before-hand for these occasional revolts. Here and there the contest breaks out into riots.

Now and then the workers are victorious, but only for a time. The real fruit of their battles lies, not in the immediate result, but in the ever expanding union of the workers. This union is helped on by the improved means of communication that are created by modern industry, and that place the workers of different localities in contact with one another. It was just this contact that was needed to centralize the numerous local struggles, all of the same character, into one national struggle between classes. But every class struggle is a political struggle. And that union, to attain which the burghers of the Middle Ages, with their miserable highways, required centuries, the modern proletarians, thanks to railways, achieve in a few years.

This organization of the proletarians into a class, and consequently into a political party, is continually being upset again by the competition between the workers themselves. But it ever rises up again, stronger, firmer, mightier. It compels legislative recognition of particular interests of the workers, by taking advantage of the divisions among the bourgeoisie itself. Thus the Ten Hours Bill in England was carried.[8]

Altogether, collisions between the classes of the old society further, in many ways, the course of development of the proletariat. The bourgeoisie finds itself involved in a constant battle: at first with the aristocracy; later on, with those portions of the bourgeoisie itself, whose interests have become antagonistic to the progress of industry; at all times, with the bourgeoisie of foreign countries. In all these battles it sees itself compelled to appeal to the proletariat, to ask for its help, and thus to drag it into the political arena. The bourgeoisie itself, therefore, supplies the proletariat with its own elements of political and general education, in other words, it furnishes the proletariat with weapons for fighting the bourgeoisie.

Further, as we have already seen, entire sections of the ruling classes are, by the advance of industry, precipitated into the proletariat, or are at least threatened in their conditions of existence. These also supply the proletariat with fresh elements of enlightenment and progress.

Finally, in times when the class struggle nears the decisive hour, the process of dissolution going on within the ruling class, in fact within the whole range of old society, assumes such a violent, glaring character, that a small section of the ruling class cuts itself adrift, and joins the revolutionary class, the class that holds the future in its hands. Just as, therefore, at an earlier period, a section of the nobility went over to the bourgeoisie, so now a portion of the bourgeoisie goes over to the proletariat, and in particular, a portion of the bourgeois ideologists, who have raised themselves to the level of comprehending theoretically the historical movement as a whole.

Of all the classes that stand face to face with the bourgeoisie today, the proletariat alone is a really revolutionary class. The other classes decay and finally disappear in the face of modern industry; the proletariat is its special and essential product.

The lower middle class, the small manufacturer, the shopkeeper, the artisan, the peasant, all these fight against the bourgeoisie, to save from extinction their existence as fractions of the middle class. They are therefore not revolutionary, but conservative. Nay more, they are reactionary, for they try to roll back the wheel of history. If by chance they are revolutionary, they are so only in view of their impending transfer into the proletariat, they thus defend not their present, but their future interests, they desert their own standpoint to place themselves at that of the proletariat.

The 'dangerous class',[9] the social scum, that passively rotting mass thrown off by the lowest layers of old society, may, here and there, be swept into the movement by a proletarian revolution; its conditions of life, however, prepare it far more for the part of a bribed tool of reactionary intrigue.

In the conditions of the proletariat, those of old society at large are already virtually swamped. The proletarian is without property; his relation to his wife and children has no longer anything in common with the bourgeois family relations; modern industrial labour, modern subjection to capital, the same in England as in France, in America as in Germany, has stripped him of every trace of national character. Law, morality, religion, are to him so many bourgeois prejudices, behind which lurk in ambush just as many bourgeois interests.

All the preceding classes that got the upper hand, sought to fortify their already acquired status by subjecting society at large to their conditions of appropriation. The proletarians cannot become masters of the productive forces of society, except by abolishing their own previous mode of appropriation, and thereby also every other previous mode of appropriation. They have nothing of their own to secure and to fortify; their mission is to destroy all previous securities for, and insurances of, individual property.

All previous historical movements were movements of minorities, or in the interest of minorities. The proletarian movement is the self-conscious, independent movement of the immense majority, in the interest of the immense majority. The proletariat, the lowest stratum of our present society, cannot stir, cannot raise itself up, without the whole superincumbent strata of official society being sprung into the air.

Though not in substance, yet in form, the struggle of the proletariat with the bourgeoisie is at first a national struggle. The proletariat of each country must, of course, first of all settle matters with its own bourgeoisie.

In depicting the most general phases of the development of the proletariat, we traced the more or less veiled civil war, raging within existing society, up to the point where that war breaks out into open revolution, and where the violent overthrow of the bourgeoisie lays the foundation for the sway of the proletariat.

Hitherto, every form of society has been based, as we have already seen, on the antagonism of oppressing and oppressed classes. But in order to oppress a class, certain conditions must be assured to it under which it can, at least, continue its slavish existence. The serf, in the period of serfdom, raised himself to membership in the commune, just as the petty bourgeois, under the yoke of feudal absolutism, managed to develop into a bourgeois. The modern labourer, on the contrary, instead of rising with the progress of industry, sinks deeper and deeper below the conditions of existence of his own class. He becomes a pauper, and pauperism develops more rapidly than population and wealth. And here it becomes evident that the bourgeoisie is unfit any longer to be the ruling class in society, and to impose its conditions of existence upon society as an overriding law. It is unfit to rule because it is incompetent to assure an existence to its slave within his slavery, because it cannot help letting him sink into such a state that it has to feed him, instead of being feed by him. Society can no longer live under this bourgeoisie, in other words, its existence is no longer compatible with society.

The essential condition for the existence, and for the sway of the bourgeois class, is the formation and augmentation of capital; the condition for capital is wage labour. Wage labour rests exclusively on competition between the labourers. The advance of industry, whose involuntary promoter is the bourgeoisie, replaces the isolation of the labourers, due to competition, by their revolutionary combination, due to association. The development of modern industry, therefore, cuts from under its feet the very foundation on which the bourgeoisie produces and appropriates products. What the bourgeoisie therefore produces, above all, are its own grave-diggers. Its fall and the victory of the proletariat are equally inevitable.

Notes

1. Clemens Lothar, prince Metternich, was the leading Austrian statesman from 1809 to 1848 and the architect of the counter-revolutionary Holy Alliance.

2. François Guizot was a French historian and *de facto* Prime Minister from 1840 to 1848 under the Orleanist 'July' monarchy of Louis Philippe.
3. By bourgeoisie is meant the class of modern capitalists, owners of the means of social production and employers of wage labour. By proletariat, the class of modern wage labourers who, having no means of production of their own, are reduced to selling their labour power in order to live [Engels].
4. That is, all *written* history. In 1847, the pre-history of society, the social organization existing previous to recorded history, was all but unknown. Since then, Haxthausen discovered common ownership of land in Russia, Maurer proved it to be the social foundation from which all Teutonic races started in history, and by and by village communities were found to be, or to have been the primitive form of society everywhere from India to Ireland. The inner organization of this primitive communistic society was laid bare, in its typical form, by Morgan's crowning discovery of the true nature of the *gens* and its relation to the *tribe*. With the dissolution of these primeval communities society begins to be differentiated into separate and finally antagonistic classes. I have attempted to retrace this process of dissolution in: *Der Ursprung der Familie, des Privateigenthums und des Staats* (*The Origin of the Family, Private Property and the State*) [Engels].
5. Guild-master, that is, a full member of a guild, a master within, not a head of a guild [Engels].
6. 'Commune' was the name taken, in France, by the nascent towns even before they had conquered, from their feudal lords and masters, local self-government and political rights as the 'third estate'. Generally speaking, for the economic development of the bourgeoisie, England is here taken as the typical country; for its political development, France [Engels].
7. In Marx's later theory of surplus value, he concluded that it is the worker's *labour power*, not his labour, that is sold to the capitalist as a commodity. (See 'Wages, Prices and Profit', in Marx and Engels, *Selected Works in Three Volumes*, Moscow, 1969.)
8. In 1846. See Engels's article 'The English Ten Hours Bill', *Articles on Britain*, Moscow, 1971, pp. 96–108.
9. i.e. the lumpenproletariat of casual labourers and unemployed, which was very extensive in the cities of nineteenth-century Europe.

FROM *THE EIGHTEENTH BRUMAIRE OF LOUIS BONAPARTE*

Karl Marx

'*C'est le triomphe complet et définitif du socialisme.*'[1] This was Guizot's characterization of 2 December. But if the overthrow of the parliamentary republic contains within itself the germ of the triumph of the proletarian revolution, its first tangible result was *the victory of Bonaparte over the Assembly, of the executive over the legislature, of force without words over the force of words*. In the Assembly the nation raised its general will to the level of law, i.e. it made the law of the ruling class its general will. It then renounced all will of its own in face of the executive and subjected itself to the superior command of an alien will, to authority. The opposition between executive and legislature expresses the opposition between a nation's heteronomy and its autonomy. France therefore seems to have escaped the despotism of a class only to fall back beneath the despotism of an individual, and indeed beneath the authority of an individual without authority. The struggle seems to have reached the compromise that all classes fall on their knees, equally mute and equally impotent, before the rifle butt.

But the revolution is thorough. It is still on its journey through purgatory. It goes about its business methodically. By 2 December 1851 it had completed one half of its preparatory work; it is now completing the other half. First of all it perfected the parliamentary power, in order to be able to overthrow it. Now, having attained this, it is perfecting the *executive power*, reducing it to its purest expression, isolating it, and pitting itself

Karl Marx (1973), *The Eighteenth Brumaire of Louis Bonaparte,* in *Political Writings, vol. 2: Surveys from Exile* ed. David Fernbach, Harmondsworth: Penguin.

against it as the sole object of attack, in order to concentrate all its forces of destruction against it. And when it has completed this, the second half of its preliminary work, Europe will leap from its seat and exultantly exclaim: 'Well worked, old mole!'[2]

The executive power possesses an immense bureaucratic and military organization, an ingenious and broadly based state machinery, and an army of half a million officials alongside the actual army, which numbers a further half million. This frightful parasitic body, which surrounds the body of French society like a caul and stops up all its pores, arose in the time of the absolute monarchy, with the decay of the feudal system, which it helped to accelerate. The seignorial privileges of the landowners and towns were transformed into attributes of the state power, the feudal dignitaries became paid officials, and the variegated medieval pattern of conflicting plenary authorities became the regulated plan of a state authority characterized by a centralization and division of labour reminiscent of a factory. The task of the first French revolution was to destroy all separate local, territorial, urban and provincial powers in order to create the civil unity of the nation. It had to carry further the centralization that the absolute monarchy had begun, but at the same time it had to develop the extent, the attributes and the number of underlings of the governmental power. Napoleon perfected this state machinery. The Legitimist and July monarchies only added a greater division of labour, which grew in proportion to the creation of new interest groups, and therefore new material for state administration, by the division of labour within bourgeois society. Every *common* interest was immediately detached from society, opposed to it as a higher, *general* interest, torn away from the self-activity of the individual members of society and made a subject for governmental activity, whether it was a bridge, a schoolhouse, the communal property of a village community, or the railways, the national wealth and the national university of France. Finally, the parliamentary republic was compelled in its struggle against the revolution to strengthen by means of repressive measures the resources and centralization of governmental power. All political upheavals perfected this machine instead of smashing it. The parties that strove in turn for mastery regarded possession of this immense state edifice as the main booty for the victor.

However, under the absolute monarchy, during the first French revolution, and under Napoleon, bureaucracy was only the means of preparing the class rule of the bourgeoisie. Under the Restoration, Louis Philippe, and the parliamentary republic, on the other hand, it was the instrument of the ruling class, however much it strove for power in its own right.

Only under the second Bonaparte does the state seem to have attained a completely autonomous position. The state machine has established itself so firmly *vis-à-vis* civil society that the only leader it needs is the head of the Society of 10 December, an adventurer who has rushed in from abroad and been chosen as leader by a drunken soldiery, which he originally bought with liquor and sausages, and to which he constantly has to throw more sausages. This explains the shamefaced despair, the feeling of terrible humiliation and degradation which weighs upon France's breast and makes her catch her breath. France feels dishonoured.

But the state power does not hover in mid-air. Bonaparte represents a class, indeed he represents the most numerous class of French society, the *small peasant proprietors*.

Just as the Bourbons were the dynasty of big landed property and the Orleans the dynasty of money, so the Bonapartes are the dynasty of the peasants, i.e. of the mass of the French people. The chosen hero of the peasantry is not the Bonaparte who submitted to the bourgeois parliament but the Bonaparte who dispersed it. For three years the towns succeeded in falsifying the meaning of the election of 10 December and swindling the peasants out of the restoration of the empire. The election of 10 December 1848 was completed only with the coup d'état of 2 December 1851.

The small peasant proprietors form an immense mass, the members of which live in the same situation but do not enter into manifold relationships with each other. Their mode of operation isolates them instead of bringing them into mutual intercourse. This isolation is strengthened by the wretched state of France's means of communication and by the poverty of the peasants. Their place of operation, the smallholding, permits no division of labour in its cultivation, no application of science and therefore no diversity of development, variety of talent, or wealth of social relationships. Each individual peasant family is almost self-sufficient; it directly produces the greater part of its own consumption and therefore obtains its means of life more through exchange with nature than through intercourse with society. The smallholding, the peasant, and the family; next door, another smallholding, another peasant, and another family. A bunch of these makes up a village, and a bunch of villages makes up a department. Thus the great mass of the French nation is formed by the simple addition of isomorphous magnitudes, much as potatoes in a sack form a sack of potatoes. In so far as millions of families live under economic conditions of existence that separate their mode of life, their interests and their cultural formation from those of the other classes and bring them into conflict with those classes, they form a class. In so far as these small peasant proprietors are merely connected on a local basis, and the identity of their interests fails to produce a feeling of community, national links, or a political organization, they do not form a class. They are therefore incapable of asserting their class interest in their own name, whether through a parliament or through a convention.[3] They cannot represent themselves; they must be represented. Their representative must appear simultaneously as their master, as an authority over them, an unrestricted governmental power that protects them from the other classes and sends them rain and sunshine from above. The political influence of the small peasant proprietors is therefore ultimately expressed in the executive subordinating society to itself.

Historical tradition produced the French peasants' belief that a miracle would occur, that a man called Napoleon would restore all their glory. And an individual turned up who pretended to be that man, because he bore the name of Napoleon, thanks to the stipulation of the Code Napoléon that '*la récherche de la paternité est interdite*'.[4] After twenty years of vagabondage and a series of grotesque adventures the prophecy was fulfilled and the man became Emperor of the French. The nephew's obsession was realized, because it coincided with the obsession of the most numerous class of the French people.

But the objection will be made: What about the peasant risings in half of France, the army's murderous forays against them, and their imprisonment and transportation *en masse*?

Since Louis XIV, France has experienced no corresponding persecution of the peasants 'for demagogic practices'.

This point should be clearly understood: the Bonaparte dynasty represents the conservative, not the revolutionary peasant: the peasant who wants to consolidate the condition of his social existence, the smallholding, not the peasant who strikes out beyond it. It does not represent the country people who want to overthrow the old order by their own energies, in alliance with the towns, but the precise opposite, those who are gloomily enclosed within this old order and want to see themselves and their smallholdings saved and given preferential treatment by the ghost of the Empire. It represents the peasant's superstition, not his enlightenment; his prejudice, not his judgement; his past, not his future; his modern Vendée, not his modern Cevennes.[5]

After the first revolution had transformed the peasants from a state of semi-serfdom into free landed proprietors, Napoleon confirmed and regulated the conditions under which they could exploit undisturbed the soil of France, which had now devolved on them for the first time, and satisfy their new-found passion for property. But the French peasant is now succumbing to his smallholding itself, to the division of the land, the form of property consolidated in France by Napoleon. It was the material conditions which made the feudal French peasant a small proprietor and Napoleon an emperor. Two generations have been sufficient to produce the inevitable consequence: a progressive deterioration of agriculture and a progressive increase in peasant indebtedness. The 'Napoleonic' form of property, which was the condition for the liberation and enrichment of the French rural population at the beginning of the nineteenth century, has developed in the course of that century into the legal foundation of their enslavement and their poverty. And precisely this law is the first of the 'Napoleonic ideas' which the second Bonaparte has to uphold. If he still shares with the peasants the illusion that the cause of their ruin is to be sought, not in the smallholding itself, but outside it, in the influence of secondary circumstances, his experiments will burst like soap bubbles at their first contact with the relations of production.

Driven on by the contradictory demands of his situation, Bonaparte, like a conjuror, has to keep the eyes of the public fixed on himself, as Napoleon's substitute, by means of constant surprises, that is to say by performing a coup d'état in miniature every day. He thereby brings the whole bourgeois economy into confusion, violates everything that seemed inviolable to the revolution of 1848, makes some tolerant of revolution and others desirous of revolution, creates anarchy itself in the name of order, and at the same time strips the halo from the state machine, profaning it and making it both disgusting and ridiculous. He repeats the cult of the Holy Tunic at Trier[6] in the form of the cult of the Napoleonic imperial mantle in Paris. But when the emperor's mantle finally falls on the shoulders of Louis Bonaparte, the bronze statue of Napoleon will come crashing down from the top of the Vendôme Column.

NOTES

1. It is the complete and final triumph of socialism.
2. Hamlet's actual words in *Hamlet* I, v, 162, are, 'Well said old mole, canst work i' th' ground so fast?' Marx's '*Brav gewühlt, alter Maulwurf*' is a condensation, with the twist that *wühlen*, besides meaning to work, grub, burrow, also means to agitate, stir up, foment discontent.
3. i.e. a revolutionary assembly like that of 1792–5.
4. Inquiry into paternity is forbidden.
5. Vendée, in Brittany, was the focus of royalist revolt during the first French revolution. Cevennes was the area of southern France in which the peasant rising of the years 1702–5 took place, the 'revolt of the Camisards'. It was a rising of Protestants for freedom of conscience, and also against fedual dues.
6. One of the sacred relics exhibited in Trier Cathedral in 1844 as part of the Catholic revival of the 1840s.

FROM *ECONOMIC AND PHILOSOPHICAL MANUSCRIPTS*

Karl Marx

The object that labour produces, its product, stands opposed to it as *something alien*, as a *power independent* of the producer. The product of labour is labour embodied and made material in an object, it is the *objectification* of labour. The realization of labour is its objectification. In the sphere of political economy this realization of labour appears as a *loss of reality* for the worker, objectification as *loss of and bondage to the object*, and appropriation as *estrangement*, as *alienation [Entäusserung]*.

So much does the realization of labour appear as loss of reality that the worker loses his reality to the point of dying of starvation. So much does objectification appear as loss of the object that the worker is robbed of the objects he needs most not only for life but also for work. Work itself becomes an object which he can only obtain through an enormous effort and with spasmodic interruptions. So much does the appropriation of the object appear as estrangement that the more objects the worker produces the fewer can he possess and the more he falls under the domination of his product, of capital.

All these consequences are contained in this characteristic, that the worker is related to the *product of his labour* as to an *alien* object. For it is clear that, according to this premise, the more the worker exerts himself in his work, the more powerful the alien, objective world becomes which he brings into being over against himself, the poorer he and his inner world become,

Karl Marx (1975), *Economic and Philosophical Manuscripts*, in *Early Writings*, tr. Rodney Livingstone and Gregor Benton, Harmondsworth: Pelican.

and the less they belong to him. It is the same in religion. The more man puts into God, the less he retains within himself. The worker places his life in the object; but now it no longer belongs to him, but to the object. The greater his activity, therefore, the fewer objects the worker possesses. What the product of his labour is, he is not. Therefore, the greater this product, the less is he himself. The externalization [*Entäusserung*] of the worker in his product means not only that his labour becomes an object, an *external* existence, but that it exists *outside him*, independently of him and alien to him, and begins to confront him as an autonomous power; that the life which he has bestowed on the object confronts him as hostile and alien.

Let us now take a closer look at *objectification*, at the production of the worker, and the *estrangement*, the *loss* of the object, of his product, that this entails.

The worker can create nothing without *nature*, without the *sensuous external world*. It is the material in which his labour realizes itself, in which it is active and from which and by means of which it produces.

But just as nature provides labour with the *means of life* in the sense that labour cannot *live* without objects on which to exercise itself, so also it provides the *means of life* in the narrower sense, namely the means of physical subsistence of the *worker*.

The more the worker *appropriates* the external world, sensuous nature, through his labour, the more he deprives himself of the *means of life* in two respects: firstly, the sensuous external world becomes less and less an object belonging to his labour, a *means of life* of his labour; and secondly, it becomes less and less a *means of life* in the immediate sense, a means for the physical subsistence of the worker.

In these two respects, then, the worker becomes a slave of his object; firstly in that he receives an *object of labour*, i.e. he receives work, and secondly in that he receives *means of subsistence*. Firstly, then, so that he can exist as a *worker*, and secondly as a *physical subject*. The culmination of this slavery is that it is only as a *worker* that he can maintain himself as a *physical subject* and only as a *physical subject* that he is a worker.

(The estrangement of the worker in his object is expressed according to the laws of political economy in the following way: the more the worker produces, the less he has to consume; the more values he creates, the more worthless he becomes; the more his product is shaped, the more misshapen the worker; the more civilized his object, the more barbarous the worker; the more powerful the work, the more powerless the worker; the more intelligent the work, the duller the worker and the more he becomes a slave of nature.)

Political economy conceals the estrangement in the nature of labour by ignoring the ***direct*** *relationship between the* ***worker*** (labour) ***and production.*** It is true that labour produces marvels for the rich, but it produces privation for the worker. It produces palaces, but hovels for the worker. It produces beauty, but deformity for the worker. It replaces labour by machines, but it casts some of the workers back into barbarous forms of labour and turns others into machines. It produces intelligence, but it produces idiocy and cretinism for the worker.

The direct relationship of labour to its products is the relationship of the worker to the objects of his production. The relationship of the rich man to the objects of production and to production itself is only a *consequence* of this first relationship, and confirms it. Later we shall consider this second aspect. Therefore when we ask what is the essential relationship of labour, we are asking about the relationship of the worker to production.

Up to now we have considered the estrangement, the alienation of the worker only from one aspect, i.e. his *relationship to the products of his labour*. But estrangement manifests itself not only in the result, but also in the *act of production*, within the *activity of production* itself. How could the product of the worker's activity confront him as something alien if it were not for the fact that in the act of production he was estranging himself from himself? After all, the product is simply the résumé of the activity, of the production. So if the product of labour is alienation, production itself must be active alienation, the alienation of activity, the activity of alienation. The estrangement of the object of labour merely summarizes the estrangement, the alienation in the activity of labour itself.

What constitutes the alienation of labour?

Firstly, the fact that labour is *external* to the worker, i.e. does not belong to his essential being; that he therefore does not confirm himself in his work, but denies himself, feels miserable and not happy, does not develop free mental and physical energy, but mortifies his flesh and ruins his mind. Hence the worker feels himself only when he is not working; when he is working he does not feel himself. He is at home when he is not working, and not at home when he is working. His labour is therefore not voluntary but forced, it is *forced labour*. It is therefore not the satisfaction of a need but a mere *means* to satisfy needs outside itself. Its alien character is clearly demonstrated by the fact that as soon as no physical or other compulsion exists it is shunned like the plague. External labour, labour in which man alienates himself, is a labour of self-sacrifice, of mortification. Finally, the external character of labour for the worker is demonstrated by the fact that it belongs not to him but to another, and that in it he belongs not to himself but to another. Just as in religion the spontaneous activity of the human imagination, the human brain and the human heart detaches itself from the individual and reappears as the alien activity of a god or of a devil, so the activity of the worker is not his own spontaneous activity. It belongs to another, it is a loss of his self.

The result is that man (the worker) feels that he is acting freely only in his animal functions – eating, drinking and procreating, or at most in his dwelling and adornment – while in his human functions he is nothing more than an animal.

It is true that eating, drinking and procreating, etc., are also genuine human functions. However, when abstracted from other aspects of human activity and turned into final and exclusive ends, they are animal.

We have considered the act of estrangement of practical human activity, of labour, from two aspects: (1) the relationship of the worker to the *product of labour* as an alien object that has power over him. This relationship is at the same time the relationship to the sensuous external world, to natural objects, as an alien world confronting him in hostile opposition. (2) The relationship of labour to the *act of production* within *labour*. This relationship is the relationship of the worker to his own activity as something which is alien and does not belong to him, activity as passivity [*Leiden*], power as impotence, procreation as emasculation, the worker's *own* physical and mental energy, his personal life – for what is life but activity? – as an activity directed against himself, which is independent of him and does not belong to him. *Self-estrangement*, as compared with the estrangement of the *object* [*Sache*] mentioned above.

We now have to derive a third feature of *estranged labour* from the two we have already looked at.

Man is a species-being, not only because he practically and theoretically makes the species – both his own and those of other things – his object, but also – and this is simply another way of saying the same thing – because he looks upon himself as the present, living species, because he looks upon himself as a *universal* and therefore free being.

Species-life, both for man and for animals, consists physically in the fact that man, like animals, lives from inorganic nature; and because man is more universal than animals, so too is the area of inorganic nature from which he lives more universal. Just as plants, animals, stones, air, light, etc., theoretically form a part of human consciousness, partly as objects of science and partly as objects of art – his spiritual inorganic nature, his spiritual means of life, which he must first prepare before he can enjoy and digest them – so too in practice they form a part of human life and human activity. In a physical sense man lives only from these natural products, whether in the form of nourishment, heating, clothing, shelter, etc. The universality of man manifests itself in practice in that universality which makes the whole of nature his *inorganic* body, (1) as a direct means of life and (2) as the matter, the object and the tool of his life activity. Nature is man's *inorganic body*, that is to say nature in so far as it is not the human body. Man *lives* from nature, i.e. nature is his *body*, and he must maintain a continuing dialogue with it if he is not to die. To say that man's physical and mental life is linked to nature simply means that nature is linked to itself, for man is a part of nature.

Estranged labour not only (1) estranges nature from man and (2) estranges man from himself, from his own active function, from his vital activity; because of this it also estranges man from his *species*. It turns his *species-life* into a means for his individual life. Firstly it estranges species-life and individual life, and secondly it turns the latter, in its abstract form, into the purpose of the former, also in its abstract and estranged form.

For in the first place labour, *life activity*, *productive life* itself appears to man only as a *means* for the satisfaction of a need, the need to preserve physical existence. But productive life is species-life. It is life-producing life. The whole character of a species, its species-character, resides in the nature of its life activity, and free conscious activity constitutes the species-character of man. Life itself appears only as a *means of life*.

The animal is immediately one with its life activity. It is not distinct from that activity; it *is* that activity. Man makes his life activity itself an object of his will and consciousness. He has conscious life activity. It is not a determination with which he directly merges. Conscious life activity directly distinguishes man from animal life activity. Only because of that is he a species-being. Or rather, he is a conscious being, i.e. his own life is an object for him, only because he is a species-being. Only because of that is his activity free activity. Estranged labour reverses the relationship so that man, just because he is a conscious being, makes his life activity, his *being* [*Wesen*], a mere means for his *existence*.

The practical creation of an *objective world*, the *fashioning* of inorganic nature, is proof that man is a conscious species-being, i.e. a being which treats the species as its own essential being or itself as a species-being. It is true that animals also produce. They build nests and dwellings, like the bee, the beaver, the ant, etc. But they produce only their own immediate needs or those of their young; they produce one-sidedly, while man produces universally; they produce only when immediate physical need compels them to do so, while man produces even when he is free from physical need and truly produces only in freedom from such need; they produce only themselves, while man reproduces the whole of nature; their products belong immediately to their physical bodies, while man freely confronts his own product. Animals produce only according to the standards and needs of the species to which they belong, while man is capable of producing according to the standards of every species and of applying to each object its inherent standard; hence man also produces in accordance with the laws of beauty.

It is therefore in his fashioning of the objective that man really proves himself to be a *species-being*. Such production is his active species-life. Through it nature appears as *his* work and his reality. The object of labour is therefore the *objectification of the species-life of man*: for man reproduces himself not only intellectually, in his consciousness, but actively and actually, and he can therefore contemplate himself in a world he himself has created. In tearing away the object of his production from man, estranged labour therefore tears away from him his *species-life*, his true species-objectivity, and transforms his advantage over animals into the disadvantage that his inorganic body, nature, is taken from him.

In the same way as estranged labour reduces spontaneous and free activity to a means, it makes man's species-life a means of his physical existence.

Consciousness, which man has from his species, is transformed through estrangement so that species-life becomes a means for him.

3. Estranged labour therefore turns *man's species-being* – both nature and his intellectual species-powers – into a being *alien* to him and a *means* of his *individual existence*. It estranges man from his own body, from nature as it exists outside him, from his spiritual essence [*Wesen*], his *human* essence.

4. An immediate consequence of man's estrangement from the product of his labour, his life activity, his species-being, is the *estrangement of man from man*. When man confronts himself, he also confronts *other* men. What is true of man's relationship to his labour, to the product of his labour and to himself, is also true of his relationship to other men, and to the labour and the object of the labour of other men.

In general, the proposition that man is estranged from his species-being means that each man is estranged from the others and that all are estranged from man's essence.

Man's estrangement, like all relationships of man to himself, is realized and expressed only in man's relationship to other men.

[. . .]

If the product of labour does not belong to the worker, and if it confronts him as an alien power, this is only possible because it belongs to *a man other than the worker*. If his activity is a torment for him, it must provide *pleasure* and enjoyment for someone else. Not the gods, not nature, but only man himself can be this alien power over men.

Consider the above proposition that the relationship of man to himself becomes *objective* and *real* for him only through his relationship to other men. If therefore he regards the product of his labour, his objectified labour, as an *alien*, *hostile* and powerful object which is independent of him, then his relationship to that object is such that another man – alien, hostile, powerful and independent of him – is its master. If he relates to his own activity as unfree activity, then he relates to it as activity in the service, under the rule, coercion and yoke of another man.

[. . .]

Thus through *estranged, alienated labour* the worker creates the relationship of another man, who is alien to labour and stands outside it, to that labour. The relation of the worker to labour creates the relation of the capitalist – or whatever other word one chooses for the master of labour – to that labour. *Private property* is therefore the product, result and necessary consequence of *alienated labour*, of the external relation of the worker to nature and to himself.

Private property thus derives from an analysis of the concept of *alienated labour*, i.e. *alienated man*, estranged labour, estranged life, *estranged man*.

It is true that we took the concept of *alienated labour* (*alienated life*) from political economy as a result of the *movement of private property*. But it is clear from an analysis of this concept that, although private property appears as the basis and cause of alienated labour, it is in fact its consequence, just as the gods were *originally* not the cause but the effect of the confusion in men's minds. Later, however, this relationship becomes reciprocal.

It is only when the development of private property reaches its ultimate point of culmination that this its secret re-emerges: namely, that it is (a) the *product* of alienated labour and (b) the *means* through which labour is alienated, the *realization of this alienation*.

This development throws light upon a number of hitherto unresolved controversies.

1. Political economy starts out from labour as the real soul of production, and yet gives nothing to labour and everything to private property. Proudhon has dealt with this contradiction by deciding for labour and against private property.[1] But we have seen that this apparent contradiction is the contradiction of *estranged labour* with itself and that political economy has merely formulated the laws of estranged labour.

It therefore follows for us that *wages* and *private property* are identical: for where the product, the object of labour, pays for the labour itself, wages are only a necessary consequence of the estrangement of labour; similarly, where wages are concerned, labour appears not as an end in itself but as the servant of wages. We intend to deal with this point in more detail later on: for the present we shall merely draw a few conclusions.

An enforced *rise in wages* (disregarding all other difficulties, including the fact that such an anomalous situation could only be prolonged by force) would therefore be nothing more than better *pay for slaves* and would not mean an increase in human significance or dignity for either the worker or the labour.

Even the *equality of wages*, which Proudhon demands, would merely transform the relation of the present-day worker to his work into the relation of all men to work. Society would then be conceived as an abstract capitalist.

Wages are an immediate consequence of estranged labour, and estranged labour is the immediate cause of private property. If the one falls, then the other must fall too.

2. It further follows from the relation of estranged labour to private property that the emancipation of society from private property, etc., from

servitude, is expressed in the *political* form of the *emancipation of the workers*. This is not because it is only a question of their emancipation, but because in their emancipation is contained universal human emancipation. The reason for this universality is that the whole of human servitude is involved in the relation of the worker to production, and all relations of servitude are nothing but modifications and consequences of this relation.

Just as we have arrived at the concept of *private property* through an analysis of the concept of *estranged, alienated labour*, so with the help of these two factors it is possible to evolve all economic *categories*, and in each of these categories, e.g. trade, competition, capital, money, we shall identify only a *particular* and *developed expression* of these basic constituents.

But before we go on to consider this configuration let us try to solve two further problems.

1. We have to determine the general *nature* of *private property*, as it has arisen out of estranged labour, in its relation to *truly human* and *social property*.

2. We have taken the *estrangement of labour*, its *alienation*, as a fact and we have analysed that fact. How, we now ask, does *man* come *to alienate his labour*, to estrange it? How is this estrangement founded in the nature of human development? We have already gone a long way towards solving this problem by *transforming* the question of the *origin* of *private property* into the question of the relationship of *alienated labour* to the course of human development. For in speaking of *private property* one imagines that one is dealing with something external to man. In speaking of labour one is dealing immediately with man himself. This new way of formulating the problem already contains its solution.

ad (1): The general nature of private property and its relationship to truly human property.

Alienated labour has resolved itself for us into two component parts which mutually condition one another, or which are merely different expressions of one and the same relationship. *Appropriation* appears as *estrangement*, as *alienation*; and *alienation* appears as *appropriation*, *estrangement* as true *admission to citizenship*.

We have considered the one aspect, *alienated* labour in relation to the *worker* himself, i.e. the *relation of alienated labour to itself*. And as product, as necessary consequence of this relationship we have found the *property relation of the non-worker* to the *worker and to labour*. *Private property* as the material, summarized expression of alienated labour embraces both relations – the *relation of the worker to labour and to the product of his labour and the non-worker* and the relation of the *non-worker to the worker* and to *the product of his labour*.

We have already seen that, in relation to the worker who *appropriates* nature through his labour, appropriation appears as estrangement, self-activity as activity for another and of another, vitality as a sacrifice of life, production of an object as loss of that object to an alien power, to an *alien* man. Let us now consider the relation between this man, who is *alien* to labour and to the worker, and the worker, labour, and the object of labour.

The first thing to point out is that everything which appears for the worker as an *activity of alienation, of estrangement*, appears for the non-worker as a *situation of alienation, of estrangement*.

Secondly, the *real, practical attitude* of the worker in production and to the product (as a state of mind) appears for the non-worker who confronts him as a *theoretical* attitude.

Thirdly, the non-worker does everything against the worker which the worker does against himself, but he does not do against himself what he does against the worker.

NOTE

1. In the pamphlet entitled *Qu'est-ce que la propriété?*, Paris, 1840.

RECENT THEORIES OF THE CAPITALIST STATE

Bob Jessop

The Classic Texts on the State

It is commonplace that Marx did not offer a theoretical analysis of the capitalist state to match the scope and rigour of *Das Kapital*. His work on the state comprises a fragmented and unsystematic series of philosophical reflections, contemporary history, journalism and incidental remarks. It is not surprising, therefore, that Marx rarely focuses directly on the complex relations between the state apparatus, state power, capital accumulation and its social preconditions. But it is less often remarked that the same is true of other classical Marxist theorists, such as Engels, Lenin, Trotsky and Gramsci. For, although they offer various acute observations on the state in general, specific historical cases, and the nature of ideological domination, they do not confront the crucial question of the differential forms of the capitalist state and their adequacy to continued accumulation in different situations. Indeed, in so far as the classic texts do focus on this issue, they do so in inconsistent ways. There are at least six different approaches, and, although they are often combined with varying degrees of consistency and mutual qualification, they involve different theoretical assumptions, principles of explanation and political implications. They must therefore be considered separately before one can draw any general conclusions about the classical approach as a whole.

Bob Jessop (1977), 'Recent theories of the capitalist state', *Cambridge Journal of Economics*, 1.

1. Marx originally treated the modern state (at least that in 19th-century Prussia) as a *parasitic* institution that played no essential role in economic production or reproduction. In his view, democratic government would be characterised by a genuine unity of state and people, whereas the modern state was an expression of the irreconcilable conflicts rooted in the egoism of civil society. In this context, the state and its officials, far from representing the common interest, tend to exploit and oppress civil society on behalf of particular sectional groups. Indeed, Marx argues that, just as corporate organisation enables the bourgeoisie and master craftsmen to defend their material interests, the state becomes the private property of officials in their struggle for self-advancement (Marx 1970: especially 44–54; see also Hunt 1975: 124). This view was elaborated in his critique of Hegel's political theories, when the young Marx was still committed to liberal radical political ideas. Nor had he then developed the conception of capitalism as a mode of production and so could not identify the specific characteristics of the capitalist state (Althusser 1969: 49–86; 1976: 151–61; Mandel 1971: pp. 52–67 and *passim*). Thereafter, although he retained the basic ideas about the *form* of the modern representative state and its separation from civil society, Marx treated it as a necessary part of the system of class domination rather than as extraneous and parasitic. The latter view can still be found in his subsequent work on Oriental despotism, however, where Marx sometimes treats the Asiatic mode of production as communal in nature and the Asiatic state as a parasitic body standing above society (see particularly Marx 1973b: pp. 471–514 *passim*). But, although the idea that the modern state is essentially parasitic is still held in anarchist circles, it was not long retained by Marx himself.

2. Marx also discusses the state and state power as *epiphenomena* (i.e. simple surface reflections) of the system of property relations and the resulting economic class struggles. This view is again largely confined to the earlier writings, but it emerges occasionally in his later work and occurs frequently in more recent Marxist analyses. It is particularly clear in Marx's early comments on law (in which legal relations are treated as mere expressions of the social relations of production), but is also apparent in more general analyses of political institutions. The most frequently cited illustration of this approach is the 1859 Preface to his *Contribution to the Critique of Political Economy*. This appears to treat law and politics as a superstructure based on the economic infrastructure, to view property relations as the legal expression of relations of production, and to ground revolution on the growing contradiction between forces and relations of production. In general, this approach considers the structure of the state as a surface reflection of a self-sufficient and self-developing economic base. And, since classes are defined in purely economic terms, the exercise of state power is seen as a surface reflection of economic struggle. It also implies that there is a perfect, one-to-one correspondence between juridico-political relations

and economic relations or, at best, some sort of 'lead' or 'lag' between them. It thus reduces the impact of the state to a simple temporal deformation of economic development (typically viewed in terms of the growth of the forces of production) and of economic class struggle (typically viewed in terms of a struggle over the distribution of the product). Thus, although state intervention can accelerate or hinder economic development, the latter is always determinant in the last instance (see particularly, Engels 1954: 253–4, and Marx and Engels 1975: 392–4).

3. Another common approach treats the state as the *factor of cohesion* in a given society. This perspective is closely identified nowadays with Poulantzas, but is also evident in the classic texts. Thus Engels views the state as an institution that emerges *pari passu* with economic exploitation. He argues that its function is to regulate the struggle between antagonistic classes through repression and concession, and thus to moderate class conflict without undermining the continued domination of the ruling class and the reproduction of the dominant mode of production (Engels 1942: 154–63 and *passim*). Lenin adopts the same view in several places (see especially Lenin 1970, *passim*). Bukharin also treats society as a system of unstable equilibrium inside which the state acts as a 'regulator' and Gramsci, albeit from a far less mechanistic position, adopts more or less the same argument on several occasions (Bukharin 1969: 150–54 and *passim*; Gramsci 1971: 206–76). The principal difficulties with this approach are twofold. Firstly, it fails to specify the nature of the state as a factor of cohesion and/or to identify the means through which the state realises this function. Hence the state is defined in functional terms and comes to include every institution which contributes to cohesion (see especially Poulantzas 1973: 44–50). It is impossible to elucidate the class nature of the state in this way. Indeed, far from leading to revolutionary conclusions, it is this view that is most often associated with the idea that the state can 'reconcile' class conflict by acting as a neutral mediator. Secondly, unless one can specify the mechanism of cohesion and its limitations, it becomes difficult to explain the emergence of revolutionary crises and the transition from one epoch to another. In this respect, this sort of approach is so obviously inadequate that it must be complemented and supported with reference to other perspectives.

4. The state is also seen as an *instrument of class rule*. This is the most common approach and is particularly evident in exegeses of Marxism – Leninism. A fundamental problem is the tendency to assume that the state as an instrument is *neutral* and can be used with equal facility and equal effectiveness by any class or social force. This approach also encounters difficulties in situations where the economically dominant class does not actually fill the key positions in the state apparatus (as cited by Marx himself in the case of the landed aristocracy ruling on behalf of capital in 19th-century Britain). The same problem occurs where the state acquires a considerable measure of independence from the dominant class owing to a more or

less temporary equilibrium in the class struggle. This situation is alleged to have occurred in the absolutist state, the Second French Empire under Louis Bonaparte, and the German Reich under Bismarck. In neither case can one explain how the state remains an instrument of class rule even though the dominant class has no immediate control over it. Similar problems occur in the study of 'dual power' in revolutionary situations and in the analysis of transitions between different modes of production.

5. A further approach in the classic Marxist texts is similar to that of orthodox institutional studies in sociology, anthropology and political science. The state is treated as a *set of institutions* and no general assumptions are made about its class character. The state is seen as a 'public power' that develops at a certain stage in the division of labour (usually identified with the emergence of a mode of production based on the exploitation of one class by another) and that involves the emergence of a distinct system of government which is monopolised by officials who specialise in administration and/or repression. This theme is evident in Engels (1942) and Lenin (1970). It can accommodate the objections to the approaches reviewed above and yet leaves open the question of their adequacy in specific situations. It implies that the functions, effects and class nature of the state cannot be determined *a priori*, but depend on the relations between its institutional structure and the class struggle in various circumstances. In the absence of such conjunctural analyses, however, the institutional approach can establish the nature of the state only through a return to more primitive formulations. Thus it tends to be associated with epiphenomenalism (the institutions mirror the economic base) and/or instrumentalism (the institutions are controlled by capital). Moreover, even when it is associated with concrete analyses, the institutional approach may simply lead to descriptive accounts without any attempt to explain what occurs.

6. It is in this context that the sixth approach is especially relevant. It examines the state as a *system of political domination* with specific effects on the class struggle. Thus, whereas the instrumentalist approach focuses on the question of 'who rules', this approach shifts attention to the forms of political representation and state intervention. It examines them as more or less adequate to securing a balance of class forces that is favourable to the long-term interests of a given class or class fraction. It is illustrated in Lenin's remark that a democratic republic is the best possible political shell for capitalism and that, once this form of state is established, no change of persons, institutions or parties can shake the political rule of capital (Lenin 1970: 296; see also Marx and Engels 1975: 350). And it is central to the discussions of the Paris Commune as the model for working-class political domination (see particularly Marx 1974, *passim*, and Lenin, 1970, *passim*). This approach is most fruitful when used in conjunction with an institutional definition of the state. For, although it avoids the difficulties associated with the other approaches reviewed above, it still needs to be

developed and supported by a concrete analysis of institutions. Otherwise it tends to become a sophisticated attempt to establish theoretical guarantees that the state in a capitalist society necessarily functions on behalf of capital. Thus, in opposition to those who argue that the internal organisation of the state can ensure that it functions to reproduce capital (e.g. Offe 1974, *passim*), it is vital to insist that state power can be more or less capitalist depending on the situation.

So nowhere in the Marxist classics do we find a well formulated, coherent and sustained theoretical analysis of the state. This is not to deny that they offer a series of acute historical generalisations and political insights nor, indeed, that they lay the foundations for a more rigorous analysis. In particular, the perspective of political domination (the sixth approach) provides an adequate starting point for studying the state and state power. But much of the renewed discussion still reflects the limitations of the other approaches and fails to develop this insight into the nature of political domination. This is apparent in various ways. Although the state is rarely treated nowadays as a simple epiphenomenon with no real influence, its forms and effects are often explained solely in terms of the 'needs' of the economy. Alternatively, the state may be connected to the economy only as an instrument in the class struggle. Both approaches can be found in association with different views about the economic base. Moreover, some recent work concentrates largely on the political struggle between capital and labour and is therefore relevant to economic questions only to the extent that they are influenced by political factors. This is not to argue that these various economic and political approaches are incorrect, but simply to suggest that one should appreciate their limitations as well as their contributions to the theory of the state. Both facets can be illustrated by considering the early work of Miliband and Poulantzas, the views of the so-called neo-Ricardian theorists, and the study of 'state monopoly capitalism'.

Variations on Some Classical Themes

Miliband and Poulantzas both focus on political and ideological struggles without reference to the economic imperatives and requirements of capital accumulation. This reflects their polemical concerns. Miliband is interested in confronting liberal theorists of democracy with the 'facts' about the social background, personal ties and shared values of economic and political elites, and about the impact of government policy on such matters as the distribution of income and wealth. He also argues that socialisation into the ideology of the ruling class is an important source of political power and social order (Miliband, 1969, *passim*). Because his principal concern is to reveal the distortions and mystifications of liberal pluralism, Miliband does not advance the Marxist analysis of the state. Indeed, he actually reproduces the liberal tendency to discuss politics in isolation from its complex articulation with economic forces. To the extent that he does relate them it is only through interpersonal connections; he neglects their mutual presupposition and interdependence on the institutional level. Thus, Miliband does not succeed in establishing the real nature of the state in capitalist society and its inherent limitations as well as advantages for capital.

Poulantzas is less concerned to disprove liberal democratic theory than to criticise the traditional Communist orthodoxy of 'state monopoly capitalism'. Thus, in opposition to the argument that the modern state is no more than a pliant tool of monopoly capital, he rejects all forms of instrumentalism and insists that the state is a complex social relation. The latter seems to mean two things. Firstly, classes should not be seen as simple economic forces existing outside and independently of the state and capable of manipulating it as a passive instrument or tool. For the political influence of classes and class fractions depends in part on the institutional structure of the state and the effects of state power. Secondly, class struggle is not confined to civil society, but is reproduced within the heart of the state apparatus itself. He also argues that the state has an objective function to perform in maintaining social cohesion so that capital accumulation can proceed unhindered (Poulantzas 1973: 44–50; 1975: 78–81 and *passim*). Thus, Poulantzas criticises Miliband for analysing the state in terms of the individual human subjects who control it, rather than in relation to its structurally determined role in capitalist society (Poulantzas 1969: 67–78).

Unfortunately, although his criticisms of Miliband's analysis and 'state monopoly capitalism' theories are both sound, Poulantzas himself does not produce a wholly satisfactory account of the capitalist state. He defines the state as the factor of cohesion but interprets this in two contrasting ways. Sometimes he suggests that a sufficient condition of cohesion is the successful organisation of a power bloc under the hegemony of monopoly capital (Poulantzas 1974: 72–88; Cutler 1971: 5–15). This suggestion completely ignores the fundamental economic constraints on the effective exercise of state power and implies that the state is an instrument of the power bloc rather than the monopoly sector alone. Elsewhere, Poulantzas adopts the reductionist view that the effects of state power are necessarily circumscribed by the dominance of capitalism so that, in the long run, they can only correspond to the interests of the dominant class (see especially Poulantzas 1969: 67–78; 1976: 63–83). This claim implies that it is totally irrelevant which class controls the state apparatus, since it must maintain cohesion by virtue of its objective function. In short, although he is closely identified with assertions about the relative autonomy of the capitalist state, Poulantzas actually oscillates between two extreme positions. Either he endows the state with complete independence from the economic base or he denies it any independence at all. Neither of these positions would be satisfactory on its own and together they render his analysis indeterminate.

In contrast to the political focus of Miliband and Poulantzas, the so-called neo-Ricardian theorists are explicitly concerned with the economic dimensions of the state. They focus on the influence of the state on the distribution of income between classes, and attempt to show how it intervenes in the economy to maintain or restore corporate profits at the expense of wages. Such action by the state is generally traced back to the pressures on profitability that stem from trade union struggles and/or international competition. The appropriate response in such situations depends on the specific form of the profits squeeze and the balance of class forces. Capital will generally attempt to manipulate the business cycle to discipline labour and reduce wage costs in the interests of corporate profit maximisation (Boddy and Crotty 1974, 1975); and/or to redistribute income to the private sector through fiscal changes, subsidies, nationalisation, devaluation, reflation, wage controls and legal restrictions on trade union activities (Glyn and Sutcliffe 1972); and/or to counter the inflationary effects of tax increases and public borrowing through cuts in public spending on the 'social wage' (Gough 1975). In contrast, the working class will attempt to resist such offensive actions by capital (Boddy and Crotty 1974: 12) and, hopefully, to transform the wages struggle and/or the opposition to the 'cuts' into a successful revolutionary movement (Glyn and Sutcliffe 1972: 189–216; Gough 1975: pp. 91–2). But the dominant position of capital in the state, and especially in the field of economic policy-making, means that it is the capitalist solution to economic crises that is imposed (Boddy and Crotty 1975, *passim*).

Such studies certainly have radical overtones and do relate state intervention to the needs of capital. But the neo-Ricardian approach is still limited in its treatment of the nature of capitalism as a mode of production and of the class character of the state. For it neglects the significance of the social relations of production and the characteristic form of capitalist exploitation through the creation and appropriation of surplus-value. This means that it tends to treat the labour process as purely technical and to relate the distribution of income to the price of labour as determined within the sphere of circulation. This places distributional struggles at the heart of neo-Ricardian analyses, rather than the struggle at the point of production, and this is reflected in the tendency to discuss state intervention in terms of income distribution and to neglect the state's fundamental role in the restructuring of production. Thus, not only does this kind of analysis imply that wage restraint and/or public spending cuts are sufficient to resolve crises, it also fails totally to confront and explain the causes, nature and limitations of growing state involvement in production itself. This is not to deny the importance of the struggle to determine wages (whether seen as the price of labour or the value of labour-power). It is to insist that an exclusive focus on one part of the circuit of capital can never provide the basis for understanding the nature of capitalist crises or state intervention.

However, despite the apparent institutional separation of the economic, political and ideological levels in capitalist societies, they are closely related. Thus economic crises necessarily have repercussions on the other levels (and vice versa) so that a restructuring of the state as a system of political domination may be a precondition of solving an economic crisis. It is in this context that concepts such as crises of political representation and ideological hegemony are particularly relevant. For these signify the dissociation of political struggle from the established organs of representation and the dissolution of hegemony, resulting in the detachment of the masses from bourgeois political and ideological leadership (Poulantzas 1974: 62–5, 71–8 and *passim*). In such situations, the bourgeois democratic republic may prove inadequate to securing the conditions necessary for accumulation. Whether it is regenerated or replaced by another form of state depends on the strategies adopted by different political forces and their relative strengths. But there can be no guarantee that new forms of domination will prove more adequate to securing such conditions or, in revolutionary situations, the conditions for a successful transition to a different form of society.

It is the merit of the neo-Gramscian school to have developed certain concepts for the analysis of specific capitalist societies and not just of capitalism considered as a pure mode of production. But its analyses are often vitiated by a systematic neglect of the economic constraints rooted in the nature of capital accumulation. For, though it is well aware of the various forms of class struggle and popular-democratic struggle, it is not as concerned with the general laws of capitalist production. This results in a certain unevenness and asymmetry in the work of the school and points to the need to integrate the different approaches.

CONCLUDING REMARKS

This review has tried to locate the position of the state in Marxist discourse and to assess the adequacy of various theoretical approaches to its study in capitalist societies. Marxist theories are heterogeneous in approach, but are unified through a common concern with specific modes of production, their conditions of existence and their effects on social formations. They are not concerned to develop a theory of the mode of production 'in general' nor, *a fortiori*, a theory of the state (or society) 'in general'. It is also debatable whether it is possible to develop a theory of the capitalist state in general. For, since capitalism exists neither in pure form nor in isolation, states in capitalist societies will necessarily differ from one another.

It is in this context that we can best appreciate the above studies. For their overall effect has been to redefine the problem of the state in capitalist society in a way that makes theoretical and political progress possible once more. They have dissolved the orthodox approaches in terms of the state as a thing or a subject that is external to the capitalist mode of production. In their place, they have focused attention on the social nature of capitalist production and its complex economic, political and ideological preconditions. This means that the state and state power must assume a central role in capital accumulation, even in those apparently counterfactual cases characterised by a neutral, *laissez-faire* state, as well as those where the state is massively involved in the organisation of production. Moreover, because the state is seen as a complex institutional system and the influence of classes is seen to depend on their forms of organisation, alliances, etc., it is also necessary to reject a crude instrumentalist approach. It is no longer a question of how pre-existing classes use the state (or the state itself acts) in defence of capitalism defined at an economic level. Henceforth it is a question of the adequacy of state power as a necessary element in the overall reproduction of the capital relation in different societies and situations. And state power in turn must be considered as a complex, contradictory effect of class (and popular-democratic) struggles, mediated through and conditioned by the institutional system of the state. In short, the effect of these studies is to reinstate and elaborate the idea that the state is a system of political domination.

But the interest of these studies is not restricted to the field of Marxist theory and politics. For the problems with which they have been grappling occur in similar forms in non-Marxist economic and political enquiries. It is not specific points of economic analysis that are at issue here, but the adequacy of certain common assumptions concerning the nature of the state, its role in economic activity, and the relevance of orthodox economic theories in the light of that role. Either the nature of the state is seen as irrelevant to economic theory as such and regarded as a factor that shapes and limits the application of economic principles in given conditions. Or, it being recognised that its exclusion from economic theory is arbitrary and unjustifiable, the state is all too often treated simply as a subject comparable to a firm or household, or as a set of neutral policy instruments applicable to various economic goals, or as the private property of rational, maximising, self-interested political actors. The precise implications of these latter approaches depend on the other assumptions with which they are combined. Thus in its theoretical guise as a subject the state may be seen as a legal sovereign that controls economic activity, as a referee or umpire that intervenes in economic disputes, as one economic agent among others, or as a political agent whose actions may promote or hinder economic performance. The instruments – goals approach is generally associated with technical disputes over the appropriate forms and direction of intervention and with political disputes about the role of the state in the allocation and redistribution of resources. And the model of '*homo politicus*' tends to be linked with claims that the self-interest of state personnel is inimical to economic growth. Now, although these approaches illuminate certain aspects of the state, they do not advance political economy in any fundamental way. For they deal at best with the surface phenomena of politics and have no theoretical means to explore the deeper connections between the state and economic development.

It is here that the recent Marxist debate has major implications for orthodox economics. For it establishes that capitalism is a specific mode of the social organisation of production and has definite historical preconditions and forms of development. It also establishes that the state has an essential role in securing these preconditions and that its institutional structure and forms of intervention must be transformed as capitalism changes and develops. The recent discussion further argues that the economic state apparatuses and their means of intervention are not neutral, but are integrated into the movement of capital and constitute a field of conflict between different interests. This means that state intervention has inherent limitations in securing the conditions for capital accumulation and is always subject to the inevitable influence of various class and popular-democratic struggles. It also means that the adequacy of particular policy instruments and general forms of intervention will vary not only with changes in economic structure but also with changes in the balance of political forces. Related to these arguments is the further point that the forms of political representation also have distinct effects on the efficacy of different forms of intervention. This in turn implies that the failure of specific policy measures or general instruments may be due to the inadequacy of the forms of political representation with which they are linked, rather than to mistaken economic analysis. It means as well that the reorganisation of the state apparatus may be necessary before economic problems or crises can be resolved. The current debate about industrial democracy, the 'social contract' and the development of tripartite or corporatist institutions is particularly germane here.

In short, the overall thrust of these studies is to suggest that the analysis of the state is not an activity irrelevant or marginal to economic theory. It is not something that can be consigned safely to another discipline within an intellectual division of labour, or to a future date in the development of economics itself. It is rather an absolute precondition of adequate economic theorising today. Economics must therefore take up the challenge of the continuing Marxist debate and counterpose its own solutions, if any, to the problems with which the latter deals. It is high time that orthodox economics renewed its traditional role as the science of political economy. Failure to do so will surely be tantamount to a self-declaration of theoretical poverty in a fundamental area of economic analysis and a primary concern of political practice.

Part 2

GRAMSCI: THEORIST OF HEGEMONY

INTRODUCTION

I. The Context

Although Gramsci stands in the Marxist tradition and was a political activist who was imprisoned by the Italian fascists, his work, to some degree, can be seen as a response to Marx and the perceived weaknesses of an overly economic approach to social theory. It is perhaps fairer to say that he was reacting against Marx's heirs, who were attempting to apply Marx and Engels in a 'scientific' way to explain laws of society. He was also responding to his own situation and his *Prison Notebooks* attempt an analysis of the weaknesses of Italian society and the reasons for the triumph of fascism. His notebooks, understandably, are far from consistent, and it is possible to develop any number of interpretations of his arguments. But if we focus on the concept of hegemony for which he is best known we can see how Gramsci's project is to combine Marxist economic analysis with a greater emphasis on the political and cultural processes. Drawing on a tradition of Italian writers, most notably Machiavelli and Croce, Gramsci attempts to develop a concept that can explain why certain groups can come to power and how they construct and maintain social, cultural and moral leadership. Against economic determinism, he argues that hegemony does not automatically derive from the dominant economic position of the ruling class, but is something that has to be actively constructed and fought for. He argues against the view that domination is primarily based on power and coercion and stresses instead the need for the leading groups to win the consent of the wider masses. This leads, among other things, to a greater emphasis on the positive role of ideas and ideology and constitutes a shifting away of the emphasis from the economic base to the superstructural level of ideology, politics and culture and to how these, as much as economic factors, are responsible for maintaining social cohesion and consent.

II. Early Work

All the selections below are taken from Gramsci's *Prison Notebooks*. Prior to imprisonment, Gramsci was a leader of the Italian Communist Party and was much concerned with how different social conditions affected the possibilities of taking power in different societies. Gramsci was of course interested in the peculiarities of the Italian situation and what possibilities the weakness of the bourgeoisie would allow the Communists. It would seem that the relative backwardness of Italian capitalism would hinder revolutionary prospects, for had not Marx written that 'no social order is ever destroyed before all the productive forces for which it is sufficient have been developed' (Marx 1975a: 426)? Yet Gramsci could look to the Russian situation to see how social change need not have to wait for a corresponding level of economic development. On the contrary, it seemed to be that the very backwardness of Russian economic development was a condition of possibility for social transformation. The young Gramsci thus took economic determinism to task, arguing that the revolution in Russia constituted a 'revolution against Marx' and that

> in Russia, Marx's *Capital* was more the book of the bourgeoisie than of the proletariat. It stood as the critical demonstration of how events should follow a pre-determined course: how in Russia a bourgeoisie had to develop, and a capitalist era had to open, with the setting up of a Western-type civilisation, before the proletariat could even think in terms of its own revolt, its own demands, its own revolution. But events have overcome ideologies. Events have exploded the critical schemas determining how the history of Russia would unfold according to the cannons of historical materialism. (Gramsci 1977: 34)

The Bolsheviks are a living breed of Marxists who conceive of the active role of classes as able to overcome economic factors. Instead of relying on pre-determined economic schemas, Gramsci stresses a more active conception of history that 'sees as the dominant factor in history, not raw economic facts, but man, men in societies, men in relation to one another, reaching agreements with one another, developing through these contacts (civilisation) a collective, social will' (Gramsci 1977: 34–5).

Yet it is not the case that Gramsci rejects economic factors as playing a significant role. Rather, he is concerned to find the right balance between economic conditions and the development of political forces, culture and ideas. This results in the development of the concept of hegemony, where the dominance of a social group is not given by economic conditions but has to be actively constructed by means of moral and political leadership.

III. The Modern Prince

Gramsci restores the active element to politics by drawing on Machiavelli and renaming the Communist Party the 'Modern Prince'. Marxism is renamed the 'philosophy of praxis', emphasising the role of meaningful human action rather than economic determinism. Machiavelli's approach is described as a 'neo-humanism', which 'bases itself entirely on the concrete action of man, who, impelled by historical necessity, works and transforms reality' (Gramsci 1971: 249).

In *The Prince* Machiavelli is concerned with how rulers might adopt a strategy to create and maintain civil unity and order. From these discussions Gramsci inherits the notion of force and consent best represented by the hybrid centaur, half animal and half human. The animal half corresponds to force, violence and authority, while the human part represents consent, civilisation and hegemony (Gramsci 1971: 170). Machiavelli distinguishes between rulership by force and rulership through the moral and intellectual power that he calls *virtù*. To become dominant and civilised, it is necessary to possess moral and intellectual authority.

The influence of Machiavelli allows Gramsci to develop his conception of Marxism as a politics of statecraft, tactics and strategy. Economic developments alone will not put the Communists in power for they need to win over the masses by moral and intellectual argument. Marxism must engage with existing consciousness if its own worldview is to gain broader acceptance. This corresponds to Machiavelli's emphasis on the need to develop a popular will. But it must be combined with the more calculating aspects of Machiavelli's advice so that the Modern Prince must assess the possibilities inherent in a given situation and decide how best to act.

IV. Hegemony: State and Civil Society, Coercion and Consent

The distinction between private and public spheres, or state and civil society, has long concerned Marxists. Whereas Marx tends to see civil society as the private sphere of property relations, Gramsci sees it as something with its own cultural and intellectual properties, a sphere into which hegemony must penetrate if it is to gain influence. Gramsci's concept of hegemony is concerned with the level of consent reached in civil society and this is often contrasted with the more coercive sphere of political society or the state. This must be a rough distinction, however, and the fragmented nature of the *Prison Notebooks* does not help in developing a consistent view on this. Perhaps the easiest way to understand this distinction is to take Gramsci's discussion of the different situations in the East (in particular Russia) and the West. Whereas in the East, a direct confrontation with the state is required, in the West it is necessary for revolutionaries to gain consent within civil society in order to confront the powerful fortresses and earthworks that the bourgeoisie has at its disposal. Gramsci reinforces this distinction by talking of two different types of strategy – the war of positions and the war of manoeuvre. The latter is a frontal assault that might be compared to the seizure of power by the Bolsheviks. In the West, with its more cohesive and integrated society, a more prolonged and tactical battle is necessary which must be conducted through the institutions of civil society.

To carry most influence social groups must work through the state, which has an ethical function in offering its apparatus for the dissemination of various ideas, norms and values. The state plays a leading and directing role in organising consent throughout civil society. As Gramsci writes, 'every state is ethical in as much as one of its most important functions is to raise the great mass of the population to a particular cultural and moral level' (Gramsci 1971: 258). However, Gramsci goes on to link this to the need to relate to the sphere of production. Therefore, although the concept of hegemony acts as a counterbalance to crude economic determinism, Gramsci does not deny the importance of the economy in shaping this process. Therefore

> the fact of hegemony presupposes that account be taken of the interests and the tendencies of the groups over which hegemony is to be exercised, and that a certain compromise equilibrium should be formed – in other words, that the leading group should make sacrifices of an economic-corporate kind . . . though hegemony is ethical-political, it must also be economic, must necessarily be based on the decisive function exercised by the leading group in the decisive nucleus of economic activity. (Gramsci 1971: 161)

V. Historical Bloc and Hegemonic Crisis

The development of a historical bloc is a long-term process whereby different social forces come together. A ruling alliance develops by incorporating some groups into a ruling bloc while offering concessions and incentives to supporting classes. However, this all takes place within a structural context – the relationship between the economic structure and the politico-ethical superstructure – so that developments at the level of culture and politics must be related back to developments at the level of production. Not just any social group can put itself forward as leading – it must have behind it the economic, political and cultural conditions that allow it to emerge as a leading force. These conditions both enable and constrain what a particular bloc can achieve.

One way of understanding this is through Gramsci's notion of the passive revolution. This indicates how social groups may strengthen their social position on the back of underlying developments in production. In Italy the industrialisation of the north and the introduction of new methods of production were radically altering social life. However, these radical changes present real threats to the stability of society. The ruling group must try to encourage social change without encouraging mass participation in social life. The revolution is passive because it reflects the weakness of the ruling bloc and the need to exclude the masses from active participation. Concessions are made in order to ward off the threat of emerging forces and outflank radical alternatives. The passive revolution is the manipulation of a developing situation by the ruling group based on taking advantage of underlying changes while absorbing the opposition. These forces often cultivate the notion of modernisation or transformation, but the real aim of the passive revolution is the maintenance of the status quo.

In analysing the situation in Italy, Gramsci is concerned with how a weak historical bloc could lead to the triumph of fascism. The Italian state was founded on a restrictive hegemonic base while the compromise between the urban industrial north and the agrarian south was responsible for a weak political unity. He explains the rise of fascism in terms of a hegemonic crisis where the masses become detached from their traditional parties and beliefs:

> At a certain point in their historical lives, social classes become detached from their traditional parties... When such crises occur, the immediate situation becomes delicate and dangerous, because the field is open for violent solutions, for the activities of unknown forces, represented by charismatic 'men of destiny'. (Gramsci 1971: 210)

The situation in Italy should therefore be seen as an example of a major hegemonic crisis or breakdown of social cohesion and consent which occurs 'either because the ruling class has failed in some major political undertaking... or because huge masses... have passed suddenly from a state of political passivity to a certain activity' (Gramsci 1971: 210). The crisis of hegemony is for Gramsci a crisis of authority and a crisis of the state. It presents major dangers but also the opportunity for a new hegemony to emerge should this be able to take advantage of the situation.

VI. Intellectuals and Production

Gramsci links the construction of hegemony to the ideological struggle to win the masses. A crucial role in this struggle goes to the intellectuals. The various social groups each have their own particular worldview or outlook and the intellectual is crucial in articulating this to wider layers. Whether this can be done depends on whether the intellectual is 'organic' – which is to say, whether the intellectuals are rooted in social strata. Gramsci is therefore employing a functional definition of intellectuals that relates them to their social role, whether in the field of production, or in that of culture, or in that of political administration. In linking the role of intellectuals to the sphere of production, Gramsci starts to investigate the role of education and training in shaping the modern worker. This links to Gramsci's ideas on more intensive work methods.

The terms 'Fordism' and 'Taylorism' describe how the production process is organised through new developments in technology and management. The Ford Motor Company introduced techniques of conveyor belt mass production which in turn created the products for a new consumer society. For Gramsci these developments have a wider social character which he describes as Americanism. Gramsci starts with how hegemony is 'born in the factory' (Gramsci 1971: 285) with the specialisation of the production and an increasingly complex division of labour requiring social education and training. Americanism requires a particular environment, social structure and type of state (Gramsci 1971: 293). The 'Fordist' state plays an active role in developing the economy and civil society. The interventionist or regulatory role of the state is backed up with underlying changes in economic production and the cooption of the organisations of the working class. Fordism, therefore, might be seen as a particular example of passive revolution:

> through the legislative intervention of the State, and by means of the corporative organisation – relatively far-reaching modifications are being introduced into the country's economic structure in order to accentuate the 'plan of production' element; in other words, that socialisation of and co-operation in the sphere of production are being increased, without however touching (or at least not going beyond the regulation and control of) individual and group appropriation of profit. (Gramsci 1971: 120)

Gramsci argues that in Italy this passive revolution is attempting to develop the productive forces of industry under the leadership of the traditional ruling classes. Gramsci analyses the development of superstructure in accordance with structure, where 'what is involved is the reorganisation of the structure and the real relations between men on the one hand and the world of the economy or of production on the other' (Gramsci 1971: 263). But at the same time, this combination of factors undermines the view that economic forces are all powerful. Economic processes are tendencies that are affected by counteracting forces (Gramsci 1995: 429); therefore Taylorism and Fordism, while confirming the importance of the economic structure, are also examples of attempts to overcome these tendential laws (Gramsci 1995: 433). The issue to be discussed now becomes the degree of success in overcoming such tendencies and the question of what replaces Fordism once it starts to fail in this task.

THE MODERN PRINCE: BRIEF NOTES ON MACHIAVELLI'S POLITICS

Antonio Gramsci

The basic thing about *The Prince* is that it is not a systematic treatment, but a 'live' work, in which political ideology and political science are fused in the dramatic form of a 'myth'. Before Machiavelli, political science had taken the form either of the Utopia or of the scholarly treatise. Machiavelli, combining the two; gave imaginative and artistic form to his conception by embodying the doctrinal, rational element in the person of a *condottiere*,[1] who represents plastically and 'anthropomorphically' the symbol of the 'collective will'. In order to represent the process whereby a given collective will, directed towards a given political objective, is formed, Machiavelli did not have recourse to long-winded arguments, or pedantic classifications of principles and criteria for a method of action. Instead he represented this process in terms of the qualities, characteristics, duties and requirements of a concrete individual. Such a procedure stimulates the artistic imagination of those who have to be convinced, and gives political passions a more concrete form.*

Antonio Gramsci (1971), 'The Modern Prince: brief notes on Machiavelli's politics', in *Selections from the Prison Notebooks*, ed. and tr. Quintin Hoare and Geoffrey Nowell Smith, London: Lawrence and Wishart.

* One will have to look through the political writers who preceded Machiavelli, to see whether there had been other examples of such personification before *The Prince*. The 'mythical' character of the book to which I have referred is due also to its conclusion; having described the ideal *condottiere*, Machiavelli here, in a passage of great artistic effect, invokes the real *condottiere* who is to incarnate him historically.[2] This passionate invocation reflects back on the entire book, and is precisely what gives it its dramatic character. L. Russo, in his *Prolegomeni*,[3] calls Machiavelli the artist of politics, and once even uses the word 'myth', but not exactly in the sense just indicated.

Machiavelli's *Prince* could be studied as an historical exemplification of the Sorelian myth[4] – i.e. of a political ideology expressed neither in the form of a cold utopia nor as learned theorising, but rather by a creation of concrete phantasy which acts on a dispersed and shattered people to arouse and organise its collective will. The utopian character of *The Prince* lies in the fact that the Prince had no real historical existence; he did not present himself immediately and objectively to the Italian people, but was a pure theoretical abstraction – a symbol of the leader and ideal *condottiere*. However, in a dramatic movement of great effect, the elements of passion and of myth which occur throughout the book are drawn together and brought to life in the conclusion, in the invocation of a prince who 'really exists'. Throughout the book, Machiavelli discusses what the Prince must be like if he is to lead a people to found a new State; the argument is developed with rigorous logic, and with scientific detachment. In the conclusion, Machiavelli merges with the people, becomes the people; not, however, some 'generic' people, but the people whom he, Machiavelli, has convinced by the preceding argument – the people whose consciousness and whose expression he becomes and feels himself to be, with whom he feels identified. The entire 'logical' argument now appears as nothing other than auto-reflection on the part of the people – an inner reasoning worked out in the popular consciousness, whose conclusion is a cry of passionate urgency. The passion, from discussion of itself, becomes once again 'emotion', fever, fanatical desire for action. This is why the epilogue of *The Prince* is not something extrinsic, tacked on, rhetorical, but has to be understood as a necessary element of the work – indeed as the element which gives the entire work its true colour, and makes it a kind of 'political manifesto'.

[...]

The modern prince, the myth-prince, cannot be a real person, a concrete individual. It can only be an organism, a complex element of society in which a collective will, which has already been recognised and has to some extent asserted itself in action, begins to take concrete form. History has already provided this organism, and it is the political party – the first cell in which there come together germs of a collective will tending to become universal and total. In the modern world, only those historico-political actions which are immediate and imminent, characterised by the necessity for lightning speed, can be incarnated mythically by a concrete individual. Such speed can only be made necessary by a great and imminent danger, a great danger which precisely fans passion and fanaticism suddenly to a white heat, and annihilates the critical sense and the corrosive irony which are able to destroy the 'charismatic' character of the *condottiere* (as happened in the Boulanger adventure).[5] But an improvised action of such a kind, by its very nature, cannot have a long-term and organic character. It will in almost all cases be appropriate to restoration and reorganisation, but not to the founding of new States or new national and social structures (as was at issue in Machiavelli's *Prince*, in which the theme of restoration was merely a rhetorical element, linked to the literary concept of an Italy descended from Rome and destined to restore the order and the power of Rome).** It will be defensive rather than capable of original creation. Its underlying assumption will be that a collective will, already in existence, has become nerveless and dispersed, has suffered a collapse which is dangerous and threatening but not definitive and catastrophic, and that it is necessary to reconcentrate and reinforce it – rather than that a new collective will must be created from scratch, to be directed towards goals which are concrete and rational, but whose concreteness and rationality have not yet been put to the critical test by a real and universally known historical experience.

The abstract character of the Sorelian conception of the myth is manifest in its aversion (which takes the emotional form of an ethical repugnance) for the Jacobins, who were certainly a 'categorical embodiment' of Machiavelli's Prince.[6] *The Modern Prince* must have a part devoted to Jacobinism (in the integral sense which this notion has had historically, and must have conceptually), as an exemplification of the concrete formation and operation of a collective will which at least in some aspects was an original, *ex novo* creation. And a definition must be given of collective will, and of political will in general, in the modern sense: will as operative awareness of historical necessity, as protagonist of a real and effective historical drama.

One of the first sections must precisely be devoted to the 'collective will', posing the question in the following terms: 'When can the conditions for awakening and developing a national-popular collective will be said to exist?'[7] Hence an historical (economic) analysis of the social structure of the given country and a 'dramatic' representation of the attempts made in the course of the centuries to awaken this will, together with the reasons for the successive failures. Why was there no absolute monarchy in Italy in Machiavelli's time? One has to go back to the Roman Empire (the language question, problem of the intellectuals, etc.), and understand the function of the mediaeval Communes, the significance of Catholicism etc[8] In short, one has to make an outline of the whole history of Italy – in synthesis, but accurate.

** It is true that Machiavelli was inspired to his political conception of the *necessity* for a unitary Italian State not only by the example and model of the great absolute monarchies of France and Spain, but also by the remembrance of Rome's past. However, it should be emphasised that this is no reason for confusing Machiavelli with the literary-rhetorical tradition. For this element is neither exclusive nor even predominant, nor is the necessity for a great national State argued from it; moreover, this very allusion to Rome is less abstract than it may seem, when it is set in its correct context of the intellectual climate of Humanism and Renaissance. In Book VII of the *Art of War* one finds: 'This province (Italy) seems born to bring dead things back to life, as we have seen occur with poetry, with painting and with sculpture' – why then should it not rediscover military skill too? etc. One would have to collect together all the other references of this kind in order to establish their exact character.

The reason for the failures of the successive attempts to create a national-popular collective will is to be sought in the existence of certain specific social groups which were formed at the dissolution of the Communal bourgeoisie; in the particular character of other groups which reflect the international function of Italy as seat of the Church and depositary of the Holy Roman Empire; and so on. This function and the position which results from it have brought about an internal situation which may be called 'economic-corporate'[9] – politically, the worst of all forms of feudal society, the least progressive and the most stagnant. An effective *Jacobin* force was always missing, and could not be constituted; and it was precisely such a Jacobin force which in other nations awakened and organised the national-popular collective will, and founded the modern States. Do the necessary conditions for this will finally exist, or rather what is the present relation between these conditions and the forces opposed to them? Traditionally the forces of opposition have been the landed aristocracy and, more generally, landed property as a whole. Italy's particular characteristic is a special '*rural bourgeoisie*',[10] a legacy of parasitism bequeathed to modern times by the disintegration as a class of the Communal bourgeoisie (the hundred cities, the cities of silence)[11] The positive conditions are to be sought in the existence of urban social groups which have attained an adequate development in the field of industrial production and a certain level of historico-political culture. Any formation of a national-popular collective will is impossible, unless the great mass of peasant farmers bursts *simultaneously* into political life. That was Machiavelli's intention through the reform of the militia, and it was achieved by the Jacobins in the French Revolution. That Machiavelli understood it reveals a precocious Jacobinism that is the (more or less fertile) germ of his conception of national revolution. All history from 1815 onwards shows the efforts of the traditional classes to prevent the formation of a collective will of this kind, and to maintain 'economic-corporate' power in an international system of passive equilibrium.

An important part of *The Modern Prince* will have to be devoted to the question of intellectual and moral reform, that is to the question of religion or world-view. In this field too we find in the existing tradition an absence of Jacobinism and fear of Jacobinism (the latest philosophical expression of such fear is B. Croce's Malthusian attitude towards religion).[12] The modern Prince must be and cannot but be the proclaimer and organiser of an intellectual and moral reform, which also means creating the terrain for a subsequent development of the national-popular collective will towards the realisation of a superior, total form of modern civilisation.

These two basic points – the formation of a national-popular collective will, of which the modern Prince is at one and the same time the organiser and the active, operative expression; and intellectual and moral reform – should structure the entire work. The concrete, programmatic points must be incorporated in the first part, that is they should result from the line of discussion '*dramatically*', and not be a cold and pedantic exposition of arguments.

Can there be cultural reform, and can the position of the depressed strata of society be improved culturally, without a previous economic reform and a change in their position in the social and economic fields? Intellectual and moral reform has to be linked with a programme of economic reform – indeed the of programme of economic reform is precisely the concrete form in which every intellectual and moral reform presents itself. The modern Prince, as it develops, revolutionises the whole system of intellectual and moral relations, in that its development means precisely that any given act is seen as useful or harmful, as virtuous or as wicked, only in so far as it has as its point of reference the modern Prince itself, and helps to strengthen or to oppose it. In men's consciences, the Prince takes the place of the divinity or the categorical imperative, and becomes the basis for a modern laicism and for a complete laicisation of all aspects of life and of all customary relationships. [1933–34: 1st version 1931–32.]

NOTES

1. The *condottieri* were leaders of mercenary armies known as companies of fortune, which roved Italy in the fourteenth and fifteenth centuries and in numerous cases took power in the cities which employed them, and founded dynasties.
2. i.e. Lorenzo de' Medici, to whom 'The Prince' is addressed, and who is invited in the famous last chapter of the work to 'make Petrarch's words come true: 'Virtù contro a furore prenderà l'arme; e fia el combatter corto, ché l'antico valore nell'italici cor non è ancor morto'. [Virtue will take up arms against fury; and may the fight be brief, since the ancient valour is not yet dead in Italian hearts]'.
3. Luigi Russo: *Prolegomeni a Machiavelli*, included in *Ritratti e disegni storici*, Bari 1937. We have not been able to trace the original place and date of publication. In another note (*Note sul Machiavelli, sulla politica e sullo stato moderno*, p. 141) Gramsci writes: 'Russo, in his *Prolegomeni*, makes *The Prince* into Machiavelli's treatise on dictatorship (moment of authority and of the individual), and *The Discourses* into his treatise on hegemony (moment of the universal and of liberty). Russo's observation is correct, although there are allusions to the moment of hegemony or consent in *The Prince* too, beside those to authority or force. Similarly, the observation is correct that there is no opposition in principle between *Principato* and republic; what is involved is rather the hypostasis of the two moments of authority and of universality'.
4. Georges Sorel (1847–1922) was the principal theorist of revolutionary syndicalism, and the author notably of *Reflections on Violence* (1906). Influenced above all by Bergson and Marx, he in his turn had an immense influence in France and Italy – e.g. on Mussolini. His work was an amalgam of extremely disparate elements, reflecting the metamorphoses through which he passed – anti-Jacobin moralist, socialist, revolutionary syndicalist, far-right (indeed near-monarchist) preacher of an anti-bourgeois authoritarian moral regeneration, sympathiser with the Bolshevik revolution. In *Reflections on Violence*, Sorel develops the idea of the General Strike as a myth – indeed 'the *myth* in which Socialism is wholly comprised, i.e. a body of images capable of evoking instinctively all the sentiments which correspond to the different manifestations of the war undertaken by Socialism against modern society'. Myths 'enclose within them all the strongest inclinations of a people, of a party, or of a class'. He contrasts myth in this sense with utopias 'which present a deceptive

mirage of the future to the people'. (Another example of myth was Mazzini's 'mad chimera', which 'did more for Italian unity than Cavour and all the politicians of his school'). The idea of the General Strike 'destroys all the theoretical consequences of every possible social policy; its partisans look upon even the most popular reforms as having a middle-class character; so far as they are concerned, nothing can weaken the fundamental opposition of the class war'. The General Strike thus focuses the 'cleavage' between the antagonistic classes, by making every individual outburst of violence into an act in the class war. 'Cleavage', for Sorel, is the equivalent of class consciousness, of the class-for-itself; e.g. 'When the governing classes, no longer daring to govern, are ashamed of their privileged situation, are eager to make advances to their enemies, and proclaim their horror of all cleavage in society, it becomes much more difficult to maintain in the minds of the proletariat this idea of cleavage without which Socialism cannot fulfil its historical role'. *Reflections on Violence*, Collier Books, 1950, pp. 124–26, 133–35, 186.

5. General Boulanger (1837–91) was French Minister of War in 1886. He symbolised the idea of *revanche* (against Germany after the Franco-Prussian War of 1870–71) in the popular consciousness. The government became afraid of his popularity, and of his tractations with monarchist forces. They dismissed him, and posted him to Clermont-Ferrand. He founded a Boulangist party, which called for a new Constituent Assembly, a military regeneration of the nation, and reform of 'the abuses of parliamentarism'. Elected with a huge majority to the National Assembly, he appeared likely to attempt a *coup* – which could well have succeeded – but in fact hesitated, and subsequently fled the country fearing imminent arrest (1889).
6. For Gramsci's conception of the relation between Machiavelli, Jacobinism and the Communist Party, see introductions to 'Notes on Italian History' and to 'The Modern Prince' (pp. 44–47 and 123–4). See too 'Material for a critical essay on Croce's two Histories', on pp. 114–118 above. On IL Risorgimento p. 155 Gramsci defines 'historical Jacobinism' as 'union of city and countryside'.
7. The notion of the 'popular-national' (or, more frequently 'national-popular') is one of the most interesting and also most widely criticised ideas in Gramsci's thought. Supposedly at the origin of the cultural policy of the PCI since the war, it is perhaps best taken as describing a sort of 'historic bloc' between national and popular aspirations in the formation of which the intellectuals, in the wide, Gramscian use of the term play an essential mediating role. It is important to stress, however, that it is a cultural concept, relating to the position of the masses within the culture of the nation, and radically alien to any form of populism or 'national socialism'.
8. For Gramsci's discussion of the 'language question', see *Gli intellettuali e l'organizzazione della cultura*, pp. 21–25, etc. In the Middle Ages, the Catholic Church fought against the use of the vernacular and for the preservation of Latin as the 'universal' language, since this was a key element in its own intellectual hegemony. Dante, for example, felt compelled to defend his use of (Florentine) Italian in the Divine Comedy. Gramsci describes the emergence of Florentine dialect as a 'noble vernacular'. 'The flowering of the Communes developed the vernaculars, and the intellectual hegemony of Florence produced a united vernacular, a noble vernacular. . . . The fall of the Communes and the advent of the Princely régime, the creation of a governing caste detached from the people, crystallised this vernacular in the same way as literary Latin had become crystallised. Italian was once again a written and not a spoken language, a language of scholars rather than a language of the nation' The language question was simplified at one level in the nineteenth century, when literary Italian finally defeated Latin as the language of learning, and when it was adopted as the language of the new Italian national state. But it persists in the existence of dialects as the 'mother-tongue' in many Italian regions even today, despite the development of the mass media and universal education in this century.

9. For the concept of economic-corporate, see 'Notes on Italian History', note 4, and also Notes on Gramsci's Terminology, p. xiii.
10. On the 'rural bourgeoisie', see note 11 following, and 'Subversive', pp. 272–5 below.
11. Gramsci defines the 'hundred cities' as 'the agglomeration into burgs (cities) of the rural bourgeoisie, and the agglomeration into peasant villages [*borgate*] of great masses of agricultural labourers and landless peasants in areas where extensive *latifundia* exist (Puglie, Sicily)'.

    D'Annunzio gave the title 'Cities of Silence' to a sequence of poems, mainly sonnets, in *Elettra*, the second book of his *Laudi*. These cities – Ferrara, Pisa, Ravenna, Rimini, Assisi, Spoleto, Gubbio, Urbino, Padova, Lucca, Pistoia, Prato, Perugia, Spello, Montefalco, Narni, Todi, Orvieto, Arezzo, Cortona, Bergamo, Carrara, Volterra, Vicenza, Brescia – all had glorious pasts but are now of secondary importance, some little more than villages with magnificent monu-mental centres as a relic of their bygone splendour.
12. Gramsci alludes to Malthus here, as he usually does, simply to indicate fear of, or contempt for, the masses. On *Il materialismo storico e la filosofia di Benedetto Croce*, pp. 224–29 he discusses Croce's attitude to religion, and the character of the 'reformation' which he represents. Gramsci criticises Croce for not understanding that 'the philosophy of praxis, with its vast mass movement, has represented and does represent an historical process similar to the Reformation, in contrast with liberalism, which reproduces a Renaissance which is narrowly limited to restricted intellectual groups.... Croce is essentially anti-confessional (we cannot call him anti-religious given his definition of religious reality) and for numerous Italian and European intellectuals his philosophy... has been a genuine intellectual and moral reform similar to the Renaissance... But Croce did not 'go to the people', did not wish to become a 'national' element (just as the men of the Renaissance – unlike the Lutherans and Calvinists – were not 'national' elements), did not wish to create a band of disciples who... could have popularised his philosophy and tried to make it into an educative element, starting in the primary school (and hence educative for the simple worker or peasant, i.e. for the simple man of the people). Perhaps this was impossible, but it was worth trying and the fact that it was not tried is certainly significant'. Gramsci goes on to criticise Croce's view that religion is appropriate for the masses, while only an élite of superior intellects are capable of a rational conception of the world. Croce was minister of education in Giolitti's 1920–21 government, and introduced a draft bill to reorganise the national educational system; this bill provided for the reintroduction of religious instruction in the primary schools – something which had not existed since the 1859 Casati Act laid the basis for the educational system of post-Risorgimento Italy. In fact, Giolitti withdrew the bill, but the main lines of it were taken up by Gentile when, as minister of education in the first Fascist government of 1922, he drew up the Gentile Act, which was passed in 1923.

    For the concept of 'intellectual and moral reform' (taken from Renan), see 'Philosophy of Praxis and Modern Culture' on pp. 388–99. It should be noted that the Italian word '*riforma*' translates both 'reform' and 'reformation' in English.

THE MODERN PRINCE: ANALYSIS OF SITUATIONS. RELATIONS OF FORCE

Antonio Gramsci

The study of how 'situations' should be analysed, in other words how to establish the various levels of the relations of force, offers an opportunity for an elementary exposition of the science and art of politics – understood as a body of practical rules for research and of detailed observations useful for awakening an interest in effective reality and for stimulating more rigorous and more vigorous political insights. This should be accompanied by the explanation of what is meant in politics by strategy and tactics, by strategic 'plan', by propaganda and agitation, by command structure[1] or science of political organisation and administration.

The elements of empirical observation which are habitually included higgledy-piggledy in works of political science (G. Mosca's *Elementi di scienza politica* may be taken as typical) ought, in so far as they are not abstract and illusory, to be inserted into the context of the relations of force, on one level or another. These levels range from the relations between international forces (one would insert here the notes written on what a great power is, on the combinations of States in hegemonic systems, and hence on the concept of independence and sovereignty as far as small and medium powers are concerned)[2] to the objective relations within society – in other words, the degree of development of productive forces; to relations

Antonio Gramsci (1971), 'The Modern Prince: Analysis of situations. Relations of force', in *Selections from the Prison Notebooks*, ed. and tr. Quintin Hoare and Geoffrey Nowell Smith, London: Lawrence and Wishart.

of political force and those between parties (hegemonic systems within the State); and to immediate (or potentially military) political relations.

Do international relations precede or follow (logically) fundamental social relations? There can be no doubt that they follow. Any organic innovation in the social structure, through its technical-military expressions, modifies organically absolute and relative relations in the international field too. Even the geographical position of a national State does not precede but follows (logically) structural changes, although it also reacts back upon them to a certain extent (to the extent precisely to which superstructures react upon the structure, politics on economics, etc.). However, international relations react both passively and actively on political relations (of hegemony among the parties). The more the immediate economic life of a nation is subordinated to international relations, the more a particular party will come to represent this situation and to exploit it, with the aim of preventing rival parties gaining the upper hand (recall Nitti's famous speech on the *technical* impossibility of revolution in Italy). From this series of facts one may conclude that often the so-called 'foreigner's party'[3] is not really the one which is commonly so termed, but precisely the most nationalistic party – which, in reality, represents not so much the vital forces of its own country, as that country's subordination and economic enslavement to the hegemonic nations or to certain of their number.* [1933–34: 1st version 1931–32.]

It is the problem of the relations between structue and superstructure which must be accurately posed and resolved if the forces which are active in the history of a particular period are to be correctly analysed, and the relation between them determined. Two principles must orient the discussion: 1. that no society sets itself tasks for whose accomplishment the necessary and sufficient conditions do not either already exist or are not at least beginning to emerge and develop; 2. that no society breaks down and can be replaced until it has first developed all the forms of life which are implicit in its internal relations.** From a reflection on these two principles, one can move on to develop a whole series of further principles of historical methodology. Meanwhile, in studying a structure, it is necessary to distinguish organic movements (relatively permanent) from movements which may be termed 'conjunctural' (and which appear as occasional, immediate, almost accidental).[4] Conjunctural phenomena too depend on organic movements to be sure, but they do not have any very far-reaching historical significance;

* An allusion to this international element which 'represses' domestic energies can be found in G. Volpe's articles published in *Corriere della Sera*, on 22 and 23 March 1932.

** 'No social order ever perishes before all the productive forces for which there is room in it have developed; and new, higher relations of production never appear before the material conditions for their existence have matured in the womb of the old society. Therefore mankind always sets itself only such tasks as it can solve; since, looking at the matter more closely, it will always be found that the task itself arises only when the material conditions for its solution already exist or are at least in the process of formation.' Marx, Preface to the *Critique of Political Economy*.

they give rise to political criticism of a minor, day-to-day character, which has as its subject top political leaders and personalities with direct governmental responsibilities. Organic phenomena on the other hand give rise to socio-historical criticism, whose subject is wider social groupings – beyond the public figures and beyond the top leaders. When an historical period comes to be studied, the great importance of this distinction becomes clear. A crisis occurs, sometimes lasting for decades. This exceptional duration means that incurable structural contradictions have revealed themselves (reached maturity), and that, despite this, the political forces which are struggling to conserve and defend the existing structure itself are making every effort to cure them, within certain limits, and to overcome them. These incessant and persistent efforts (since no social formation will ever admit that it has been superseded) form the terrain of the 'conjunctural', and it is upon this terrain that the forces of opposition organise. These forces seek to demonstrate that the necessary and sufficient conditions already exist to make possible, and hence imperative, the accomplishment of certain historical tasks (imperative, because any falling short before an historical duty increases the necessary disorder, and prepares more serious catastrophes). (The demonstration in the last analysis only succeeds and is 'true' if it becomes a new reality, if the forces of opposition triumph; in the immediate, it is developed in a series of ideological, religious, philosophical, political, and juridical polemics, whose concreteness can be estimated by the extent to which they are convincing, and shift the previously existing disposition of social forces.)

A common error in historico-political analysis consists in an inability to find the correct relation between what is organic and what is conjunctural. This leads to presenting causes as immediately operative which in fact only operate indirectly, or to asserting that the immediate causes are the only effective ones. In the first case there is an excess of 'economism', or doctrinaire pedantry; in the second, an excess of 'ideologism'. In the first case there is an overestimation of mechanical causes, in the second an exaggeration of the voluntarist and individual element. The distinction between organic 'movements' and facts and 'conjunctural' or occasional ones must be applied to all types of situation; not only to those in which a regressive development or an acute crisis takes place, but also to those in which there is a progressive development or one towards prosperity, or in which the productive forces are stagnant. The dialectical nexus between the two categories of movement, and therefore of research, is hard to establish precisely. Moreover; if error is serious in historiography, it becomes still more serious in the art of politics, when it is not the reconstruction of past history but the construction of present and future history which is at stake.***

*** Failure to consider the immediate moment of 'relations of force' is linked to residues of the vulgar liberal conception – of which syndicalism is a manifestation which thought itself more

One's own baser and more immediate desires and passions are the cause of error, in that they take the place of an objective and impartial analysis – and this happens not as a conscious 'means' to stimulate to action, but as self-deception. In this case too the snake bites the snake-charmer – in other words the demagogue is the first victim of his own demagogy.

[...]

Meanwhile, in the 'relation of forces' various moments or levels must be distinguished, and they are fundamentally the following:

1. A relation of social forces which is closely linked to the structure, objective, independent of human will, and which can be measured with the systems of the exact or physical sciences. The level of development of the material forces of production provides a basis for the emergence of the various social classes, each one of which represents a function and has a specific position within production itself. This relation is what it is, a refractory reality: nobody can alter the number of firms or their employees, the number of cities or the given urban population, etc. By studying these fundamental data it is possible to discover whether in a particular society there exist the necessary and sufficient conditions for its transformation – in other words, to check the degree of realism and practicability of the various ideologies which have been born on its own terrain, on the terrain of the contradictions which it has engendered during the course of its development.

2. A subsequent moment is the relation of political forces; in other words, an evaluation of the degree of homogeneity, self-awareness, and organisation attained by the various social classes. This moment can in its turn be analysed and differentiated into various levels, corresponding to the various moments of collective political consciousness, as they have manifested themselves in history up till now. The first and most elementary of these is the economic-corporate level: a tradesman feels *obliged* to stand by another tradesman, a manufacturer by another manufacturer, etc., but the tradesman does not yet feel solidarity with the manufacturer; in other words, the members of the professional group are conscious of its unity and homogeneity, and of the need to organise it, but in the case of the wider social group this is not yet so. A second moment is that in which consciousness is reached of the solidarity of interests among all the members of a social class – but

advanced when in reality it was taking a step backward. In fact the vulgar liberal conception, stressing relations between political forces organised in the various forms of party (newspaper readerships, parliamentary and local elections, the mass organisations of parties and trade unions in the strict sense), was more advanced than syndicalism, which gave primordial importance to the fundamental socio-economic relation and only to that. The vulgar liberal conception took implicit account of this socio-economic relation too (as many signs clearly indicate), but it insisted besides on the relation of political forces – which was an expression of the former and in reality contained it. These residues of the vulgar liberal conception can be traced in a whole series of works purporting to be connected with the philosophy of praxis, and have given rise to infantile forms of optimism and folly.

still in the purely economic field. Already at this juncture the problem of the State is posed – but only in terms of winning politico-juridical equality with the ruling groups: the right is claimed to participate in legislation and administration, even to reform these – but within the existing fundamental structures. A third moment is that in which one becomes aware that one's own corporate interests, in their present and future development, transcend the corporate limits of the purely economic class, and can and must become the interests of other subordinate groups too. This is the most purely political phase, and marks the decisive passage from the structure to the sphere of the complex superstructures; it is the phase in which previously germinated ideologies become 'party', come into confrontation and conflict, until only one of them, or at least a single combination of them, tends to prevail, to gain the upper hand, to propagate itself throughout society – bringing about not only a unison of economic and political aims, but also intellectual and moral unity, posing all the questions around which the struggle rages not on a corporate but on a 'universal' plane, and thus creating the hegemony of a fundamental social group over a series of subordinate groups. It is true that the State is seen as the organ of one particular group, destined to create favourable conditions for the latter's maximum expansion. But the development and expansion of the particular group are conceived of, and presented, as being the motor force of a universal expansion, of a development of all the 'national' energies. In other words, the dominant group is coordinated concretely with the general interests of the subordinate groups, and the life of the State is conceived of as a continuous process of formation and superseding of unstable equilibria (on the juridical plane) between the interests of the fundamental group and those of the subordinate groups – equilibria in which the interests of the dominant group prevail, but only up to a certain point, i.e. stopping short of narrowly corporate economic interest.

In real history these moments imply each other reciprocally – horizontally and vertically, so to speak – i.e. according to socio-economic activity (horizontally) and to country (vertically), combining and diverging in various ways. Each of these combinations may be represented by its own organised economic and political expression. It is also necessary to take into account the fact that international relations intertwine with these internal relations of nation-states, creating new, unique and historically concrete combinations. A particular ideology, for instance, born in a highly developed country, is disseminated in less developed countries, impinging on the local interplay of combinations.**** This relation between international forces and national forces is further complicated by the existence within

**** Religion, for example, has always been a source of such national and international ideological-political combinations, and so too have the other international organisations – Freemasonry, Rotarianism, the Jews, career diplomacy. These propose political solutions of diverse historical origin, and assist their victory in particular countries – functioning as international political parties which operate within each nation with the full concentration of the international forces. A religion, every State of several structurally diverse territorial sectors, with diverse relations of force at all levels (thus the Vendée[5] was allied with the forces of international reaction, and represented them in the heart of French territorial unity; similarly Lyons in the French Revolution represented a particular knot of relations, etc.).

3. The third moment is that of the relation of military forces, which from time to time is directly decisive. (Historical development oscillates continually between the first and the third moment, with the mediation of the second.) But this too is not undifferentiated, nor is it susceptible to immediate schematic definition. Here too, two levels can be distinguished: the military level in the strict or technical military sense, and the level which may be termed politico-military.

[. . .]

But the most important observation to be made about any concrete analysis of the relations of force is the following: that such analyses cannot and must not be ends in themselves (unless the intention is merely to write a chapter of past history), but acquire significance only if they serve to justify a particular practical activity, or initiative of will. They reveal the points of least resistance, at which the force of will can be most fruitfully applied; they suggest immediate tactical operations; they indicate how a campaign of political agitation may best be launched, what language will best be understood by the masses, etc. The decisive element in every situation is the permanently organised and long-prepared force which can be put into the field when it is judged that a situation is favourable (and it can be favourable only in so far as such a force exists, and is full of fighting spirit). Therefore the essential task is that of systematically and patiently ensuring that this force is formed, developed, and rendered ever more homogeneous, compact, and self-aware. This is clear from military history, and from the care with which in every period armies have been prepared in advance to be able to make war at any moment. The great Powers have been great precisely because they were at all times prepared to intervene effectively in favourable international conjunctures – which were precisely favourable because there was the concrete possibility of effectively intervening in them. [1933–34: 1st version 1931–32.]

NOTES

1. *Organica* has no exact equivalent in English – it means the organisation of armed forces, their division into different arms and corps, their system of ranks, etc.
2. See *Note sul Machiavelli, sulla politica e sullo Stato moderno*, pp. 141 and 167 ff.

---

freemasonry, Rotary, Jews, etc., can be subsumed into the social category of 'intellectuals', whose function, on an international scale, is that of mediating the extremes, of 'socialising' the technical discoveries which provide the impetus for all activities of leadership, of devising compromises between, and ways out of, extreme solutions.

3. Term used especially of communist parties by the nationalist Right, and, in an earlier period, of parties influenced by the ideas of the French Revolution. The latter – Mazzini's Action Party is a good example – did in fact often have links with liberals in other countries.
4. On *Passato e presente* pp. 148–9 Gramsci wrote: 'The conjuncture can be defined as the set of circumstances which determine the market in a given phase, provided that these are conceived of as being in movement, i.e. as constituting a process of ever-changing combinations, a process which is the economic cycle . . . In Italian the meaning of 'favourable or unfavourable economic situation (*occasione*)' remains attached to the word 'conjuncture'. Difference between 'situation' and 'conjuncture': the conjuncture is the set of immediate and ephemeral characteristics of the economic situation . . . Study of the conjuncture is thus more closely linked to immediate politics, to 'tactics' and agitation, while the 'situation' relates to 'strategy' and propaganda, etc.'
5. From 1793–96 royalist priests and landowners fomented peasant guerrilla warfare against the Republic in the Vendée region in Western France.

FROM 'STATE AND CIVIL SOCIETY'

Antonio Gramsci

POLITICAL STRUGGLE AND MILITARY WAR

In the East the State was everything, civil society was primordial and gelatinous; in the West, there was a proper relation between State and civil society, and when the State trembled a sturdy structure of civil society was at once revealed. The State was only an outer ditch, behind which there stood a powerful system of fortresses and earthworks: more or less numerous from one State to the next, it goes without saying – but this precisely necessitated an accurate reconnaissance of each individual country.

Bronstein's theory can be compared to that of certain French syndicalists on the General Strike, and to Rosa [Luxemburg]'s theory in the work translated by Alessandri. Rosa's book and theories anyway influenced the French syndicalists, as is clear from some of Rosmer's[1] articles on Germany in *Vie Ouvrière* (first series in pamphlet form). It partly depends too on the theory of spontaneity. [1930–32]

THE TRANSITION FROM THE WAR OF MANŒUVRE (FRONTAL ATTACK) TO THE WAR OF POSITION – IN THE POLITICAL FIELD AS WELL

This seems to me to be the most important question of political theory that the post-war period has posed, and the most difficult to solve correctly. It is related to the problems raised by Bronstein [Trotsky], who in one way

Antonio Gramsci (1971), 'State and civil society', in *Selections from the Prison Notebooks*, ed. and tr. Quintin Hoare and Geoffrey Nowell Smith, London: Lawrence and Wishart.

or another can be considered the political theorist of frontal attack in a period in which it only leads to defeats. This transition in political science is only indirectly (mediately) related to that which took place in the military field, although certainly a relation exists and an essential one. The war of position demands enormous sacrifices by infinite masses of people. So an unprecedented concentration of hegemony is necessary, and hence a more 'interventionist' government, which will take the offensive more openly against the oppositionists and organise permanently the 'impossibility' of internal disintegration – with controls of every kind, political, administrative, etc., reinforcement of the hegemonic 'positions' of the dominant group, etc. All this indicates that we have entered a culminating phase in the political-historical situation, since in politics the 'war of position', once won, is decisive definitively. In politics, in other words, the war of manœuvre subsists so long as it is a question of winning positions which are not decisive, so that all the resources of the State's hegemony cannot be mobilised. But when, for one reason or another, these positions have lost their value and only the decisive positions are at stake, then one passes over to siege warfare; this is concentrated, difficult, and requires exceptional qualities of patience and inventiveness. In politics, the siege is a reciprocal one, despite all appearances, and the mere fact that the ruler has to muster all his resources demonstrates how seriously he takes his adversary. [1930–32]

'A resistance too long prolonged in a besieged camp is demoralising in itself. It implies suffering, fatigue, loss of rest, illness and the continual presence not of the acute danger which tempers but of the chronic danger which destroys.' Karl Marx: Eastern Question. 14 September 1855.

[...]

PROBLEM OF THE 'COLLECTIVE MAN' OR OF 'SOCIAL CONFORMISM'[2]

Educative and formative role of the State. Its aim is always that of creating new and higher types of civilisation; of adapting the 'civilisation' and the morality of the broadest popular masses to the necessities of the continuous development of the economic apparatus of production; hence of evolving even physically new types of humanity. But how will each single individual succeed in incorporating himself into the collective man, and how will educative pressure be applied to single individuals so as to obtain their consent and their collaboration, turning necessity and coercion into 'freedom'? Question of the 'Law': this concept will have to be extended to include those activities which are at present classified as 'legally neutral', and which belong to the domain of civil society; the latter operates without 'sanctions' or compulsory 'obligations', but nevertheless exerts a collective pressure and obtains objective results in the form of an evolution of customs, ways of thinking and acting, morality, etc.

Political concept of the so-called 'Permanent Revolution', which emerged before 1848 as a scientifically evolved expression of the Jacobin experience from 1789 to Thermidor.[3] The formula belongs to an historical period in which the great mass political parties and the great economic trade unions did not yet exist, and society was still, so to speak, in a state of fluidity from many points of view: greater backwardness of the countryside, and almost complete monopoly of political and State power by a few cities or even by a single one (Paris in the case of France); a relatively rudimentary State apparatus, and greater autonomy of civil society from State activity; a specific system of military forces and of national armed services; greater autonomy of the national economies from the economic relations of the world market, etc. In the period after 1870, with the colonial expansion of Europe, all these elements change: the internal and international organisational relations of the State become more complex and massive, and the Forty-Eightist formula of the 'Permanent Revolution' is expanded and transcended in political science by the formula of 'civil hegemony'. The same thing happens in the art of politics as happens in military art: war of movement increasingly becomes war of position, and it can be said that a State will win a war in so far as it prepares for it minutely and technically in peacetime. The massive structures of the modern democracies, both as State organisations, and as complexes of associations in civil society, constitute for the art of politics as it were the 'trenches' and the permanent fortifications of the front in the war of position: they render merely 'partial' the element of movement which before used to be 'the whole' of war, etc.

This question is posed for the modern States, but not for backward countries or for colonies, where forms which elsewhere have been superseded and have become anachronistic are still in vigour. The question of the value of ideologies must also be studied in a treatise of political science. [1933–34]

[. . .]

The State

We are still on the terrain of the identification of State and government – an identification which is precisely a representation of the economic-corporate form, in other words of the confusion between civil society and political society. For it should be remarked that the general notion of State includes elements which need to be referred back to the notion of civil society (in the sense that one might say that State = political society + civil society, in other words hegemony protected by the armour of coercion). In a doctrine of the State which conceives the latter as tendentially capable of withering away and of being subsumed into regulated society, the argument is a fundamental one. It is possible to imagine the coercive element of the State withering away by degrees, as ever-more conspicuous elements of regulated society (or ethical State or civil society) make their appearance.

The expressions 'ethical State' or 'civil society' would thus mean that this 'image' of a State without a State was present to the greatest political and legal thinkers, in so far as they placed themselves on the terrain of pure science (pure utopia, since based on the premise that all men are really equal and hence equally rational and moral, i.e. capable of accepting the law spontaneously, freely, and not through coercion, as imposed by another class, as something external to consciousness).

It must be remembered that the expression 'nightwatchman' for the liberal State comes from Lassalle, i.e. from a dogmatic and non-dialectical statalist (look closely at Lassalle's doctrines on this point and on the State in general, in contrast with Marxism). In the doctrine of the State as regulated society, one will have to pass from a phase in which 'State' will be equal to 'government', and 'State' will be identified with 'civil society', to a phase of the State as nightwatchman – i.e. of a coercive organisation which will safeguard the development of the continually proliferating elements of regulated society, and which will therefore progressively reduce its own authoritarian and forcible interventions. Nor can this conjure up the idea of a new 'liberalism', even though the beginning of an era of organic liberty be imminent. [1930–32]

If it is true that no type of State can avoid passing through a phase of economic-corporate primitivism, it may be deduced that the content of the political hegemony of the new social group which has founded the new type of State must be predominantly of an economic order: what is involved is the reorganisation of the structure and the real relations between men on the one hand and the world of the economy or of production on the other. The superstructural elements will inevitably be few in number, and have a character of foresight and of struggle, but as yet few 'planned' elements. Cultural policy will above all be negative, a critique of the past; it will be aimed at erasing from the memory and at destroying. The lines of construction will as yet be 'broad lines', sketches, which might (and should) be changed at all times, so as to be consistent with the new structure as it is formed. This precisely did not happen in the period of the mediaeval communes; for culture, which remained a function of the Church, was precisely anti-economic in character (i.e. against the nascent capitalist economy); it was not directed towards giving hegemony to the new class, but rather to preventing the latter from acquiring it. Hence Humanism and the Renaissance were reactionary, because they signalled the defeat of the new class, the negation of the economic world which was proper to it, etc. [1931–32]

[. . .]

Organisation of National Societies

I have remarked elsewhere that in any given society nobody is disorganised and without party, provided that one takes organisation and party in a broad and not a formal sense. In this multiplicity of private associations (which are of two kinds: natural, and contractual or voluntary) one or more predominates relatively or absolutely – constituting the hegemonic apparatus of one social group over the rest of the population (or civil society): the basis for the State in the narrow sense of the governmental-coercive apparatus.

It always happens that individuals belong to more than one private association, and often to associations which are objectively in contradiction to one another. A totalitarian[4] policy is aimed precisely: 1. at ensuring that the members of a particular party find in that party all the satisfactions that they formerly found in a multiplicity of organisations, i.e. at breaking all the threads that bind these members to extraneous cultural organisms; 2. at destroying all other organisations or at incorporating them into a system of which the party is the sole regulator. This occurs: 1. when the given party is the bearer of a new culture – then one has a progressive phase; 2. when the given party wishes to prevent another force, bearer of a new culture, from becoming itself 'totalitarian' – then one has an objectively regressive and reactionary phase, even if that reaction (as invariably happens) does not avow itself, and seeks itself to appear as the bearer of a new culture.

[. . .]

STATE AND PARTIES

The function of hegemony or political leadership exercised by parties can be estimated from the evolution of the internal life of the parties themselves. If the State represents the coercive and punitive force of juridical regulation of a country, the parties – representing the spontaneous adhesion of an *élite* to such a regulation, considered as a type of collective society to which the entire mass must be educated – must show in their specific internal life that they have assimilated as principles of moral conduct those rules which in the State are legal obligations. In the parties necessity has already become freedom, and thence is born the immense political value (i.e. value for political leadership) of the internal discipline of a party, and hence the value as a criterion of such discipline in estimating the growth potential of the various parties. From this point of view the parties can be considered as schools of State life. Elements of party life: character (resistance to the pressures of surpassed cultures), honour (fearless will in maintaining the new type of culture and life), dignity (awareness of operating for a higher end), etc. [1930–32]

NOTES

1. Alfred Rosmer was a revolutionary syndicalist during the First World War, and edited *La Vie Ouvrière* together with Pierre Monatte. They were both among the first leaders of the PCF, and Rosmer was editor of *Humanité* from 1923 to 1924. He was expelled in 1926 for supporting the Joint Opposition in the Russian Party.

2. See too *Note sul Machiavelli, sulla politica e sullo Stato Moderno* pp. 150–51: 'Tendency to conformism in the contemporary world, more widespread and deeper than in the past: the standardisation of thought and action assumes national or even continental proportions. The economic basis of the 'collective man': big factories, Taylorisation, rationalisation, etc. . . . On social 'conformism', it should be stressed that the problem is not a new one, and that the alarm expressed by certain intellectuals is merely comic. Conformism has always existed: what is involved today is a struggle between 'two conformisms', i.e. a struggle for hegemony, a crisis of civil society. The old intellectual and moral leaders of society feel the ground slipping from under their feet; they perceive that their 'sermons' have become precisely mere 'sermons', i.e. external to reality, pure form without any content, shades without a spirit. This is the reason for their reactionary and conservative tendencies; for the particular form of civilisation, culture and morality which they represented is decomposing, and they loudly proclaim the death of all civilisation, all culture, all morality; they call for repressive measures by the State, and constitute resistance groups cut off from the real historical process, thus prolonging the crisis, since the eclipse of a way of living and thinking cannot take place without a crisis. The representatives of the new order in gestation, on the other hand, inspired by 'rationalistic' hatred for the old, propagate utopias and fanciful schemes. What is the point of reference for the new world in gestation? The world of production; work. The greatest utilitarianism must go to found any analysis of the moral and intellectual institutions to be created and of the principles to be propagated. Collective and individual life must be organised with a view to the maximum yield of the productive apparatus. The development of economic forces on new bases and the progressive installation of the new structure will heal the contradictions which cannot fail to exist, and, when they have created a new 'conformism' from below, will permit new possibilities for self-discipline, i.e. for freedom, including that of the individual.'
3. See 'Notes on Italian History', note 49.
4. It is important to realise that Gramsci does not use this word in the pejorative sense which it has acquired in bourgeois ideology today – it is a quite neutral term for him, meaning approximately 'all-embracing and unifying'. We have sometimes translated it by 'global'.

THE INTELLECTUALS

Antonio Gramsci

The Formation of the Intellectuals

Are intellectuals an autonomous and independent social group, or does every social group have its own particular specialised category of intellectuals? The problem is a complex one, because of the variety of forms assumed to date by the real historical process of formation of the different categories of intellectuals.

The most important of these forms are two:

1. Every social group, coming into existence on the original terrain of an essential function in the world of economic production, creates together with itself, organically, one or more strata[1] of intellectuals which give it homogeneity and an awareness of its own function not only in the economic but also in the social and political fields. The capitalist entrepreneur creates alongside himself the industrial technician, the specialist in political economy, the organisers of a new culture, of a new legal system, etc. It should be noted that the entrepreneur himself represents a higher level of social elaboration, already characterised by a certain directive [*dirigente*][2] and technical (i.e. intellectual) capacity: he must have a certain technical capacity, not only in the limited sphere of his activity and initiative but in other spheres as well, at least in those which are closest to economic production. He must be an organiser of masses of men; he must be an organiser of the

Antonio Gramsci (1971), 'The intellectuals', in *Selections from the Prison Notebooks*, ed. and tr. Quintin Hoare and Geoffrey Nowell Smith, London: Lawrence and Wishart.

'confidence' of investors in his business, of the customers for his product, etc.

2. If not all entrepreneurs, at least an *élite* amongst them must have the capacity to be an organiser of society in general, including all its complex organism of services, right up to the state organism, because of the need to create the conditions most favourable to the expansion of their own class; or at the least they must possess the capacity to choose the deputies (specialised employees) to whom to entrust this activity of organising the general system of relationships external to the business itself. It can be observed that the 'organic' intellectuals which every new class creates alongside itself and elaborates in the course of its development, are for the most part 'specialisations' of partial aspects of the primitive activity of the new social type which the new class has brought into prominence.*

[. . .]

What are the 'maximum' limits of acceptance of the term 'intellectual'? Can one find a unitary criterion to characterise equally all the diverse and disparate activities of intellectuals and to distinguish these at the same time and in an essential way from the activities of other social groupings? The most widespread error of method seems to me that of having looked for this criterion of distinction in the intrinsic nature of intellectual activities, rather than in the ensemble of the system of relations in which these activities (and therefore the intellectual groups who personify them) have their place within the general complex of social relations. Indeed the worker or proletarian, for example, is not specifically characterised by his manual or instrumental work, but by performing this work in specific conditions and in specific social relations (apart from the consideration that purely physical labour does not exist and that even Taylor's phrase of 'trained gorilla'[4] is a metaphor to indicate a limit in a certain direction: in any physical work, even the most degraded and mechanical, there exists a minimum of technical qualification, that is, a minimum of creative intellectual activity.) And we have already observed that the entrepreneur, by virtue of his very function, must have to some degree a certain number of qualifications of an intellectual nature although his part in society is determined not by these, but by the general social relations which specifically characterise the position of the entrepreneur within industry.

* Mosca's *Elementi di Scienza Politica* (new expanded edition, 1923) are worth looking at in this connection. Mosca's so-called 'political class'[3] is nothing other than the intellectual category or the dominant social group. Mosca's concept of 'political class' can be connected with Pareto's concept of the *élite*, which is another attempt to interpret the historical phenomenon of the intellectuals and their function in the life of the state and of society. Mosca's book is an enormous hotch-potch, of a sociological and positivistic character, plus the tendentiousness of immediate politics which makes it less indigestible and livelier from a literary point of view.

All men are intellectuals, one could therefore say: but not all men have in society the function of intellectuals.**

When one distinguishes between intellectuals and non-intellectuals, one is referring in reality only to the immediate social function of the professional category of the intellectuals, that is, one has in mind the direction in which their specific professional activity is weighted, whether towards intellectual elaboration or towards muscular-nervous effort. This means that, although one can speak of intellectuals, one cannot speak of non-intellectuals, because non-intellectuals do not exist. But even the relationship between efforts of intellectual-cerebral elaboration and muscular-nervous effort is not always the same, so that there are varying degrees of specific intellectual activity. There is no human activity from which every form of intellectual participation can be excluded: *homo faber* cannot be separated from *homo sapiens*.[5] Each man, finally, outside his professional activity, carries on some form of intellectual activity, that is, he is a 'philosopher', an artist, a man of taste, he participates in a particular conception of the world, has a conscious line of moral conduct, and therefore contributes to sustain a conception of the world or to modify it, that is, to bring into being new modes of thought.

The problem of creating a new stratum of intellectuals consists therefore in the critical elaboration of the intellectual activity that exists in everyone at a certain degree of development, modifying its relationship with the muscular-nervous effort towards a new equilibrium, and ensuring that the muscular-nervous effort itself, in so far as it is an element of a general practical activity, which is perpetually innovating the physical and social world, becomes the foundation of a new and integral conception of the world. The traditional and vulgarised type of the intellectual is given by the man of letters, the philosopher, the artist. Therefore journalists, who claim to be men of letters, philosophers, artists, also regard themselves as the 'true' intellectuals. In the modern world, technical education, closely bound to industrial labour even at the most primitive and unqualified level, must form the basis of the new type of intellectual.

[...]

Thus there are historically formed specialised categories for the exercise of the intellectual function. They are formed in connection with all social groups, but especially in connection with the more important, and they undergo more extensive and complex elaboration in connection with the dominant social group. One of the most important characteristics of any group that is developing towards dominance is its struggle to assimilate and to conquer 'ideologically' the traditional intellectuals, but this assimilation and conquest is made quicker and more efficacious the more the group in question succeeds in simultaneously elaborating its own organic intellectuals.

** Thus, because it can happen that everyone at some time fries a couple of eggs or sews up a tear in a jacket, we do not necessarily say that everyone is a cook or a tailor.

The enormous development of activity and organisation of education in the broad sense in the societies that emerged from the medieval world is an index of the importance assumed in the modern world by intellectual functions and categories. Parallel with the attempt to deepen and to broaden the 'intellectuality' of each individual, there has also been an attempt to multiply and narrow the various specialisations. This can be seen from educational institutions at all levels, up to and including the organisms that exist to promote so-called 'high culture' in all fields of science and technology.

School is the instrument through which intellectuals of various levels are elaborated. The complexity of the intellectual function in different states can be measured objectively by the number and gradation of specialised schools: the more extensive the 'area' covered by education and the more numerous the 'vertical' 'levels' of schooling, the more complex is the cultural world, the civilisation, of a particular state. A point of comparison can be found in the sphere of industrial technology: the industrialisation of a country can be measured by how well equipped it is in the production of machines with which to produce machines, and in the manufacture of ever more accurate instruments for making both machines and further instruments for making machines, etc. The country which is best equipped in the construction of instruments for experimental scientific laboratories and in the construction of instruments with which to test the first instruments, can be regarded as the most complex in the technical-industrial field, with the highest level of civilisation, etc. The same applies to the preparation of intellectuals and to the schools dedicated to this preparation; schools and institutes of high culture can be assimilated to each other. In this field also, quantity cannot be separated from quality. To the most refined technical-cultural specialisation there cannot but correspond the maximum possible diffusion of primary education and the maximum care taken to expand the middle grades numerically as much as possible. Naturally this need to provide the widest base possible for the selection and elaboration of the top intellectual qualifications – i.e. to give a democratic structure to high culture and top-level technology – is not without its disadvantages: it creates the possibility of vast crises of unemployment for the middle intellectual strata, and in all modern societies this actually takes place.

[. . .]

The relationship between the intellectuals and the world of production is not as direct as it is with the fundamental social groups but is, in varying degrees, 'mediated' by the whole fabric of society and by the complex of superstructures, of which the intellectuals are, precisely, the 'functionaries'. It should be possible both to measure the 'organic quality' [*organicità*] of the various intellectual strata and their degree of connection with a fundamental social group, and to establish a gradation of their functions and of the superstructures from the bottom to the top (from the structural base upwards). What we can do, for the moment, is to fix two major superstructural 'levels': the one that can be called 'civil society', that is the ensemble of organisms commonly called 'private', and that of 'political society', or 'the State'. These two levels correspond on the one hand to the function of 'hegemony' which the dominant group exercises throughout society and on the other hand to that of 'direct domination' or command exercised through the State and 'juridical' government. The functions in question are precisely organisational and connective. The intellectuals are the dominant group's 'deputies' exercising the subaltern functions of social hegemony and political government. These comprise:

1. The 'spontaneous' consent given by the great masses of the population to the general direction imposed on social life by the dominant fundamental group; this consent is 'historically' caused by the prestige (and consequent confidence) which the dominant group enjoys because of its position and function in the world of production.
2. The apparatus of state coercive power which 'legally' enforces discipline on those groups who do not 'consent' either actively or passively. This apparatus is, however, constituted for the whole of society in anticipation of moments of crisis of command and direction when spontaneous consent has failed.

This way of posing the problem has as a result a considerable extension of the concept of intellectual, but it is the only way which enables one to reach a concrete approximation of reality. It also clashes with preconceptions of caste. The function of organising social hegemony and state domination certainly gives rise to a particular division of labour and therefore to a whole hierarchy of qualifications in some of which there is no apparent attribution of directive or organisational functions. For example, in the apparatus of social and state direction there exist a whole series of jobs of a manual and instrumental character (non-executive work, agents rather than officials or functionaries).[6] It is obvious that such a distinction has to be made just as it is obvious that other distinctions have to be made as well. Indeed, intellectual activity must also be distinguished in terms of its intrinsic characteristics, according to levels which in moments of extreme opposition represent a real qualitative difference – at the highest level would be the creators of the various sciences, philosophy, art, etc., at the lowest the most humble 'administrators' and divulgators of pre-existing, traditional, accumulated intellectual wealth.***

*** Here again military organisation offers a model of complex gradations between subaltern officers, senior officers and general staff, not to mention the NCO's, whose importance is greater than is generally admitted. It is worth observing that all these parts feel a solidarity and indeed that it is the lower strata that display the most blatant *esprit de corps*, from which they derive a certain 'conceit' which is apt to lay them open to jokes and witticisms.

In the modern world the category of intellectuals, understood in this sense, has undergone an unprecedented expansion. The democratic-bureaucratic system has given rise to a great mass of functions which are not all justified by the social necessities of production, though they are justified by the political necessities of the dominant fundamental group. Hence Loria's[7] conception of the unproductive 'worker' (but unproductive in relation to whom and to what mode of production?), a conception which could in part be justified if one takes account of the fact that these masses exploit their position to take for themselves a large cut out of the national income. Mass formation has standardised individuals both psychologically and in terms of individual qualification and has produced the same phenomena as with other standardised masses: competition which makes necessary organisations for the defence of professions, unemployment, over-production in the schools, emigration, etc.

NOTES

1. The Italian word here is '*ceti*' which does not carry quite the same connotations as 'strata', but which we have been forced to translate in that way for lack of alternatives. It should be noted that Gramsci tends, for reasons of censorship, to avoid using the word class in contexts where its Marxist overtones would be apparent, preferring (as for example in this sentence) the more neutral 'social group'. The word 'group', however, is not always a euphemism for 'class', and to avoid ambiguity Gramsci uses the phrase 'fundamental social group' when he wishes to emphasise the fact that he is referring to one or other of the major social classes (bourgeoisie, proletariat) defined in strict Marxist terms by its position in the fundamental relations of production. Class groupings which do not have this fundamental role are often described as 'castes' (aristocracy, etc.). The word 'category', on the other hand, which also occurs on this page, Gramsci tends to use in the standard Italian sense of members of a trade or profession, though also more generally. Throughout this edition we have rendered Gramsci's usage as literally as possible (see note on Gramsci's Terminology, p. xiii).
2. See note on Gramsci's Terminology.
3. Usually translated in English as 'ruling class', which is also the title of the English version of Mosca's *Elementi* (G. Mosca, *The Ruling Class*, New York 1939). Gaetano Mosca (1858–1941) was, together with Pareto and Michels, one of the major early Italian exponents of the theory of political *élites*. Although sympathetic to fascism, Mosca was basically a conservative, who saw the *élite* in rather more static terms than did some of his fellows.
4. For Frederick Taylor and his notion of the manual worker as a 'trained gorilla', see Gramsci's essay *Americanism and Fordism*.
5. i.e. Man the maker (or tool-bearer) and Man the thinker.
6. '*Funzionari*': in Italian usage the word is applied to the middle and higher echelons of the bureaucracy. Conversely 'administrators' ('*amministratori*') is used here (end of paragraph) to mean people who merely 'administer' the decisions of others. The phrase 'non-executive work' is a translation of '[*impiego*] *di ordine e non di concetto*' which refers to distinctions within clerical work.
7. For Loria see 'Problems of Marxism', note 108. The notion of the 'unproductive labourer' is not in fact an invention of Loria's but has its origins in Marx's definitions of productive and unproductive labour in *Capital*, which Loria, in his characteristic way, both vulgarised and claimed as his own discovery.

FROM 'AMERICANISM AND FORDISM'

Antonio Gramsci

Rationalism of Production and Work

The expression 'consciousness of purpose' might appear humorous to say the least to anyone who recalls Taylor's phrase about the 'trained gorilla'.[1] Taylor is in fact expressing with brutal cynicism the purpose of American society – developing in the worker to the highest degree automatic and mechanical attitudes, breaking up the old psycho-physical nexus of qualified professional work, which demands a certain active participation of intelligence, fantasy and initiative on the part of the worker, and reducing productive operations exclusively to the mechanical, physical aspect. But these things, in reality, are not original or novel: they represent simply the most recent phase of a long process which began with industrialism itself. This phase is more intense than preceding phases, and manifests itself in more brutal forms, but it is a phase which will itself be superseded by the creation of a psycho-physical nexus of a new type, both different from its pre-decessors and undoubtedly *superior*. A forced selection will ineluctably take place; a part of the old working class will be pitilessly eliminated from the world of labour, and perhaps from the world *tout court*.

It is from this point of view that one should study the 'puritanical' initiative of American industrialists like Ford. It is certain that they are not concerned with the 'humanity' or the 'spirituality' of the worker, which are immediately smashed. This 'humanity and spirituality' cannot be realised

Antonio Gramsci (1971), 'Americanism and Fordism', in *Selections from the Prison Notebooks*, ed. and tr. Quintin Hoare and Geoffrey Nowell Smith, London: Lawrence and Wishart.

except in the world of production and work and in productive 'creation'. They exist most in the artisan, in the 'demiurge',[2] when the worker's personality was reflected whole in the object created and when the link between art and labour was still very strong. But it is precisely against this 'humanism' that the new industrialism is fighting. 'Puritanical' initiatives simply have the purpose of preserving, outside of work, a certain psycho-physical equilibrium which prevents the physiological collapse of the worker, exhausted by the new method of production. This equilibrium can only be something purely external and mechanical, but it can become internalised if it is proposed by the worker himself, and not imposed from the outside, if it is proposed by a new form of society, with appropriate and original methods. American industrialists are concerned to maintain the continuity of the physical and muscular-nervous efficiency of the worker. It is in their interests to have a stable, skilled labour force, a permanently well-adjusted complex, because the human complex (the collective worker) of an enterprise is also a machine which cannot, without considerable loss, be taken to pieces too often and renewed with single new parts.

The element of so-called high wages also depends on this necessity. It is the instrument used to select and maintain in stability a skilled labour force suited to the system of production and work. But high wages are a double-edged weapon. It is necessary for the worker to spend his extra money 'rationally' to maintain, renew and, if possible, increase his muscular-nervous efficiency and not to corrode or destroy it.

[...]

HIGH WAGES

It is an obvious reflection that so-called high wages are a transitory form of remuneration. Adaptation to the new methods of production and work cannot take place simply through social compulsion. This is a 'prejudice' which is widespread in Europe and even more so in Japan, which cannot fail before long to have serious consequences for the physical and psychic health of the workers. It is, furthermore, a prejudice which has its roots only in the endemic unemployment which has been a feature of the post-war period. If the situation were 'normal', the apparatus of coercion needed to obtain the desired result would involve more than just high wages. Coercion has therefore to be ingeniously combined with persuasion and consent. This effect can be achieved, in forms proper to the society in question, by higher remuneration such as to permit a particular living standard which can maintain and restore the strength that has been worn down by the new form of toil. But no sooner have the new methods of work and production been generalised and diffused, the new type of worker been created universally and the apparatus of material production further perfected, no sooner has this happened than the excessive 'turnover' has automatically to be restricted by widespread unemployment, and high wages disappear. In reality American high-wage industry is still exploiting a monopoly granted to it by the fact that it has the initiative with the new methods. Monopoly wages correspond to monopoly profits. But the monopoly will necessarily be first limited and then destroyed by the further diffusion of the new methods both within the United States and abroad (compare the Japanese phenomenon of low-priced goods), and high wages will disappear along with enormous profits. Also it is well known that high wages are of necessity connected with a labour aristocracy and are not granted to all American workers.

The whole Fordian ideology of high wages is a phenomenon derived from an objective necessity of modern industry when it has reached a certain stage of development. It is not a primary phenomenon – which does not however exonerate one from studying its importance and the repercussions that the ideology can have on its own account. Meanwhile, what is meant by 'high wages'? Are the wages paid by Ford high only in relation to the average American wage? Or are they high as a price to be paid for the labouring power expended by Ford's employees in production and with those methods of work? It doesn't seem that any systematic research has been done on this, but that alone could provide a conclusive answer. The research is difficult, but the reasons why it is difficult are in themselves an indirect answer to the problem. The answer is difficult because the skilled labour force at Ford is extremely unstable and as a result it is not possible to establish an average for 'rational' turnover among Ford workers for the purpose of comparison with the average in other industries. But why is it unstable? Why on earth should a worker prefer lower wages than those paid by Ford? Does this not mean that the so-called 'high wages' are less capable of reconstituting the labour power expended than the lower wages paid by other firms? The instability of the labour force demonstrates that as far as Ford's is concerned the normal conditions of workers' competition for jobs (wage differentials) are effective only to a limited degree. The different level of average wages is not effective, nor is the pressure of the reserve army of the unemployed. This means that in dealing with Ford a new element must be looked for, and this new element will be the origin both of the high wages and of the other phenomena referred to (instability, etc.). The new element must be looked for in this fact alone: that Ford's industry requires a discrimination, a qualification, in its workers, which other industries do not yet call for, a new type of qualification, a form of consumption of labour power and a quantity of power consumed in average hours which are the same numerically but which are more wearying and exhausting than elsewhere and which, in the given conditions of society as it is, the wages are not sufficient to recompense and make up for.

Once these reasons have been established, the problem arises: whether the type of industry and organisation of work and production typical of Ford is rational; whether, that is, it can and should be generalised, or whether, on the other hand, we are not dealing with a malignant phenomenon which must be fought against through trade-union action and through legislation? In other words, whether it is possible, with the material and moral pressure of society and of the State, to lead the workers as a mass to undergo the entire process of psycho-physical transformation so that the average type of Ford worker becomes the average type of worker in general? Or whether this is impossible because it would lead to physical degeneration and to deterioration of the species, with the consequent destruction of all labour power? It seems possible to reply that the Ford method is rational, that is, that it should be generalised; but that a long process is needed for this, during which a change must take place in social conditions and in the way of life and the habits of individuals. This, however, cannot take place through coercion alone, but only through tempering compulsion (self-discipline) with persuasion. Persuasion should also take the form of high wages, which offer the possibility of a better standard of living, or more exactly perhaps, the possibility of realising a standard of living which is adequate to the new methods of production and work which demand a particular degree of expenditure of muscular and nervous energy.

To a limited but none the less important degree, phenomena similar to those created on a large scale by Fordism have been and still are occurring in certain branches of industry and in certain not yet 'Fordised' establishments. To build up an organic and well-articulated skilled labour force in a factory or a team of specialised workers, has never been easy. Once the labour force or the team has been built up, its components, or a part of them, sometimes not only finish up enjoying monopoly wages but are not dismissed from work in the event of a temporary check in production. It would be uneconomic to allow the elements of an organic whole so laboriously built up to be dispersed, because it would be almost impossible to bring them together again, while on the other hand reconstructing it with new elements, chosen haphazardly, would involve not inconsiderable effort and expense. This is a limitation on the law of competition determined by the reserve army and by unemployment, and this limitation has always been at the origin of the formation of privileged labour aristocracies. Since there has never functioned and does not function any law of perfect parity of systems and production and work methods valid for all firms in a specific branch of industry, it follows that every firm is, to a greater or less degree, 'unique' and will form a labour force with qualifications proper to its own particular requirements. Little manufacturing and working secrets, or 'fiddles', practised by this labour force, which in themselves seem insignificant, can, when repeated an infinite number of times, assume immense economic importance. A particular case of this can be observed in the organisation of work in the docks, particularly in ports where there is an imbalance between loading and unloading of goods or where seasonal pile-ups of goods alternate with seasons which are entirely dead. There has to be a skilled labour force which is permanently available (which does not absent itself from the place of work) to deal with the minimum of seasonal or other work, and this leads to the formation of a kind of closed shop with high wages and other privileges, opposed to the mass of 'casual' workers. The same thing happens in agriculture, in the relationship between tenant farmers and '*braccianti*'[3] and also in many industries which have 'dead' seasons, either for reasons inherent in the industry itself (as with the clothing industry) or because of the inefficient organisation of the wholesale trade which does its buying according to a pattern of its own which is not properly geared to the pattern of production.

NOTES

1. This phrase, whose revealing 'tactlessness' instantly attracted the attention of commentators, occurs on p. 40 of Frederick Taylor's *The Principles of Scientific Management* (1911), where the author writes: 'This work [pig-iron handling] is so crude and elementary in its nature that the writer firmly believes that it would be possible to train an intelligent gorilla so as to become a more efficient pig-iron handler than any man could be.' Frederick Taylor (1856–1915) was an American engineer and pioneer of scientific management.

   For Gramsci's analysis of the significance of 'Taylorism', see also 'Taylorism and the Mechanisation of the Worker' and Introduction to this Section.
2. 'demiurge': from the Greek, meaning a handicraftsman, but with the extended sense, in Platonic philosophy, of 'creator of the world'.
3. '*braccianti*': landless agricultural labourers, who are not fixed wage earners but are hired by the day according to the work to be done. The problems of organising in a single movement 'braccianti' and small tenant farmers, with their obviously conflicting immediate interests, were particularly acute in the Romagna and the Po Valley.

Part 3

DURKHEIM AND FUNCTIONALISM

INTRODUCTION

I. Understanding Society

This selection focuses mainly on the work of the French sociologist Émile Durkheim but will take the story further by discusing the functionalist sociology of Talcott Parsons. Durkheim and Parsons share an emphasis on social cohesion, equilibrium, regulation, integration and organisation. Society is seen as an organism that maintains itself while its institutions and practices are seen in terms of their function in performing a social requirement.

Society is prior to the individual and forms an organic whole: 'society is not the mere sum of individuals, but the system formed by their association represents a specific reality which has its own characteristics' (Durkheim 1982: 129). One of the ways in which Durkheim expresses this is through the idea of the collective conscience or collective habits, which 'are expressed in definite forms such as legal or moral rules, popular sayings, or facts of social structure . . . they constitute a fixed object, a constant standard which is always to hand for the observer' (Durkheim 1982: 82). Durkheim talks of collective representations as the condensation of the beliefs and values of a society – 'what collective representations express is the way in which the group thinks of itself in its relationships with the objects which affect it' (Durkheim 1982: 40).

Durkheim describes his study of the form and structure of society as a social morphology. He describes three different levels, which may be listed as:

1. morphology – the substratum of collective life – volume, distribution and density of population, material objects – instruments, machines, raw materials, etc.
2. institutions – the normative sphere – more or less formal legal and moral rules and norms, morals, religious dogmas, political forms, economics, professional roles, collective habits and routines.
3. collective representations – symbolic – societal values and ideals, various opinions, legends, myths, religious representations, emerging values and opinions.

II. Religion and the Collective Conscience

Durkheim's views on religion are well known. He argues that it performs an essential social function in maintaining social cohesion through belief systems. Through collective representations we get a conception of ourselves, of each other and of our relations with the natural world. They are based on cooperation between people and are the combination of different ideas and feelings that have accumulated (Durkheim 1995: 15). The collective or common conscience describes the beliefs and sentiments that are shared in common by members of society. The French term '*conscience*' implies both conscience and consciousness. It is not an expression of individual consciousness but something objective that develops according to its own laws. With the development of a collective conscience our morality is universalised. Thus religion serves to impose a uniformity of beliefs and actions in that 'all known religions have been systems of ideas that tend to embrace the universality of things and to give us a representation of the world as a whole' (Durkheim 1995: 140).

Religions contain a set of representations and modes of ritual conduct that provide a basis for collective action and understanding. They are specifically systems of ideas, attitudes and actions towards sacred things that unifies the social group. A basic social function of religion is to maintain the separation between the sacred and profane by laying down a system of beliefs, rules and prohibitions:

> *A religion is a unified system of beliefs and practices relative to sacred things, that is to say, things set apart and forbidden – beliefs and practices which united into one single moral community called a Church, all those who adhere to them.* (Durkheim 1995: 44)

Durkheim argues that primitive religions have greater moral and intellectual uniformity, acting as the main basis of social solidarity. Members of the group recognise their duties and obligations towards each other, obligations that may include aid, vengeance and mourning. Therefore

> religious conceptions aim above all to express and explain not what is exceptional and abnormal but what is constant and regular. As a

> general rule, the gods are used far less to account for monstrosity, oddity, and anomaly than for the normal march of the universe. (Durkheim 1995: 26)

Like Weber, Durkheim believes the modern world becomes increasingly rationalistic, with the changing nature of belief systems leading to more diverse and complex social processes. But this is not seen negatively although it does present new problems – particularly of moral cohesiveness. However, 'it is the division of labor which, more and more, fills the role that was formerly filled by the common conscience. It is the principal bond of social aggregates of higher types' (Durkheim 1964: 173).

III. Solidarity and the Division of Labour

Durkheim defines social solidarity as the system of bonds and relations that tie us together and link us to the social whole. *The Division of Labour in Society* starts by examining less advanced societies where mechanical solidarity prevails. By this he means that the collective conscience is strong with no distinction between the individual and collective conscience. As the extract states, members share the same perceptions and functions and solidarity is based on likeness. Religion is the dominant belief system that unites people through common practices. Shared beliefs and sentiments allow the individual to have little autonomy. Durkheim describes this as a segmental structure, with society made up of small groups or segments organised into tribes with close proximity to one another. The structure of these segmental societies is like the rings of an earthworm, which are integrated into one body. As societies become more advanced the segments turn into organs with more specialised functions. Advanced societies are characterised by industrialisation and increased division of labour with specialised functions and autonomous social bodies. Solidarity now comes from occupation rather than kinship and social links are based on contracts. Common beliefs and practices start eroding and there emerges a more political and legal form of centralised power with specialised judicial and administrative functions. Organic solidarity is based on these more specialised social relations, with individuals linked more to each other rather than to society as a whole. As organic solidarity increases, society becomes more and more based on the interdependence of its members, whether through economic activities or though other specialised functions such as political or legal ones. However, increasingly specialised functions means there is less shared understanding. In place of collective states, individual personality becomes more and more important.

Durkheim's work also distinguishes between penal and contractual law. Penal law is about doing harm, either physically or through restricting freedom or reducing social honour. Penal law is more in keeping with mechanical solidarity and is a response to crimes that go against the common conscience or against prevailing social rules, common customs or core beliefs. Repressive force is used in proportion to the given offence and is a severe and swift 'public vindication'. The collective population is mobilised in moral outrage so that punishment expresses a 'unanimous aversion' to the crime, and 'serves to heal the wounds made upon collective sentiments' (Durkheim 1964: 108). The origin of the penal-repressive approach is religious and it serves to maintain collective sentiments in order to preserve power of social cohesion. Punishment's 'true function is to maintain social cohesion intact, while maintaining all its vitality in the common conscience' (Durkheim 1964: 108).

By contrast, in modern society organic solidarity binds people together through contracts rather than through the common conscience. Judicial law is based on contracts between individual parties rather than between individuals and society. Written law prescribes obligations to others and establishes the sanctions if violated. It is less about the cohesion of society as a whole, more about specialised or restitutive sanctions which aim to return things to their normal state and to re-establish what has been disturbed. Restitutive sanctions are based on specialised social institutions which become autonomous as a consequence of the developed division of labour.

Durkheim also has in mind a system of moral regulation that accompanies the division of labour. Class struggles and other social disturbances reflect a lack of social cohesion, due to the growth of new divisions of economic functions outpacing the development of corresponding forms of moral regulation. Whereas for Marx, economic conflict is a fundamental aspect of capitalist society, for Durkheim it is the product of unregulated economic expansion.

An example of this is what Durkheim calls the anomic division of labour, which is particularly prevalent during crises and commercial failure. Social cohesion is affected as social solidarity breaks down and individuals cannot understand the functions of society as a whole. With the anomic division of labour it becomes difficult to maintain relations between people. Another case is termed the forced division of labour, which occurs when jobs are allocated on the basis of unequal power relations rather than through free choice. In Durkheim's view, strong social solidarity is spontaneous, therefore with a forced division of labour individuals cannot enjoy their natural place in the social system. Crisis, therefore, is not primarily economic but moral, as is reflected in the process of anomie or normlessness. The resolution of these problems lies not with a change in the social order but with social reform and reconstruction. The division of labour leads to new laws and beliefs that have to be coordinated.

IV. Suicide and Anomie

Suicide is regarded as a pathological response to the civilisation of society. Its causes are not psychological but are located within society. The act of suicide is a consequence of a social condition and suicide often corresponds to a serious upheaval in the organic conditions of society. In Durkheim's view, 'suicide varies inversely with the degree of integration of the social groups of which the individual forms a part' (Durkheim 1951: 208). Social integration refers to bonds between the individual and society. These bonds are commonly held views and values that act as a check on individualism and focuses the individual outside the self. Social bonds act to impose restrictions and constraints on people, regulating individual wants and needs. Without them, we get anomic and egoistic forms of suicide.

Egoistic suicide occurs when the individual is not sufficiently integrated and it is a result of too much individuation and a weakening of the social fabric. If the individual is thrown to their own resources there is a greater chance of suicide. Individuals retreat into themselves and detach themselves from society. By contrast, altruistic suicide results from too much social integration. The bond between the individual and society is excessively strong owing to such things as customs or social honour. Suicide is almost like a social duty or obligation, where pressure is brought upon the individual by society to avoid disgrace.

As religion plays less of a role in the life of individuals, social bonds get weaker and attachment to the community declines. With Protestantism, the religious act of confession is replaced with self-reflection and ritual is minimised. This self-reflection loosens the hold of religious doctrine and encourages greater self-reliance and hence egoism. The problem is that this egoism comes at the expense of social integration in that once the obligations of religious teaching are questioned, social cohesion starts to break down. While older forms of regulation like religion and the family start to fail, new functional substitutes may not be forthcoming, leading to social disequilibrium and anomie. Anomie refers to the absence of law, deregulation or the failure of regulating norms. Rapid economic change may give rise to new interests that have yet to reach equilibrium. Durkheim links anomic suicide to shifts in the regulatory mechanisms in society, in particular those responsible for social equilibrium. In modern society free enterprise and the spirit of competition replace religion as the dominant social institution. Economic development frees social activity from regulation by replacing religion and removing social limits. As religion is replaced by economic and industrial ends, desires get expressed through material wants. In modern societies these desires increase but social restraints are reduced.

V. North American Functionalism

Durkheim influences the structural-functionalism of later generations and we can find in his concept of anomie the basis for the work of North American sociologists such as Parsons and Robert Merton. They look at how these moral rules form the basis of social life and how they function to control or discipline our impulses. Drawing on Durkheim's distinction between the normal integrated society and the pathological conditions that deviate from this, functionalism distinguishes between healthy and pathological forms of social organisation. Social cohesion comes from socialised conformity to particular social rules and cultural norms. This internalised moral order relates to the collective conscience or system of common values beyond the individual level, which forms the basis of social order and collective solidarity.

Parsons outlines an evolutionary theory of social development with systems adapting to their environment. Society is self-regulating with a kind of adjustment mechanism that keeps it in a state of stable equilibrium:

> Every social system is a *functioning entity*. That is, it is a system of interdependent structures and processes such that it tends to maintain a relative stability and distinctiveness of pattern and behaviour as an entity . . . To this extent it is analogous to an organism. (Parsons 1954: 143)

Parsons's work is notorious for its awkward style and many distinctions and categories. One of Parsons's distinctions is between the social system divided into the personality system (and the process of socialisation), the cultural system (of normative structures and need-dispositions) and the realm of symbolic meanings. Culture is assessed in terms of its usefulness for system maintenance, as is social solidarity. When discussing the social system Parsons says that it must satisfy certain functional prerequisites if it is to survive. These four needs or requirements are:

1. Each system must adapt to its environment (adaption).
2. Each must have a means of mobilising its resources to achieve its goals and obtain gratification (goal attainment).
3. The system must maintain internal coordination of its parts and develop ways of dealing with deviance. It must hold itself together (integration).
4. The system must maintain itself in a state of equilibrium (pattern maintenance).

Social actors should be mobilised in accordance with requirements of the role system. The psychological aspect of social life is examined in terms of the dispositions of social agents, their internalisation of social norms and their performance of a role. People act according to their need-dispositions and their internalisation of cultural patterns.

The socialisation process involves mechanisms of value acquisition, instruction, reward and punishment. The moral code provides the basis for social cohesion and a lack of conformity with these moral norms constitutes the central 'strain' in the social system – that is to say, the problem of deviance. The conformity–deviance dimension is a functional problem inherent in socially structured systems of social action, particularly in relation to cultural values. Conflicts are viewed in relation to institutions and strains are the product of changes in the institutional complex. Therefore social cohesion is based on maintaining a dynamic equilibrium while deviance is seen as a disturbance of the equilibrium of this interactive system – something that is developed further in Merton's work. This looks at how social structures develop mechanisms that articulate different obligations and values while articulating social status through the allocation of different roles. Merton's 'primary aim is to discover how some *social structures exert a definite pressure upon certain persons in the society to engage in non-conforming rather than conforming conduct*' (Merton 1957: 132). Culture is something that imposes on people from the outside and, as with Parsons, is seen as a set of norms governing behaviour of a social group. Social disorganisation may come from conflicting values, conflicting interests, conflicting status and social roles, and faulty socialisation and social communication. Social cohesion is viewed in terms of the regulatory capacity of society while conflict or dissensus is a result of the breakdown of this capacity. One explanation is that society's overemphasis on material goals or monetary success leads to the failure of the regulatory capacity of society. With people located differently within the opportunity structure, gaps emerge between aspirations and attainment. This breakdown is Merton's way of understanding anomie. His account is particularly relevant to North American society and the way the system fetishises money as a sign of success while blaming the worse off rather than the structure for failure.

The theories of Parsons and Merton were developed during a period of economic expansion and reflect this with their emphasis on stability and order. But there were underlying threats in the form of anxieties about the Soviet Union and the dangers posed to social order by rapid economic growth. The functionalists look at how modern society is ordered and how conflict might be avoided by better regulation.

FROM *THE ELEMENTARY FORMS OF THE RELIGIOUS LIFE*

Émile Durkheim

No doubt, when all we do is consider the formulas literally, these religious beliefs and practices appear disconcerting, and our inclination might be to write them off to some sort of inborn aberration. But we must know how to reach beneath the symbol to grasp the reality it represents and that gives the symbol its true meaning. The most bizarre or barbarous rites and the strangest myths translate some human need and some aspect of life, whether social or individual. The reasons the faithful settle for in justifying those rites and myths may be mistaken, and most often are; but the true reasons exist nonetheless, and it is the business of science to uncover them.

Fundamentally, then, there are no religions that are false. All are true after their own fashion: All fulfill given conditions of human existence, though in different ways. Granted, it is not impossible to rank them hierarchically. Some can be said to be superior to others, in the sense that they bring higher mental faculties into play, that they are richer in ideas and feelings, that they contain proportionately more concepts than sensations and images, and that they are more elaborately systematized. But the greater complexity and higher ideal content, however real, are not sufficient to place the corresponding religions into separate genera. All are equally religious, just as all living beings are equally living beings, from the humblest plastid to man. If I address myself to primitive religions, then, it is not with any ulterior motive of disparaging religion in general: these religions are to be respected no less than the others. They fulfill the same needs, play

Émile Durkheim (1995), *The Elementary Forms of the Religious Life*, New York: Free Press.

the same role, and proceed from the same causes; therefore, they can serve just as well to elucidate the nature of religious life and, it follows, to solve the problem I wish to treat.

Still, why give them a kind of priority? Why choose them in preference to others as the subject of my study? This choice is solely for reasons of method.

First of all, we cannot arrive at an understanding of the most modern religions without tracing historically the manner in which they have gradually taken shape. Indeed, history is the only method of explanatory analysis that can be applied to them. History alone enables us to break down an institution into its component parts, because it shows those parts to us as they are born in time, one after the other. Second, by situating each part of the institution within the totality of circumstances in which it was born, history puts into our hands the only tools we have for identifying the causes that have brought it into being. Thus, whenever we set out to explain something human at a specific moment in time – be it a religious belief, a moral rule, a legal principle, an aesthetic technique, or an economic system – we must begin by going back to its simplest and most primitive form. We must seek to account for the features that define it at that period of its existence and then show how it has gradually developed, gained in complexity, and become what it is at the moment under consideration.

If it is useful to know what a given religion consists of; it is far more important to examine what religion is in general. This is a problem that has always intrigued philosophers, and not without reason: it is of interest to all humanity. Unfortunately, the method philosophers ordinarily use to solve it is purely one of dialectic: all they do is analyze the idea they have of religion, even if they have to illustrate the results of that mental analysis with examples borrowed from those religions that best suit their model. But while this method must be abandoned, the problem of definition remains; and philosophy's great service has been to prevent it from being settled once and for all[1] by the disdain of the savants. The problem can in fact be approached in another way. Since all religions may be compared, all being species within the same genus, some elements are of necessity common to them all. By that I mean not only the outward and visible features that they all equally exhibit and that make it possible to define religion in a provisional way at the beginning of research. The discovery of these apparent signs is relatively easy, for the observation required does not go beyond the surface of things. But these external resemblances presuppose deeper ones. At the foundation of all systems of belief and all cults, there must necessarily be a certain number of fundamental representations and modes of ritual conduct that, despite the diversity of forms that the one and the other may have taken on, have the same objective meaning everywhere and everywhere fulfill the same functions. It is these enduring elements that constitute what is eternal and human in religion. They are the whole objective content of the idea that is expressed when *religion* in general is spoken of.

How, then, can those elements be uncovered?

Surely it is not by observing the complex religions that have arisen in the course of history. Each of those religions is formed from such a variety of elements that it is very hard to distinguish what is secondary to them from what is primary, and what is essential from what is accessory. Simply consider religions like those of Egypt, India, or classical antiquity! Each is a dense tangle of many cults that can vary according to localities, temples, generations, dynasties, invasions, and so on. Popular superstitions intermingle in them with the most sophisticated dogmas. Neither religious thinking nor religious practice is shared equally among the mass of the faithful. The beliefs as well as the rites are taken in different ways, depending on men, milieux, and circumstances. Here it is priests, there monks, elsewhere the laity; here, mystics and rationalists, theologians and prophets, and so on. Under such conditions, it is difficult to perceive what might be common to all. It is indeed possible to find ways of studying some particular phenomenon fruitfully – such as prophetism, monasticism, or the mysteries – through one or another of those systems in which it is especially well developed. But how can one find the common basis of religious life under the luxuriant vegetation that grows over it? How can one find the fundamental states characteristic of the religious mentality in general through the clash of theologies, the variations of ritual, the multiplicity of groupings, and the diversity of individuals?

The case is altogether different in the lower societies. The lesser development of individuality, the smaller scale of the group, and the homogeneity of external circumstances all contribute to reducing the differences and variations to a minimum. The group regularly produces an intellectual and moral uniformity of which we find only rare examples in the more advanced societies. Everything is common to everyone. The movements are stereotyped; everyone executes the same ones in the same circumstances; and this conformity of conduct merely translates that of thought. Since all the consciousnesses are pulled along in the same current, the individual type virtually confounds itself with the generic type. At the same time that all is uniform, all is simple. What could be more basic than those myths composed of a single theme, repeated endlessly, or than those rites composed of a small number of movements, repeated until the participants can do no more. Neither the popular nor the priestly imagination has yet had the time or the means to refine and transform the basic material of ideas and religious practices; reduced to essentials, that material spontaneously presents itself to examination, and discovering it calls for only a minimal effort. Inessential, secondary, and luxurious developments have not yet come to hide what is primary.* Everything is boiled down to what is absolutely indispensable,

* This is not to say, of course, that primitive cults do not go beyond bare essentials. Quite the contrary, as we will see, religious beliefs and practices that do not have narrowly utilitarian aims

to that without which there would be no religion. But the indispensable is also the fundamental, in other words, that which it is above all important for us to know.

[. . .]

But primitive religions do not merely allow us to isolate the constituent elements of religion; their great advantage is also that they aid in its explanation. Because the facts are simpler, the relations between them are more apparent. The reasons men invoke to explain their actions to themselves have not yet been refined and revamped by sophisticated thought: they are closer and more akin to the motives that caused those actions. To understand a delusion properly and to be able to apply the most appropriate treatment, the doctor needs to know what its point of departure was. That event is the more easily detected the nearer to its beginnings the delusion can be observed. Conversely, the longer a sickness is left to develop, the more that original point of departure slips out of view. This is so because all sorts of interpretations have intervened along the way, and the tendency of those interpretations is to repress the original state into the unconscious and to replace it with other states through which the original one is sometimes not easy to detect. The distance between a systematized delusion and the first impressions that gave birth to it is often considerable. The same applies to religious thought. As it progresses historically, the causes that called it into existence, though still at work, are seen no more except through a vast system of distorting interpretations. The popular mythologies and the subtle theologies have done their work: they have overlaid the original feelings with very different ones that, although stemming from primitive feelings of which they are the elaborated form, nevertheless allow their true nature to show only in part. The psychological distance between the cause and the effect, and between the apparent cause and the effective cause, has become wider and more difficult for the mind to overcome. The remainder of this work will be an illustration and a test of this methodological point. We will see how, in the primitive religions, the religious phenomenon still carries the visible imprint of its origins. It would have been much more difficult for us to infer those origins by considering more developed religions alone.

Thus, the study I undertake is a way of taking up again the old problem of the origin of religions *but under new conditions*. Granted, if by origin one means an absolute first beginning, there is nothing scientific about the question, and it must be resolutely set aside. There is no radical instant when religion began to exist, and the point is not to find a roundabout way

are found in every religion (Bk.III, chap. 4, §2). This nonutilitarian richness is indispensable to religious life, and of its very essence. But it is by far less well developed in the lower religions than in the others, and this fact will put us in a better position to determine its raison d'être.

of conveying ourselves there in thought. Like every other human institution, religion begins nowhere. So all speculations in this genre are righly discredited; they can consist of only subjective and arbitrary constructions without checks of any sort. The problem I pose is altogether different. I would like to find a means of discerning the ever-present causes on which the most basic forms of religious thought and practice depend. For the reasons just set forth, the causes are more easily observable if the societies in which they are observed are less complex. That is why I seek to get closer to the origins.** The reason is not that I ascribe special virtues to the lower religions. Quite the contrary, they are crude and rudimentary; so there can be no question of making them out to be models of some sort, which the later religions would only have had to reproduce. But their very lack of elaboration makes them instructive, for in this way they become useful experiments in which the facts and the relations among facts are easier to detect. To uncover the laws of the phenomena he studies, the physicist seeks to simplify those phenomena and to rid them of their secondary characteristics. In the case of institutions, nature spontaneously makes simplifications of the same kind at the beginning of history. I wish only to put those simplifications to good use. Doubtless, I will be able to obtain only very elementary facts by this method. When I have accounted for them, to the extent this will be possible, the novelties of all kinds that have been produced in the course of evolution will still not be explained. But although I would not dream of denying the importance of the problems such novelties pose, I think those problems benefit by being treated at the proper time, and there is good reason not to tackle them until after those whose study I have undertaken.

[. . .]

The general conclusion of the chapters to follow is that religion is an eminently social thing. Religious representations are collective representations that express collective realities; rites are ways of acting that are born only in the midst of assembled groups and whose purpose is to evoke, maintain, or recreate certain mental states of those groups. But if the categories are of religious origin, then they must participate in[2] what is common to all religion: they, too, must be social things, products of collective thought. At the very least – since with our present understanding of these matters, radical and exclusive theses are to be guarded against – it is legitimate to say that they are rich in social elements.

** It will be seen that I give the word 'origins', like the word 'primitive', an entirely relative sense. I do not mean by it an absolute beginning but the simplest social state known at present – the state beyond which it is at present impossible for us to go. When I speak about origins and the beginnings of history or religious thought, this is the sense in which those phrases must be understood.

NOTES

1. Swain rendered Durkheim's *prescrit* as 'suppressed', as if he had written *proscrit*.
2. The phrase 'participate in', which occurs frequently, has usually not been replaced with simpler possibilities such as 'partakes of' or 'shares in' because the notion of participation that can be seen in the sentence 'Jesus participated in divine and human nature' must be borne in mind, together with an argument in which Durkheim was engaged. Lucien Lévy-Bruhl, whose book *Les Fonctions mentales dans les sociétés inférieures* Durkheim criticizes, considered 'participations' to exemplify the inherent illogic of 'primitive' thought. Durkheim held just the opposite.

FROM *THE DIVISION OF LABOUR IN SOCIETY*

Émile Durkheim

From 'The Function of the Division of Labour: Organic Solidarity'

III.

[. . .]

There is in the consciousness of each one of us two consciousnesses: one that we share in common with our group in its entirety, which is consequently not ourselves, but society living and acting within us; the other that, on the contrary, represents us alone in what is personal and distinctive about us, what makes us an individual.[1] The solidarity that derives from similarities is at its *maximum* when the collective consciousness completely envelops our total consciousness, coinciding with it at every point. At that moment our individuality is zero. That individuality cannot arise until the community fills us less completely. Here there are two opposing forces, the one centripetal, the other centrifugal, which cannot increase at the same time. We cannot ourselves develop simultaneously in two so opposing directions. If we have a strong inclination to think and act for ourselves we cannot be strongly inclined to think and act like other people. If the ideal is to create for ourselves a special, personal image, this cannot mean to be like everyone else. Moreover, at the very moment when this solidarity exerts its effect, our personality, it may be said by definition, disappears, for we are no longer ourselves, but a collective being.

Émile Durkheim (1984), *The Division of Labour in Society*, tr. W. D. Halls, Basingstoke: Macmillan.

The social molecules that can only cohere in this one manner cannot therefore move as a unit save in so far as they lack any movement of their own, as do the molecules of inorganic bodies. This is why we suggest that this kind of solidarity should be called mechanical. The word does not mean that the solidarity is produced by mechanical and artificial means. We only use this term for it by analogy with the cohesion that links together the elements of raw materials, in contrast to that which encompasses the unity of living organisms. What finally justifies the use of this term is the fact that the bond that thus unites the individual with society is completely analogous to that which links the thing to the person. The individual consciousness, considered from this viewpoint, is simply a dependency of the collective type, and follows all its motions, just as the object possessed follows those which its owner imposes upon it. In societies where this solidarity is highly developed the individual, as we shall see later, does not belong to himself; he is literally a thing at the disposal of society. Thus, in these same social types, personal rights are still not yet distinguished from 'real' rights.

The situation is entirely different in the case of solidarity that brings about the division of labour. Whereas the other solidarity implies that individuals resemble one another, the latter assumes that they are different from one another. The former type is only possible in so far as the individual personality is absorbed into the collective personality; the latter is only possible if each one of us has a sphere of action that is peculiarly our own, and consequently a personality. Thus the collective consciousness leaves uncovered a part of the individual consciousness, so that there may be established in it those special functions that it cannot regulate. The more extensive this free area is, the stronger the cohesion that arises from this solidarity. Indeed, on the one hand each one of us depends more intimately upon society the more labour is divided up, and on the other, the activity of each one of us is correspondingly more specialised, the more personal it is. Doubtless, however circumscribed that activity may be, it is never completely original. Even in the exercise of our profession we conform to usages and practices that are common to us all within our corporation. Yet even in this case, the burden that we bear is in a different way less heavy than when the whole of society bears down upon us, and this leaves much more room for the free play of our initiative. Here, then, the individuality of the whole grows at the same time as that of the parts. Society becomes more effective in moving in concert, at the same time as each of its elements has more movements that are peculiarly its own. This solidarity resembles that observed in the higher animals. In fact each organ has its own special characteristics and autonomy, yet the greater the unity of the organism, the more marked the individualisation of the parts. Using this analogy, we propose to call 'organic' the solidarity that is due to the division of labour.

[...]

IV

The following propositions sum up this first part of our work.

Social life is derived from a dual source, the similarity of individual consciousnesses and the social division of labour. In the first case the individual is socialised because, lacking any individuality of his own, he is mixed up with his fellows in the same collective type. In the second case it is because, whilst his physiognomy and his activities are personal to him, distinguishing him from others, he depends upon them to the very extent that he is distinguished from them, and consequently upon the society that is the result of their combining together.

The similarity of consciousnesses gives rise to legal rules which, under the threat of repressive measures, impose upon everybody uniform beliefs and practices. The more pronounced the similarity, the more completely social life is mixed up with religious life, and the closer economic institutions are to communism.

The division of labour gives rise to legal rules that determine the nature and relationships of the function thus divided up, but the infringement of the rules entails only measures of reparation lacking any expiatory character.

Each set of legal rules moreover is accompanied by a set of rules that are purely moral. Where penal law is very voluminous common morality is very extensive. This means that there are a host of collective practices placed under the protection of public opinion. Where restitutory law is very developed, for each profession a professional morality exists. Within the same group of workers a public opinion exists, diffused throughout this limited body, which despite the lack of any legal sanctions, is nevertheless obeyed. There are customs and usages common to the same group of functionaries which none can infringe without incurring the reprimand of the corporation.[2] Yet this morality is distinguished from the previous one by differences analogous to those that separate the two corresponding species of laws. This morality is in fact localised within a limited area of society. Moreover, the repressive character of the sanctions attached to it is appreciably less severe. Professional faults give rise to a disapproval much weaker than attacks upon public morality.

However, the rules of professional morality and law are categorical, like the others. They force the individual to act in accordance with ends that are not for his own, to make concessions, to agree to compromises, to take into account interests superior to his own. Consequently even where society rests wholly upon the division of labour, it does not resolve itself into a myriad of atoms juxtaposed together, between which only external and transitory contact can be established. The members are linked by ties that extend well beyond the very brief moment when the act of exchange is being accomplished. Each one of the functions that the members exercise is constantly dependent upon others and constitutes with them a solidly linked system. Consequently the nature of the task selected derives from duties that are permanent. Because we fulfil this or that domestic or social function we are caught up in a network of obligations from which we have no right to disengage ourselves. There is above all one organ in regard to which our state of dependence continues to grow: this is the state. The points where we come into contact with it are multiplied, as well as the occasions when it is charged with reminding us of the sentiment of our common solidarity.

Thus altruism is not destined to become, as Spencer would wish, a kind of pleasant ornament of our social life, but one that will always be its fundamental basis. How indeed could we ever do without it? Men cannot live together without agreeing, and consequently without making mutual sacrifices, joining themselves to one another in a strong and enduring fashion. Every society is a moral society. In certain respects this feature is even more pronounced in organised societies. Because no individual is sufficient unto himself, it is from society that he receives all that is needful, just as it is for society that he labours. Thus there is formed a very strong feeling of the state of dependence in which he finds himself: he grows accustomed to valuing himself at his true worth, viz., to look upon himself only as a part of the whole, the organ of an organism. Such sentiments are of a kind not only to inspire those daily sacrifices that ensure the regular development of everyday social life but even on occasion acts of utter renunciation and unbounded abnegation. For its part society learns to look upon its constituent members no longer as things over which it has rights, but as co-operating members with whom it cannot do without and towards whom it has duties. Thus it is wrong to oppose a society that derives from a community of beliefs to one whose foundation is co-operation, by granting only the first a moral character and seeing in the latter only an economic grouping. In reality, co-operation has also its intrinsic morality. There is only reason to believe, as we shall later see more clearly, that in our present-day societies this morality has still not developed to the extent which from now onwards is necessary for them.

But this morality is not of the same nature as the other. The latter is strong only if the individual is weak. Made up of rules practised by all without distinction, it receives from this universal, uniform practice an authority that makes it something superhuman, removing it more or less from argument. The other, by contrast, develops as the individual personality grows stronger. However regulated a function may be, it always leaves plenty of room for individual initiative. Even many of the obligations that are subject to penalties in this way have their origin in a choice by the will. It is we who choose our profession and even certain of our domestic functions. Doubtless once our resolve has ceased to be internal and been translated externally into social consequences, we are bound by it: duties are imposed upon us that we have not expressly wished. Yet it is through a voluntary act that they arose. Finally, because these rules of conduct relate not to the conditions of ordinary life but to different forms of professional activity, they have for this reason a more temporal character which, so to speak, whilst retaining all their obligatory force, makes them more accessible to the actions of men.

There are thus two great currents in social life, to which correspond two types of structure that are no less different.

Of these currents, the one that has its origin in social similarities flows at first alone, and has no competition. At that time it mingles with the very life of society. Then gradually it becomes channelled and becomes less apparent, whilst the second continues to grow bigger. Likewise to segmentary structure is more and more overshadowed by the other, but without ever disappearing completely.

[...]

FROM 'THE ABNORMAL FORMS: CONCLUSION'

I

If there is one rule of conduct whose moral character is undisputed, it is that which decrees that we should realise in ourselves the essential features of the collective type. It is among lower peoples that it attains the greatest inflexibility. There the first duty is to resemble everyone else, to have nothing that is personal, whether as regards beliefs or practices. In the more advanced societies, the similarities that are required are fewer in number. However, as we have seen, some exist, the absence of which constitutes for us a state of moral error. Doubtless crime comprises a lesser number of different categories. But today as formerly, if the criminal is the object of reprobation, it is because he is not like us. Likewise, on a lower plane, acts that are merely immoral and prohibited as such are those that display dissimilarities that are less profound, although still serious. Moreover, is it not this rule that common morality expresses, although in somewhat different language, when it ordains that a man should be a man in every sense of the word, that is, possess all the ideas and sentiments that constitute a human consciousness? Undoubtedly if one follows this formula to the letter, the man it prescribes for us would be man in general, and not one of this or that social species. But in reality that human consciousness that we must realise within ourselves in its entirety is nothing other than the collective consciousness of the group of which we form part. For of what can it be made up, if not of the ideas and sentiments to which we are most attached? Where should we turn to look for the characteristics of our model if it is not within ourselves and around us? If we believe that this collective ideal is that of the whole of humanity, it is because it has become sufficiently abstract and general to appear to suit all men without distinction. Yet in fact every people forms regarding this alleged type of humanity a particular conception that derives from its personal temperament. Each one represents it in his own image. Even the moralist who believes he is able, by the power of thought, to withdraw himself from the influence of surrounding ideas, cannot succeed in doing so. For he is entirely permeated by them and, whatever he does, it is they that he discovers once more at the conclusion of his deductions. This is why every nation has a school of moral philosophy that is in harmony with its character.

On the other hand, we have shown that the function of this rule was to forestall any disturbance of the common consciousness and, consequently, of social solidarity. It cannot perform this role save on condition that it possesses a moral character. It is impossible for offences against the most fundamental of the collective sentiments to be tolerated without society disintegrating. But such offences must be combated with the aid of that particularly energetic reaction associated with moral rules.

Now the opposite rule, which decrees that we should specialise, has exactly the same function. It is also necessary for the cohesion of societies, at least from a certain time onwards in their evolution. Doubtless, the solidarity that it ensures differs from the former one. But if it is different, it is no less indispensable. Higher societies cannot maintain their equilibrium unless work is divided up. The attraction of like for like suffices less and less to produce this effect. If therefore the moral character of the first of these rules is necessary for it to be able to perform its role, this necessity is no less for the second rule. They both correspond to the same social need and satisfy it only in different ways because the conditions of existence within societies themselves differ. Consequently, without our needing to speculate on the prime foundation of ethics, we can induce the moral value of the one from the moral value of the other. If from certain viewpoints, there is truly antagonism between them, it is not because they serve different ends. On the contrary, it is because they lead to the same aim, but by opposing routes. Thus it is not necessary to choose between them once and for all, nor to condemn the one in the name of the other. What must be done is to give to each one, at each moment of history, the place that is fitting.

We may perhaps be able to generalise even more.

The necessities of our subject have in fact obliged us to classify moral rules and to review the main species among them. Thus we are better able than we were at the outset to perceive, or at the very least to conjecture, not merely the external signs but the internal character that is common to them all and that can serve to define them. We have split them into two kinds: rules with a repressive sanction, which is either diffuse or organised, and rules with a restitutory sanction. We have seen that the former express the conditions of that solidarity *sui generis* which derives from resemblances, and to which we have given the name mechanical solidarity. The latter, those of negative solidarity,[3] we have termed organic solidarity. Thus we may state generally that the characteristic of moral rules is that they enunciate the basic conditions of social solidarity. Law and morality represent the totality of bonds that bind us to one another and to society, which shape the mass of individuals into a cohesive aggregate. We may say that what is moral is everything that is a source of solidarity, everything that forces man to take account of other people, to regulate his actions by something other than the promptings of his own egoism, and the more numerous and strong these ties are, the more solid is the morality. We can see how inaccurate it is to define it, as has often been done, in terms of freedom. It rather consists much more in a state of dependence. Far from it serving to emancipate the individual, disengaging him from the surrounding environment, its essential function, on the contrary, is to be the integrating element in a whole, and in consequence it removes from the individual some of his freedom of movement. It is true that occasionally we meet souls who are not without nobility but who find this idea of dependence intolerable. Yet this is because they do not perceive the source from where flows their own morality, because that source is too deep. Conscience is a poor judge of what occurs in the depths of one's being, because it does not penetrate that far.

Thus society is not, as has often been believed, some happening that is a stranger to morality, or which has only secondary reprecussions upon it. It is not a mere juxtaposition of individuals who, upon entering into it, bring with them an intrinsic morality. Man is only a moral being because he lives in society, since morality consists in solidarity with the group, and varies according to that solidarity. Cause all social life to vanish, and moral life would vanish at the same time, having no object to cling to. The state of nature of the eighteenth-century Philosophes is, if not immoral, at least *amoral*, a fact that Rousseau himself recognised. For that reason, moreover, we do not fall back upon the formula that expresses morality as a function of social interest. Doubtless society cannot exist if its parts are not solidly bound to one another, but solidarity is only one of the conditions for its existence. There are many others no less necessary, which are not moral. Moreover, it can be that, within this network of the ties that go to make up morality, there are some that are not useful in themselves, or whose strength bears no relationship to their degree of usefulness. The idea of the useful does not therefore come into our definition as an essential element of it.

As for what is termed individual morality, if by this is meant a set of duties in relation to which the individual would be both subject and object, which would bind him only to himself and would consequently subsist even if he were alone, this is an abstract conception that has no foundation in reality. Morality, at all levels, is never met with save in the state of society and has never varied save as a function of social conditions. Thus to ask what morality might become if societies did not exist is to depart from the facts and to enter the realm of gratuitous hypothesis and unverifiable fantasy. In reality the duties of the individual to himself are duties to society. They correspond to certain collective sentiments which it is no more permissible to offend when the offended person and the offender are one and the same person than when they are two distinct individuals. For example, today there is in every healthy consciousness a very active feeling of respect for human dignity, to which we are obliged to make our behaviour conform both in our relationship with ourselves and in our relationship with others – this is indeed all that is essential in the kind of morality termed individual. Any action that offends it is blamed, even when the doer and the sufferer of the offence are one and the same person. This is why, in Kant's formula, we must respect human personality wherever we meet it, that is, within ourselves and within our fellow-beings. This is because the sentiment of which it is the object is no less offended in the one case than in the other.

Not only does the division of labour exhibit that character by which we define morality, but it increasingly tends to become the essential condition for social solidarity. As evolution advances, the bonds that attach the individual to his family, to his native heath, to the traditions that the past has bequeathed him, to the collective practices of the group – all these become loosened. Being more mobile, the individual changes his environment more easily, leaves his own people to go and live a more autonomous life elsewhere, works out for himself his ideas and sentiments. Doubtless all trace of common consciousness does not vanish because of this. At the very least there will always subsist that cult of the person and individual dignity about which we have just spoken, which today is already the unique rallying-point for so many minds. But how insignificant this is if we consider the ever-increasing scope of social life and, consequently, of the individual consciousness! As the latter becomes more expansive, as the intelligence becomes even better equipped, and activity more varied, for morality to remain unchanged, that is, for the individual to be bound to the group even so strongly as once he was, the ties that bind him must be reinforced, becoming more numerous. Thus if only those ties were forged that were based on similarities, the disappearance of the segmentary type of society would be accompanied by a steady decline in morality. Man would no longer be held adequately under control. He would no longer feel around him and above him that salutary pressure of society that moderates his egoism, making of him a moral creature. This it is that constitutes the moral value of the division of labour. Through it the individual is once more made aware of his dependent state *vis-à-vis* society. It is from society that proceed those forces that hold him in check and keep him within bounds. In short, since the division of labour becomes the predominant source of social solidarity, at the same time it becomes the foundation of the moral order.

We may thus state literally that in higher societies our duty lies not in extending the range of our activity but in concentrating it, in making it more specialised. We must limit our horizons, select a definite task, and involve ourselves utterly, instead of making ourselves, so to speak, a finished work of art, one that derives all its value from itself rather than from the services it renders. Finally, this specialisation must be carried the farther the more society is of a higher species. No other limits can be placed upon it.[4] Undoubtedly we must also work towards realising within ourselves the collective type, in so far as it exists. There are common sentiments and ideas without which, as one says, one is not a man. The rule prescribing that we should specialise remains limited by the opposite rule. We conclude that it is not good to push specialisation as far as possible, but only as far as necessary. The weight to be given to these two opposing necessities is determined by experience and cannot be calculated *a priori*. It suffices for us to have shown that the latter is no different in nature from the former, but that it is also moral and that, moreover, this duty becomes ever more important and urgent, because the general qualities we have discussed suffice less and less to socialise the individual.

Thus it is not without reason that public sentiment is continually distancing itself even more markedly from the dilettante, and even from those who, too much absorbed with a culture that is exclusively general, shrink from allowing themselves to be wholly caught up with the professional organisation. This is in fact because they do not adhere closely enough to society or, if one likes, society does not hold on to them closely enough. They elude it, and precisely because they do not feel it with the sense of vividness and continuity needed, they are unaware of all the obligations laid upon them by their condition as social beings. The general idea to which they are attached being, for reasons we have given, formal and fluctuating, it cannot draw them very much outside themselves. Without a determinate goal one does not cling to very much, so that one can scarcely lift oneself out of a more or less refined egoism. On the other hand, he who has dedicated himself to a definite task is reminded at every moment of the common sentiment of solidarity through the thousand and one duties of professional morality.[5]

II

Yet does not the division of labour, by rendering each one of us an incomplete being, not entail some curtailment of the individual personality? This criticism has often been made.

Firstly, let us note that it is difficult to see why it might be more in accord with the logic of human nature to develop more superficially rather than in depth. Why should a more extensive activity, one that is more dispersed, be superior to one more concentrated and circumscribed? Why should more dignity attach to being complete and mediocre than in leading a more specialised kind of life but one more intense, particularly if we can recapture in this way what we have lost, through our association with others who possess what we lack and who make us complete beings? We start from the principle that man must realise his nature as man – as Aristotle said, accomplish his *οἰχέίον ἔργον*. But at different moments in history this nature does not remain constant; it is modified with societies. Among lower peoples, the act that connotes a man is to resemble his fellows, to realise within himself all the characteristics of the collective type which, even more than today, was then confused with the human type. In more advanced societies man's nature is mainly to be a part of society; consequently the act that connotes a man is for him to play his part as one organ of society.

There is something more: far from the progress of specialisation whittling away the individual personality, this develops with the division of labour.

Indeed to be a person means to be an autonomous source of action. Thus man only attains this state to the degree that there is something within him that is his and his alone, that makes him an individual, whereby he is more than the mere embodiment of the generic type of his race and group. It will in any case be objected that he is endowed with free will, and that this is sufficient upon which to base his personality. But whatever this freedom may consist of – and it is the subject of much argument – it is not this impersonal, invariable, metaphysical attribute that can serve as the sole basis for the empirical, variable and concrete personality of individuals. That personality cannot be formed by the entirely abstract capacity to choose between two opposites. This faculty must be exercised in relation to ends and motives that are peculiar to the person acting. In other words the stuff of which his consciousness is made up must have a personal character. Now we have seen in the second book of this study that is an outcome that occurs progressively as the division of labour itself progresses. The disappearance of the segmentary type of society, at the same time as it necessitates greater specialisation, frees the individual consciousness in part from the organic environment that supports it, as it does from the social environment that envelops it. This dual emancipation renders the individual more independent in his own behaviour. The division of labour itself contributes to this liberating effect. Individual natures become more complex through specialising; by this very fact they are partly shielded against the effects of the collectivity and the influences of heredity, which can scarcely enforce themselves except in simple, general matters.

Thus, as a consequence of a veritable illusion, one could occasionally believe that the personality was more whole, so long as it had not been breached by the division of labour. Doubtless, viewing from the outside the variety of occupations that the individual embarks upon, it may seem that the personality then develops more freely and completely. But in reality the activity he displays is not his own. It is society, it is the race, which act in and through him; he is only the intermediary through which they are realised. His liberty is only apparent, his personality is borrowed. Since the life of societies is in certain respects less regular, we imagine that original talents can more easily come to light, that it is easier for each individual to follow his own tastes, that greater room is left for the free play of fantasy. Yet this is to forget that personal sentiments are then very rare. If the motives governing conduct do not occur with the same regularity as they do today, they do not cease to be collective, and consequently impersonal. The same is true for the actions they inspire. We have moreover shown above how the activity becomes richer and more intense the more specialised it becomes.[6]

Thus the advance of the individual personality and that of the division of labour depend on one and the same cause. Thus also it is impossible to will the one without willing the other. Nowadays no one questions the obligatory nature of the rule that ordains that we should exist as a person, and this increasingly so.

One final consideration will show to what extent the division of labour is linked to our whole moral life.

It has long been a dream cherished by men to succeed at last in achieving as a reality the ideal of human brotherhood. Peoples raise their voices to wish for a state of affairs where war would no longer govern international relations, where relationships between societies would be regulated peacefully as are already those between individuals, and where all men would co-operate in the common task and live the same life. Although these aspirations are partly neutralised by others that relate to the particular society of which we form part, they remain very strong and are continually gathering strength. However, they cannot be satisfied unless all men form part of one and the same society, subject to the same laws. For, just as private conflicts can only be contained by the regulatory action of a society that embraces all individuals, so inter-social conflicts can only be contained by the regulatory action of a society that embraces all societies. The only power that can serve to moderate individual egoism is that of the group; the only one that can serve to moderate the egoism of groups is that of another group that embraces them all.

Really, once the problem has been posed in these terms, we must acknowledge that this ideal is not on the verge of being realised in its entirety. Between the different types of society coexisting on earth there are too many intellectual and moral divergences to be able to live in a spirit of brotherhood in the same society. Yet what is possible is that societies of the same species should come together, and it is indeed in this direction that our society appears to be going. We have seen already that there is tending to form, above European peoples, in a spontaneous fashion, a European society that has even now some feeling of its own identity and the beginnings of an organisation.[7] If the formation of one single human society is for ever ruled out – and this has, however, not yet been demonstrated[8] at least the formation of larger societies will draw us continually closer to that goal. Moreover, these facts do not at all contradict the definition we have given of morality. If we cling to humanity and ought to continue to do so, it is because it is a society in the process of realising itself in this way, one to which we are solidly bound.[9]

Yet we know that more extensive societies cannot be formed without the development of the division of labour. Without a greater specialisation of functions not only could they not sustain their equilibrium, but the increase in the number of elements in competition would also automatically suffice to bring about that state. Even more would this be the case, for an increase in volume does not generally occur without an increase in population density. Thus we may formulate the following proposition: the ideal of human brotherhood cannot be realised unless the division of labour progresses. We must choose: either we must abandon our dream, if we refuse to limit our individual activity any further; or we can pursue the consummation of our dream, but only on the condition just stated.

III

Yet if the division of labour produces solidarity, it is not only because it makes each individual an agent of exchange, to use the language of the economists.[10] It is because it creates between men a whole system of rights and duties joining them in a lasting way to one another. Just as social similarities give rise to a law and a morality that protect them, so the division of labour gives rise to rules ensuring peaceful and regular co-operation between the functions that have been divided up. If economists have believed that this would produce enough solidarity, however it came about, and in consequence have maintained that human societies could and should resolve themselves into purely economic associations, it is because they believed that only individual and temporary interests were at stake. Thus, in order to evaluate the interests that conflict and ascertain how they should be balanced, that is, to determine the conditions in which exchange should take place, individuals alone are competent. Moreover, since these interests are continually developing, there is no room for any permanent regulatory system. But from every viewpoint such a conception is inadequate and does not fit the facts. The division of labour does not present individuals to one another, but social functions. Society has an interest in the interplay of those functions: depending on whether they co-operate regularly or not, society will be healthy or sick. Its existence is therefore dependent upon them, all the more intimately bound up with them the more they are divided. This is why it cannot let them remain in an indeterminate state; moreover, they determine one another. It is like this that rules arise which increase in number the more labour is divided – rules whose absence makes organic solidarity either impossible or imperfect.

But the mere existence of rules is not sufficient: they must also be just. For this the external conditions of competition should be equal. If, on the other hand, we call to mind that the collective consciousness is increasingly reduced to the cult of the individual, we shall see that the characteristic of morality in organised societies, as compared to segmentary societies, is that it possesses something more human, and consequently more rational, about it. It does not cause our activity to depend upon ends that do not directly concern us. It does not make us the servants of some ideal powers completely different in nature from ourselves, powers who follow their own course without heeding the interests of men. It requires us only to be charitable and just towards our fellow-men, to fulfil our task well, to work towards a state where everyone is called to fulfil the function he performs best and will receive a just reward for his efforts. The rules constituting this morality have no constraining power preventing their being fully examined. Because they are better made for us and, in a certain sense, by us, we are freer in relation to them. We seek to understand them and are less afraid to change them. Moreover, we must be careful not to esteem such an ideal defective on the pretext that it is too down-to-earth, too easily within our grasp. An ideal is no more lofty because it is more transcendent, but because it opens up broader vistas to us. It is not important that such an ideal should soar high above us – to an extent that it becomes foreign to us. But it is important that it should open up for our activity a long-term perspective – and such an ideal is far from being on the point of realisation. We feel only too well how laborious a task it is to erect such a society, one in which each individual will have the place he merits and will be rewarded according to his deserts, where everyone will consequently co-operate spontaneously both for the common good and that of the individual. Likewise no morality is superior to all others because its imperatives are couched in a drier, more authoritarian manner, or because it is immune from reflective thinking. Doubtless it must be capable of linking us to something other than ourselves. But there is no need for it to fetter us to the point that it immobilises us.

It has been rightly stated[11] that morality – and this must include both theory and the practice of ethics – is in the throes of an appalling crisis. What we have expounded can help us to understand the causes and nature of this sickness. Over a very short space of time very profound changes have occurred in the structure of our societies. They have liberated themselves from the segmentary model with a speed and in proportions without precedent in history. Thus the morality corresponding to this type of society has lost influence, but without its successor developing quickly enough to occupy the space left vacant in our consciousness. Our beliefs have been disturbed. Tradition has lost its sway. Individual judgement has thrown off the yoke of the collective judgement. On the other hand, the functions that have been disrupted in this period of trial have had no time to adjust to one another. The new life that all of a sudden has arisen has not been able to organise itself thoroughly. Above all, it has not been organised so as to satisfy the need for justice that has been aroused even more passionately in our hearts. If this is so, the remedy for the ill is nevertheless not to seek to revive traditions and practices that no longer correspond to present-day social conditions, and that could only subsist in a life that would be artificial, one only of appearance. We need to put a stop to this anomie, and to find ways of harmonious co-operation between those organs that still clash discordantly together. We need to introduce into their relationships a greater justice by diminishing those external inequalities that are the source of our ills. Our disease is therefore not, as occasionally we appear to believe, of an intellectual order, but linked to deeper causes. We are not suffering because we no longer know on what theoretical idea should be sustained the morality we have practised up to now. The cause is that certain elements of this morality have been irretrievably undermined, and the morality we require is only in the process of taking shape. Our anxiety does not arise because the criticism of scientists has demolished the traditional explanation handed down to us regarding our duties. Consequently it is not a new philosophical system that will ever be capable of dispelling that anxiety. Rather is it because certain of these duties no longer being grounded on reality, a loosening of ties has occurred that can only stop when a new discipline has become established and consolidated itself. In short, our first duty at the present time is to fashion a morality for ourselves. Such a task cannot be improvised in the silence of the study. It can arise only of its own volition, gradually, and under the pressure of internal causes that render it necessary. What reflection can and must do is to prescribe the goal that must be attained. That is what we have striven to accomplish.

NOTES

1. L. H. Morgan, *Ancient Society* (London, 1877) p. 81.
2. Moreover, this rebuke, like any moral punishment, is translated into external action (disciplinary punishments, dismissal of employees, loss of relationships, etc.).
3. Cf. *supra*, Book I, Chapter III, § II.
4. However, there is perhaps another limit about which we need not speak, since it rather concerns individual hygiene. It might be maintained that, as a result of our organic and psychological make-up, the division of labour cannot go beyond a certain limit without disorders ensuing. Without going into the question, let us however note that the extreme specialisation that the biological functions have attained does not seem to substantiate this hypothesis. Furthermore, even in the domain of psychological and social functions, through historical development, has not the division of labour between man and woman been carried to its ultimate limit? Have not whole abilities been lost by the latter, and is the converse not also true? Why should the same phenomenon not occur between persons of the same sex? Undoubtedly time is always needed for the organism to adapt to these changes, but we cannot see why a day should come when this adaptation will become impossible.
5. Among the practical consequences that could be drawn from the proposition we have just established, there is one that concerns pedagogy. As regards education one always reasons as if the moral foundation of man was made up of generalities. We have just seen that this is in no way true. Man is destined to fulfil a special function in the social organism, and consequently he must learn in advance how to play his part as one organ. An education is necessary for this, just as it is for him to learn to play his part as a man, as is said. Moreover, we do not mean that the child should be brought up prematurely for a particular occupation, but he should be induced to like limited tasks and well-defined horizons. This aptitude is very different from that of general matters and cannot be awakened by the same means.
6. Cf. *supra*, pp. 214 ff. and p. 252.
7. Cf. pp. 222–3.
8. There is nothing that demonstrates that the intellectual and moral diversity of societies is destined to continue. The ever greater expansion of higher societies, whereby

the absorption or elimination of less advanced societies occurs, is tending in any case to lessen that diversity.

9. Thus the duties we have towards society do not take precedence over those we have towards our country. For the latter is the sole society that is at present realised of which we form part. The other is hardly more than a *desideratum*, whose realisation is not even certain.
10. The term is that of de Molinari, *La morale économique*, p. 248.
11. Cf. Beaussire, *Les principes de la morale*, introduction.

FROM *SUICIDE*

Émile Durkheim

We have thus successively set up the three following propositions:

> *Suicide varies inversely with the degree of integration of religious society.*
> *Suicide varies inversely with the degree of integration of domestic society.*
> *Suicide varies inversely with the degree of integration of political society.*

This grouping shows that whereas these different societies have a moderating influence upon suicide, this is due not to special characteristics of each but to a characteristic common to all. Religion does not owe its efficacy to the special nature of religious sentiments, since domestic and political societies both produce the same effects when strongly integrated. This, moreover, we have already proved when studying directly the manner of action of different religions upon suicide.[1] Inversely, it is not the specific nature of the domestic or political tie which can explain the immunity they confer, since religious society has the same advantage. The cause can only be found in a single quality possessed by all these social groups, though perhaps to varying degrees. The only quality satisfying this condition is that they are all strongly integrated social groups. So we reach the general conclusion: suicide varies inversely with the degree of integration of the social groups of which the individual forms a part.

Émile Durkheim (1951), *Suicide*, tr. John Spanlding and George Simpson, New York: Free Press.

But society cannot disintegrate without the individual simultaneously detaching himself from social life, without his own goals becoming preponderant over those of the community, in a word without his personality tending to surmount the collective personality. The more weakened the groups to which he belongs, the less he depends on them, the more he consequently depends only on himself and recognizes no other rules of conduct than what are founded on his private interests. If we agree to call this state egoism, in which the individual ego asserts itself to excess in the face of the social ego and at its expense, we may call egoistic the special type of suicide springing from excessive individualism.

But how can suicide have such an origin?

First of all, it can be said that, as collective force is one of the obstacles best calculated to restrain suicide, its weakening involves a development of suicide. When society is strongly integrated, it holds individuals under its control, considers them at its service and thus forbids them to dispose wilfully of themselves. Accordingly it opposes their evading their duties to it through death. But how could society impose its supremacy upon them when they refuse to accept this subordination as legitimate? It no longer then possesses the requisite authority to retain them in their duty if they wish to desert; and conscious of its own weakness, it even recognizes their right to do freely what it can no longer prevent. So far as they are the admitted masters of their destinies, it is their privilege to end their lives. They, on their part, have no reason to endure life's sufferings patiently. For they cling to life more resolutely when belonging to a group they love, so as not to betray interests they put before their own. The bond that unites them with the common cause attaches them to life and the lofty goal they envisage prevents their feeling personal troubles so deeply. There is, in short, in a cohesive and animated society a constant interchange of ideas and feelings from all to each and each to all, something like a mutual moral support, which instead of throwing the individual on his own resources, leads him to share in the collective energy and supports his own when exhausted.

But these reasons are purely secondary. Excessive individualism not only results in favoring the action of suicidogenic causes, but it is itself such a cause. It not only frees man's inclination to do away with himself from a protective obstacle, but creates this inclination out of whole cloth and thus gives birth to a special suicide which bears its mark. This must be clearly understood for this is what constitutes the special character of the type of suicide just distinguished and justifies the name we have given it. What is there then in individualism that explains this result?

It has been sometimes said that because of his psychological constitution, man cannot live without attachment to some object which transcends and survives him, and that the reason for this necessity is a need we must have not to perish entirely. Life is said to be intolerable unless some reason for existing is involved, some purpose justifying life's trials. The individual alone is not a sufficient end for his activity. He is too little. He is not only hemmed in spatially; he is also strictly limited temporally. When, therefore, we have no other object than ourselves we cannot avoid the thought that our efforts will finally end in nothingness, since we ourselves disappear. But annihilation terrifies us. Under these conditions one would lose courage to live, that is, to act and struggle, since nothing will remain of our exertions. The state of egoism, in other words, is supposed to be contradictory to human nature and, consequently, too uncertain to have chances of permanence.

In this absolute formulation the proposition is vulnerable. If the thought of the end of our personality were really so hateful, we could consent to live only by blinding ourselves voluntarily as to life's value. For if we may in a measure avoid the prospect of annihilation we cannot extirpate it; it is inevitable, whatever we do. We may push back the frontier for some generations. force our name to endure for some years or centuries longer than our body; a moment, too soon for most men, always comes when it will be nothing. For the groups we join in order to prolong our existence by their means are themselves mortal; they too must dissolve, carrying with them all our deposit of ourselves. Those are few whose memories are closely enough bound to the very history of humanity to be assured of living until its death. So, if we really thus thirsted after immortality, no such brief perspectives could ever appease us. Besides, what of us is it that lives? A word, a sound, an imperceptible trace, most often anonymous,[2] therefore nothing comparable to the violence of our efforts or able to justify them to us. In actuality, though a child is naturally an egoist who feels not the slightest craving to survive himself, and the old man is very often a child in this and so many other respects, neither ceases to cling to life as much or more than the adult; indeed we have seen that suicide is very rare for the first fifteen years and tends to decrease at the other extreme of life. Such too is the case with animals, whose psychological constitution differs from that of men only in degree. It is therefore untrue that life is only possible by its possessing its rationale outside of itself.

Indeed, a whole range of functions concern only the individual; these are the ones indispensable for physical life. Since they are made for this purpose only, they are perfected by its attainment. In everything concerning them, therefore, man can act reasonably without thought of transcendental purposes. These functions serve by merely serving him. In so far as he has no other needs, he is therefore self-sufficient and can live happily with no other objective than living. This is not the case, however, with the civilized adult. He has many ideas, feelings and practices unrelated to organic needs. The roles of art, morality, religion, political faith, science itself are not to repair organic exhaustion nor to provide sound functioning of the organs. All this supra-physical life is built and expanded not because of the demands of the cosmic environment but because of the demands of the social environment. The influence of society is what has aroused in us the sentiments of sympathy and solidarity drawing us toward others; it is society which, fashioning us in its image, fills us with religious, political and moral beliefs that control our actions. To play our social role we have striven to extend our intelligence and it is still society that has supplied us with tools for this development by transmitting to us its trust fund of knowledge.

Through the very fact that these superior forms of human activity have a collective origin, they have a collective purpose. As they derive from society they have reference to it; rather they are society itself incarnated and individualized in each one of us. But for them to have a raison d'être in our eyes, the purpose they envisage must be one not indifferent to us. We can cling to these forms of human activity only to the degree that we cling to society itself. Contrariwise, in the same measure as we feel detached from society we become detached from that life whose source and aim is society. For what purpose do these rules of morality, these precepts of law binding us to all sorts of sacrifices, these restrictive dogmas exist, if there is no being outside us whom they serve and in whom we participate? What is the purpose of science itself? If its only use is to increase our chances for survival, it does not deserve the trouble it entails. Instinct acquits itself better of this role; animals prove this. Why substitute for it a more hesitant and uncertain reflection? What is the end of suffering, above all? If the value of things can only be estimated by their relation to this positive evil for the individual, it is without reward and incomprehensible. This problem does not exist for the believer firm in his faith or the man strongly bound by ties of domestic or political society. Instinctively and unreflectively they ascribe all that they are and do, the one to his Church or his God, the living symbol of the Church, the other to his family, the third to his country or party. Even in their sufferings they see only a means of glorifying the group to which they belong and thus do homage to it. So, the Christian ultimately desires and seeks suffering to testify more fully to his contempt for the flesh and more fully resemble his divine model. But the more the believer doubts, that is, the less he feels himself a real participant in the religious faith to which he belongs, and from which he is freeing himself; the more the family and community become foreign to the individual, so much the more does he become a mystery to himself, unable to escape the exasperating and agonizing question: to what purpose?

If, in other words, as has often been said, man is double, that is because social man superimposes himself upon physical man. Social man necessarily presupposes a society which he expresses and serves. If this dissolves, if we no longer feel it in existence and action about and above us, whatever is social in us is deprived of all objective foundation. All that remains is an artificial combination of illusory images, a phantasmagoria vanishing at the least reflection; that is, nothing which can be a goal for our action. Yet this social man is the essence of civilized man; he is the masterpiece of existence. Thus we are bereft of reasons for existence; for the only life to which we could cling no longer corresponds to anything actual; the only existence still based upon reality no longer meets our needs. Because we have been initiated into a higher existence, the one which satisfies an animal or a child can satisfy us no more and the other itself fades and leaves us helpless. So there is nothing more for our efforts to lay hold of, and we feel them lose themselves in emptiness. In this sense it is true to say that our activity needs an object transcending it. We do not need it to maintain ourselves in the illusion of an impossible immortality; it is implicit in our moral constitution and cannot be even partially lost without this losing its raison d'être in the same degree. No proof is needed that in such a state of confusion the least cause of discouragement may easily give birth to desperate resolutions. If life is not worth the trouble of being lived, everything becomes a pretext to rid ourselves of it.

But this is not all. This detachment occurs not only in single individuals. One of the constitutive elements of every national temperament consists of a certain way of estimating the value of existence. There is a collective as well as an individual humor inclining peoples to sadness or cheerfulness, making them see things in bright or sombre lights. In fact, only society can pass a collective opinion on the value of human life; for this the individual is incompetent. The latter knows nothing but himself and his own little horizon; thus his experience is too limited to serve as a basis for a general appraisal. He may indeed consider his own life to be aimless; he can say nothing applicable to others. On the contrary, without sophistry, society may generalize its own feeling as to itself, its state of health or lack of health. For individuals share too deeply in the life of society for it to be diseased without their suffering infection. What it suffers they necessarily suffer. Because it is the whole, its ills are communicated to its parts. Hence it cannot disintegrate without awareness that the regular conditions of general existence are equally disturbed. Because society is the end on which our better selves depend, it cannot feel us escaping it without a simultaneous realization that our activity is purposeless. Since we are its handiwork, society cannot be conscious of its own decadence without the feeling that henceforth this work is of no value. Thence are formed currents of depression and disillusionment emanating from no particular individual but expressing society's state of disintegration. They reflect the relaxation of social bonds, a sort of collective asthenia, or social malaise, just as individual sadness, when chronic, in its way reflects the poor organic state of the individual. Then metaphysical and religious systems spring up which, by reducing these obscure sentiments to formulae, attempt to prove to men the senselessness of life and that it is self-deception to believe that it has purpose. Then new moralities originate which, by elevating facts to ethics, commend suicide or at least tend in that direction by suggesting a minimal existence. On their appearance they seem to have been created out of whole cloth by their makers who are sometimes blamed for the pessimism of their doctrines. In reality they are an effect rather than a cause; they merely symbolize in abstract language and systematic form the physiological distress of the body social.[3] As these currents are collective, they have, by virtue of their origin, an authority which they impose upon the individual and they drive him more vigorously on the way to which he is already inclined by the state of moral distress directly aroused in him by the disintegration of society. Thus, at the very moment that, with excessive zeal, he frees himself from the social environment, he still submits to its influence. However individualized a man may be, there is always something collective remaining – the very depression and melancholy resulting from this same exaggerated individualism. He effects communion through sadness when he no longer has anything else with which to achieve it.

Hence this type of suicide well deserves the name we have given it. Egoism is not merely a contributing factor in it; it is its generating cause. In this case the bond attaching man to life relaxes because that attaching him to society is itself slack. The incidents of private life which seem the direct inspiration of suicide and are considered its determining causes are in reality only incidental causes. The individual yields to the slightest shock of circumstance because the state of society has made him a ready prey to suicide.

NOTES

1. See Book II, Ch. 2.
2. We say nothing of the ideal protraction of life involved in the belief in immortality of the soul, for (1) this cannot explain why the family or attachment to political society preserves us from suicide; and (2) it is not even this belief which forms religion's prophylactic influence, as we have shown above.
3. This is why it is unjust to accuse these theorists of sadness of generalizing personal impressions. They are the echo of a general condition.

Part 4

WEBER AND RATIONALISM

INTRODUCTION

I. Leadership and Legitimation

Weber's definition of politics draws heavily on the idea of leadership and the power to dominate. His three general forms of leadership are defined as charismatic, traditional and legal-rational domination. These in turn can be said to illustrate the ways in which different forms of society cohere and the different ways in which consensus and legitimacy are established.

Charismatic leadership is an unpredictable form of rule that is unable to provide lasting social cohesion. It is based on the appeal of a great figure or personality, for example a prophet, warrior or political demagogue, who can exhibit extraordinary qualities. These must be demonstrated by bringing success or prosperity to the community. This brings about personal and emotional loyalty, which inevitably makes it more unstable than a rule-governed form of leadership.

With traditional authority, cohesion and consent depend upon established social customs, conventions, norms, practices and structures rather than charismatic personality. The monarch or religious leader does not rule by virtue of magical powers or personal qualities but through established tradition or routine. Consensus is based on an 'established belief in the sanctity of immemorial traditions' (Weber 1978: 215). Cohesion is maintained through a feeling of common purpose and the belief that the authority of the leader derives from an established way of doing things. Feudal forms of traditionalism depend upon a set of obligations and rights. Eventually, with a separating out of powers and spheres of interest, a third, legal-rational, model starts to emerge.

Here leadership is based on rules not rulers. Leadership is established through regulations and procedures with consensus resting on 'belief in the legitimacy of enacted rules and the right of those elevated to authority under such rules to issue commands' (Weber 1978: 215). Legal-rationality accompanies the growth of industrialisation, the development of the nation-state, and the modernisation of society more generally. Authority of command derives from the position of office, with the new leaders of society being bureaucratic officials, office holders and managers. Rule is by virtue of rationally established norms, enactments, decrees and regulations. Office holders and officials form a hierarchy of command. Administrative staff are separated from the ownership of the means of production and administration so that their authority and legitimacy derives solely from their social function and position.

II. BUREAUCRACY

Legal-rational society claims legitimacy from the belief in the formal correctness of rules while those who enact them are considered a legitimate authority. Weber's essay on bureaucracy printed here focuses on perhaps the dominant feature of legal-rational society. Although he shows how bureaucracy has been a feature of nearly all societies, it finds its greatest expression in modern society with its technical and economic basis. The decisive factor in the rise of bureaucracy is its technical superiority and precision. It offers an almost machine-like efficiency and a technical superiority, eliminating all personal, irrational and emotional elements. This brings a new degree of stability and cohesion since, unlike previous forms of domination which rely on more volatile personal and political relations, bureaucracy represents a continuous form of administration carried out by trained professionals who operate 'impartially' according to prescribed rules. The more complex and specialised nature of modern culture demands the personally detached and 'objective' expert. The growing complexity of administrative tasks and expansion of their scope need the technical superiority of those who have training and experience.

Weber writes that modern officialdom concerns fixed and official jurisdictional areas that are ordered by rules, laws and administrative regulations. Duties are fulfilled by those who have the appropriate qualifications and authority operates through the bureaucratic structures in a hierarchical way. In this hierarchy officials are selected according to merit and expertise and they are trained to fulfil a particular function. For Weber a vitally important aspect of this type of bureaucracy is the separation of the office holder from the means of administration. This makes the bureaucrat dependent on their office and makes them fully identify with their position. The bureaucrat strives to improve their rank within the organisation and thereby enhance their salary, status and social esteem.

Bureaucracy becomes a form of domination based on the concentration of the material means of management. The masses become dependent on its functioning, as may be seen from the operation of the institutions of the modern state: the health and welfare systems, the educational establishment, the political parties and trade unions and other such bodies. It carries over into the realm of politics, with mass democracy being based less on the dominant personality, or on the membership, but on the party apparatus with its professional staff and administrators. While legal-rational society is often accompanied by mass democracy, Weber argues that real power is concentrated in the hands of a few specialists.

III. Legal-rational Society and the Protestant Ethic

Modern society is based on the instrumental rationality of formal rules, procedures and calculated acts. In contrast to Marx's emphasis on the development of the mode of production, for Weber modernity is characterised by the process of rationalisation across all aspects of society, including markets, law, education, government, political parties and trade unions. The development of capitalism is therefore seen within the context of wider trends such as the development of rational administration and governance, the advance of technology, and the development of a disciplined labour market. Capitalism becomes dominant because it develops within an already existing rational way of life. It is more the case, therefore, that rationalisation develops capitalism rather than capitalism being responsible for rationalisation, although the two processes become interlinked.

Weber regards the market economy as the most impersonal sphere of practical life. Being based on the rational and purposeful pursuit of one's interests, it has a matter-of-factness about it that is alien to fraternal relations. Modern capitalist society requires a certain type of personality best suited to rational-purposeful activity. This personality must be based on bourgeois values and a 'capitalist spirit' best suited to the economic activities of the marketplace. But whereas many Marxists have argued that social ideas, attitudes and values are determined by social conditions, Weber suggests this might be the other way round.

This capitalist spirit is explored in Weber's most famous work, *The Protestant Ethic and the Spirit of Capitalism.* He tries to answer why capitalism developed most successfully in the countries in northern Europe and North America, concluding that in these countries the values and beliefs of the Protestant religion are most conducive to capitalist development. The Protestant ethic is based on the belief that self-denial and self-control are the best guarantee of salvation and that through everyday worldly activity we show our devotion to God. This necessarily leads to the adoption of a rational and active worldview which is best suited to the development of capitalism. It emphasises the importance of hard work, a frugal lifestyle and individual responsibility. It was also single-mindedly directed towards the achievement of economic success. Anxiety caused by the question of salvation led to a regulated and responsible lifestyle which in actual fact legitimated profit-making, accumulation, economic specialisation and other activities crucial to the development of a capitalist economy. As Weber says,

> the emphasis on the ascetic importance of a fixed calling provided an ethical justification of the modern specialised division of labour. In a similar way the providential interpretation of profit making justified the activities of the business man . . . it has the highest ethical appreciation of the sober, middle-class, self-made man. (Weber 1992: 163)

By promoting rational conduct, the Protestant ethic accelerates a process of modernisation that eventually undermines the religious viewpoint. The process of modernisation and rationalisation demystifies the world and elevates science and technology to new levels of importance. The world becomes more secure through non-religious knowledge like science and rationality so that there is less need for religion to provide security, meaning and explanation.

IV. POLITICS AND POWER

A clue to Weber's rather authoritarian notion of leadership lies with the fact that his three types of leadership are synonymous with his three types of domination. Domination, in turn, is synonymous with relations of power, discipline and obedience.

> By *power* is meant that opportunity existing within a social relationship which permits one to carry out one's own will even against resistance and regardless of the basis on which this opportunity rests.
>
> By *domination* is meant the opportunity to have a command of a given specified content obeyed by a given group of persons. By 'discipline' will be meant the opportunity to obtain prompt, and automatic obedience in a predictable form from a given group of persons because of their practiced orientation toward a command. (Weber 1993: 117)

These notions do not seem very promising in terms of developing a theory of consent. It seems that behind even a consensual relationship lies the threat of force. This certainly comes across in Weber's well-known words on the state as 'a human community that (successfully) claims the *monopoly of the legitimate use of physical force* within a given territory' (Weber 1991: 78). However, while every state might be founded on force, the modern state at least seeks to legitimate this legally – 'the state is a relation of men dominating men, a relation supported by means of legitimate (i.e. considered to be legitimate) violence' (Weber 1991: 78). Therefore legitimacy is an important part of domination although the criticism might now be that Weber tends to conflate legitimation and domination as if they are one and the same thing.

Moving to Weber's conception of the nation provides more of a sense of social consent. Whereas his definition of the state concentrates on force and political ends, the nation is regarded more as a cultural community depending on long-standing customs, traditions, values and symbols. The people of a nation are brought together through a common history, cultural heritage, language, ethnic origin and common sentiments and feelings. This cultural aspect of social cohesion combines group values with a common political destiny so that 'the significance of the 'nation' is usually anchored in the superiority, or at least the irreplaceability, of the culture values that are to be preserved and developed only through the cultivation of the peculiarity of the group' (Weber 1991: 176). This conception is linked, though, to Weber's view that all politics is conflict and struggle and all cultural entities must fight to establish and maintain themselves. The nation implies 'a specific sentiment of solidarity in the face of other groups' (Weber 1991: 172). In Weber's own case, this carried over into support for German nationalism and imperialism. His reasoning was that in order for a cultural community to develop, it must extend its influence on the world stage. With the modern nation-state, cultural heritage and political organisation must be backed up with military power and prestige. It becomes a community of memories, political destiny and common struggles. A strong and assertive German foreign policy would reflect a maturing of national consciousness and political leadership. The relations of domination get transferred to the world stage.

V. Class, Status, Party

The extract from Weber's *Class, Status, Party* defines the economic order as the way goods and services are distributed and used. He agrees with Marx that this is largely determined by class, but his definition of class differs in defining it according to ownership of material goods and skills. Weber accepts the Marxist view that the class struggle, the economic situation and the relation to material goods determines the 'life chances' that people have, but he differs from Marx in relating class situation to market situation so that a person's fate is determined by their chances in the market. Class therefore becomes the shared interests that a group of individuals may have as a result of their market position with market position being understood as opportunities for earning income and consuming goods.

Stratification of social groups takes place according to their life chances or opportunities in relation to such things as employment, income, skills, education, health and living conditions. Class refers to common life chances represented by possession of goods and opportunities for income. Weber adds to class the notion of status so that ' "classes" are stratified according to their relations to the production and acquisition of goods; whereas "status groups" are stratified according to the principles of their *consumption* of goods as represented by special "styles of life"' (Weber 1991: 193). Differences in status involve such things as the level of prestige, honour or social standing attached to different groups. One group may have a higher status than another due to birth or ethnicity or occupational status and it is on this basis that a group may be rewarded or prohibited in social life. Status is something that affects market position and stratification according to status is linked to access to ideal and material goods and opportunities, something that is determined according to the way that social honour is distributed between groups. This would explain distinctions between types of workers, for example between blue-collar and white-collar workers, who enjoy a higher social prestige. Within modern societies, where the monopolisation of managerial leadership and decision-making occurs, the 'middle classes' – the intellectuals, civil servants and other white-collar workers – enjoy a high social status that is not reducible to the question of class or economic situation. This is also reflected through lifestyle and patterns of consumption and taste.

Groups may attempt to advance their social position though appeals to shared values and interests, but it may be that some form of conflict or struggle is necessary. In this case, groups organise themselves into parties which bring together those people with common aims or interests and direct them towards a common goal. Parties may organise people according to class situation or status or something looser. Parties act to achieve goals – usually to secure power for their leaders and attain material advantages for their members. They represent an organised form of activity that is bound up with questions of class, status and interests and which presupposes a comprehensive level of socialisation and a political framework of communal action. These parties may well struggle to achieve a level of domination, but Weber makes clear that this is domination within the existing system. Thus struggles may take place over particular interests and values, but a wider social consensus based on social values and an existing political framework is taken as given.

VI. Weber's Pessimism

Because of his views on bureaucracy, Weber is pessimistic about genuine mass democracy. Since mass democracy requires the large-scale organisation of political institutions and parties, the democratic ideals inevitably come into conflict with the bureaucratic party machine. Ultimately it is not the politicians but the bureaucrats (or politician-bureaucrats) who run the country. Those who are in overall control are those who control the means of organisation. In fact, not only do routine changes in government not make much difference to the structure of society, but more drastic changes such as those advocated by the socialists would make little difference either. Revolution would not remove bureaucracy; it would merely take it over.

Weber's talk 'Politics as a Vocation' contains some very negative comments on modern democracy, which allows people the chance to select a leader, but not much more. The people certainly do not rule themselves. The best hope for the people lies in the election of a charismatic leader and here we find the influence of Nietzsche on Weber's thought. The only hope of escaping the rationalisation of society is through the creative powers of a leading individual.

While Marx looks to collective political struggle, Weber's concern is with individual freedom and autonomy. Weber is concerned with the struggle to preserve liberal values and individual freedoms. Rationalised forms of instrumental action impose themselves on the individual and exert a kind of disciplinary power that regulates the lives of human beings and imposes an abstract and meaningless form of social conduct. The rationalisation of modern society represents an iron cage that imprisons the individual. Therefore 'the fate of our times is characterised by rationalisation and intellectualisation and, above all, by the "disenchantment of the world"' (Weber 1991: 155). Modernity comes to signify a loss of meaning, a fragmentation of social life and a lack of social unity. As the world becomes increasingly disenchanted, individuals are thrown back on themselves and forced to construct their own meanings and context. The self-sufficient individual becomes the only true and real social entity. The essence of human freedom is the capacity to choose ends and the nature of social action is determined by the relation of the subject to its own meanings and intentions.

The contemporary extract is taken from Derek Sayer's book *Capitalism and Modernity* and it draws a number of comparisons between Weber and Marx. It emphasises the point that it is rationalisation rather than capitalism that forms the basis of the modern world. And whereas Marx focuses on the separation of the worker from the means of production, Weber looks at how we are separated from a whole range of social activities. In particular, focus is on the office and the role of bureaucracy. Sayer goes on to discuss this in relation to developments around the fall of communism in eastern Europe and he concludes by raising a number of problems connected to human emancipation and social change. He concludes that Weber's pessimism is too deep rooted, but it nevertheless raises important questions that need to be answered.

FROM 'POLITICS AS A VOCATION'

Max Weber

What do we understand by politics? The concept is extremely broad and comprises any kind of *independent* leadership in action. One speaks of the currency policy of the banks, of the discounting policy of the Reichsbank, of the strike policy of a trade union; one may speak of the educational policy of a municipality or a township, of the policy of the president of a voluntary association, and, finally, even of the policy of a prudent wife who seeks to guide her husband. Tonight, our reflections are, of course, not based upon such a broad concept. We wish to understand by politics only the leadership, or the influencing of the leadership, of a *political* association, hence today, of a *state*.

But what is a 'political' association from the sociological point of view? What is a 'state'? Sociologically, the state cannot be defined in terms of its ends. There is scarcely any task that some political association has not taken in hand, and there is no task that one could say has always been exclusive and peculiar to those associations which are designated as political ones: today the state, or historically, those associations which have been the predecessors of the modern state. Ultimately, one can define the modern state sociologically only in terms of the specific *means* peculiar to it, as to every political association, namely, the use of physical force.

'Every state is founded on force,' said Trotsky at Brest-Litovsk. That is indeed right. If no social institutions existed which knew the use of violence,

Max Weber (1948), 'Politics as a vocation', in H. H. Gerth and C. Wright Mills (eds), *From Max Weber*, London and Boston: Routledge and Kegan Paul.

then the concept of 'state' would be eliminated, and a condition would emerge that could be designated as 'anarchy,' in the specific sense of this word. Of course, force is certainly not the normal or the only means of the state – nobody says that – but force is a means specific to the state. Today the relation between the state and violence is an especially intimate one. In the past, the most varied institutions – beginning with the sib – have known the use of physical force as quite normal. Today, however, we have to say that a state is a human community that (successfully) claims the *monopoly of the legitimate use of physical force* within a given territory. Note that 'territory' is one of the characteristics of the state. Specifically, at the present time, the right to use physical force is ascribed to other institutions or to individuals only to the extent to which the state permits it. The state is considered the sole source of the 'right' to use violence. Hence, 'politics' for us means striving to share power or striving to influence the distribution of power, either among states or among groups within a state.

This corresponds essentially to ordinary usage. When a question is said to be a 'political' question, when a cabinet minister or an official is said to be a 'political' official, or when a decision is said to be 'politically' determined, what is always meant is that interests in the distribution, maintenance, or transfer of power are decisive for answering the questions and determining the decision or the official's sphere of activity. He who is active in politics strives for power either as a means in serving other aims, ideal or egoistic, or as 'power for power's sake', that is, in order to enjoy the prestige-feeling that power gives.

Like the political institutions historically preceding it, the state is a relation of men dominating men, a relation supported by means of legitimate (i.e. considered to be legitimate) violence. If the state is to exist, the dominated must obey the authority claimed by the powers that be. When and why do men obey? Upon what inner justifications and upon what external means does this domination rest?

To begin with, in principle, there are three inner justifications, hence basic *legitimations* of domination.

First, the authority of the 'eternal yesterday', i.e. of the mores sanctified through the unimaginably ancient recognition and habitual orientation to conform. This is 'traditional' domination exercised by the patriarch and the patrimonial prince of yore.

There is the authority of the extraordinary and personal *gift of grace* (charisma), the absolutely personal devotion and personal confidence in revelation, heroism, or other qualities of individual leadership. This is 'charismatic' domination, as exercised by the prophet or – in the field of politics – by the elected war lord, the plebiscitarian ruler, the great demagogue, or the political party leader.

Finally, there is domination by virtue of 'legality,' by virtue of the belief in the validity of legal statute and functional 'competence' based on rationally created *rules*. In this case, obedience is expected in discharging statutory obligations. This is domination as exercised by the modern 'servant of the state' and by all those bearers of power who in this respect resemble him.

It is understood that, in reality, obedience is determined by highly robust motives of fear and hope – fear of the vengeance of magical powers or of the power-holder, hope for reward in this world or in the beyond – and besides all this, by interests of the most varied sort. Of this we shall speak presently. However, in asking for the 'legitimations' of this obedience, one meets with these three 'pure' types: 'traditional', 'charismatic', and 'legal.'

These conceptions of legitimacy and their inner justifications are of very great significance for the structure of domination. To be sure, the pure types are rarely found in reality. But today we cannot deal with the highly complex variants, transitions, and combinations of these pure types, which problems belong to 'political science'. Here we are interested above all in the second of these types: domination by virtue of the devotion of those who obey the purely personal 'charisma' of the 'leader'. For this is the root of the idea of a *calling* in its highest expression.

Devotion to the charisma of the prophet, or the leader in war, or to the great demagogue in the *ecclesia* or in parliament, means that the leader is personally recognized as the innerly 'called' leader of men. Men do not obey him by virtue of tradition or statute, but because they believe in him. If he is more than a narrow and vain upstart of the moment, the leader lives for his cause and 'strives for his work.'[1] The devotion of his disciples, his followers, his personal party friends is oriented to his person and to its qualities.

Charismatic leadership has emerged in all places and in all historical epochs. Most importantly in the past, it has emerged in the two figures of the magician and the prophet on the one hand, and in the elected war lord, the gang leader and *condotierre* on the other hand. *Political* leadership in the form of the free 'demagogue' who grew from the soil of the city state is of greater concern to us; like the city state, the demagogue is peculiar to the Occident and especially to Mediterranean culture. Furthermore, political leadership in the form of the parliamentary 'party leader' has grown on the soil of the constitutional state, which is also indigenous only to the Occident.

These politicians by virtue of a 'calling', in the most genuine sense of the word, are of course nowhere the only decisive figures in the cross-currents of the political struggle for power. The sort of auxiliary means that are at their disposal is also highly decisive. How do the politically dominant powers manage to maintain their domination? The question pertains to any kind of domination, hence also to political domination in all its forms, traditional as well as legal and charismatic.

Organized domination, which calls for continuous administration, requires that human conduct be conditioned to obedience towards those masters who claim to be the bearers of legitimate power. On the other hand, by virtue of this obedience, organized domination requires the control of those material goods which in a given case are necessary for the use of physical violence. Thus, organized domination requires control of the personal executive staff and the material implements of administration.

The administrative staff, which externally represents the organization of political domination, is, of course, like any other organization, bound by obedience to the power-holder and not alone by the concept of legitimacy, of which we have just spoken. There are two other means, both of which appeal to personal interests: material reward and social honor. The fiefs of vassals, the prebends of patrimonial officials, the salaries of modern civil servants, the honor of knights, the privileges of estates, and the honor of the civil servant comprise their respective wages. The fear of losing them is the final and decisive basis for solidarity between the executive staff and the power-holder. There is honor and booty for the followers in war; for the demagogue's following, there are 'spoils' – that is, exploitation of the dominated through the monopolization of office – and there are politically determined profits and premiums of vanity. All of these rewards are also derived from the domination exercised by a charismatic leader.

To maintain a dominion by force, certain material goods are required, just as with an economic organization. All states may be classified according to whether they rest on the principle that the staff of men themselves *own* the administrative means, or whether the staff is 'separated' from these means of administration. This distinction holds in the same sense in which today we say that the salaried employee and the proletarian in the capitalistic enterprise are 'separated' from the material means of production. The power-holder must be able to count on the obedience of the staff members, officials, or whoever else they may be. The administrative means may consist of money, building, war material, vehicles, horses, or whatnot. The question is whether or not the power-holder himself directs and organizes the administration while delegating executive power to personal servants, hired officials, or personal favorites and confidants, who are non-owners, i.e. who do not use the material means of administration in their own right but are directed by the lord. The distinction runs through all administrative organizations of the past.

These political associations in which the material means of administration are autonomously controlled, wholly or partly, by the dependent administrative staff may be called associations organized in '*estates*'. The vassal in the feudal association, for instance, paid out of his own pocket for the administration and judicature of the district enfeoffed to him. He supplied his own equipment and provisions for war, and his sub-vassals did likewise. Of course, this had consequences for the lord's position of power, which only rested upon a relation of personal faith and upon the fact that the legitimacy of his possession of the fief and the social honor of the vassal were derived from the overlord.

[...]

The most modern forms of party organizations stand in sharp contrast to this idyllic state in which circles of notables and, above all, members of parliament rule. These modern forms are the children of democracy, of mass franchise, of the necessity to woo and organize the masses, and develop the utmost unity of direction and the strictest discipline. The rule of notables and guidance by members of parliament ceases. 'Professional' politicians *outside* the parliaments take the organization in hand. They do so either as 'entrepreneurs' – the American boss and the English election agent are, in fact, such entrepreneurs – or as officials with a fixed salary. Formally, a fargoing democratization takes place. The parliamentary party no longer creates the authoritative programs, and the local notables no longer decide the selection of candidates. Rather assemblies of the organized party members select the candidates and delegate members to the assemblies of a higher order. Possibly there are several such conventions leading up to the national convention of the party. Naturally power actually rests in the hands of those who, within the organization, handle the work *continuously*. Otherwise, power rests in the hands of those on whom the organization in its processes depends financially or personally – for instance, on the Maecenases or the directors of powerful political clubs of interested persons (Tammany Hall). It is decisive that this whole apparatus of people – characteristically called a 'machine' in Anglo-Saxon countries – or rather those who direct the machine, keep the members of the parliament in check. They are in a position to impose their will to a rather far-reaching extent, and that is of special significance for the selection of the party leader. The man whom the machine follows now becomes the leader, even over the head of the parliamentary party. In other words, the creation of such machines signifies the advent of *plebiscitarian* democracy.

The party following, above all the party official and party entrepreneur, naturally expect personal compensation from the victory of their leader – that is, offices or other advantages. It is decisive that they expect such advantages from their leader and not merely from the individual member of parliament. They expect that the demagogic effect of the leader's *personality* during the election fight of the party will increase votes and mandates and thereby power, and, thereby, as far as possible, will extend opportunities to their followers to find the compensation for which they hope. Ideally, one of their mainsprings is the satisfaction of working with loyal personal devotion for a man, and not merely for an abstract program of a party consisting of mediocrities. In this respect, the 'charismatic' element of all leadership is at work in the party system.

In very different degrees this system made headway, although it was in constant, latent struggle with local notables and the members of parliament who wrangled for influence. This was the case in the bourgeois parties, first, in the United States, and, then, in the Social Democratic party, especially of Germany. Constant setbacks occur as soon as no genrally recognized leader exists, and, even when he is found, concessions of all sorts must be made to the vanity and the personal interest of the party notables. The machine may also be brought under the domination of the party officials in whose hands the regular business rests. According to the view of some Social Democratic circles, their party had succumbed to this 'bureaucratization'. But 'officials' submit relatively easily to a leader's personality if it has a strong demagogic appeal. The material and the ideal interests of the officials are intimately connected with the effects of party power which are expected from the leader's appeal, and besides, inwardly it is *per se* more satisfying to work for a leader. The ascent of leaders is far more difficult where the notables, along with the officials, control the party, as is usually the case in the bourgeois parties. For ideally the notables make 'their way of life' out of the petty chairmanships or committee memberships they hold. Resentment against the demagogue as a *homo novus*, the conviction of the superiority of political party 'experience' (which, as a matter of fact, actually is of considerable importance), and the ideological concern for the crumbling of the old party traditions – these factors determine the conduct of the notables. They can count on all the traditionalist elements within the party. Above all, the rural but also the petty bourgeois voter looks for the name of the notable familiar to him. He distrusts the man who is unknown to him. However, once this man has become successful, he clings to him the more unwaveringly.

[...]

Politics is a strong and slow boring of hard boards. It takes both passion and perspective. Certainly all historical experience confirms the truth – that man would not have attained the possible unless time and again he had reached out for the impossible. But to do that a man must be a leader, and not only a leader but a hero as well, in a very sober sense of the word. And even those who are neither leaders nor heroes must arm themselves with that steadfastness of heart which can brave even the crumbling of all hopes. This is necessary right now, or else men will not be able to attain even that which is possible today. Only he has the calling for politics who is sure that he shall not crumble when the world from his point of view is too stupid or too base for what he wants to offer. Only he who in the face of all this can say 'In spite of all!' has the calling for politics.

NOTE

1. *Trachtet nach seinem Werk.*

FROM 'BUREAUCRACY'

Max Weber

I. Characteristics of Bureaucracy

Modern officialdom functions in the following specific manner:

I. There is the principle of fixed and official jurisdictional areas, which are generally ordered by rules, that is, by laws or administrative regulations.

1. The regular activities required for the purposes of the bureaucratically governed structure are distributed in a fixed way as official duties.

2. The authority to give the commands required for the discharge of these duties is distributed in a stable way and is strictly delimited by rules concerning the coercive means, physical, sacerdotal, or otherwise, which may be placed at the disposal of officials.

3. Methodical provision is made for the regular and continuous fulfilment of these duties and for the execution of the corresponding rights; only persons who have the generally regulated qualifications to serve are employed.

In public and lawful government these three elements constitute 'bureaucratic authority'. In private economic domination, they constitute bureaucratic 'management'. Bureaucracy, thus understood, is fully developed in political and ecclesiastical communities only in the modern state, and, in the private economy, only in the most advanced institutions of capitalism. Permanent and public office authority, with fixed jurisdiction, is not the historical rule but rather the exception. This is so even in large political

Max Weber (1948), 'Bureaucracy', in H. H. Gerth and C. Wright Mills (eds), *from Max Weber*, London and Boston: Routledge and Kegan Paul.

structures such as those of the ancient Orient, the Germanic and Mongolian empires of conquest, or of many feudal structures of state. In all these cases, the ruler executes the most important measures through personal trustees, table-companions, or court-servants. Their commissions and authority are not precisely delimited and are temporarily called into being for each case.

II. The principles of office hierarchy and of levels of graded authority mean a firmly ordered system of super- and subordination in which there is a supervision of the lower offices by the higher ones. Such a system offers the governed the possibility of appealing the decision of a lower office to its higher authority, in a definitely regulated manner. With the full development of the bureaucratic type, the office hierarchy is monocratically organized. The principle of hierarchical office authority is found in all bureaucratic structures: in state and ecclesiastical structures as well as in large party organizations and private enterprises. It does not matter for the character of bureaucracy whether its authority is called 'private' or 'public'.

When the principle of jurisdictional 'competency' is fully carried through, hierarchical subordination – at least in public office – does not mean that the 'higher' authority is simply authorized to take over the business of the 'lower'. Indeed, the opposite is the rule. Once established and having fulfilled its task, an office tends to continue in existence and be held by another incumbent.

III. The management of the modern office is based upon written documents ('the files'), which are preserved in their original or draught form. There is, therefore, a staff of subaltern officials and scribes of all sorts. The body of officials actively engaged in a 'public' office, along with the respective apparatus of material implements and the files, make up a 'bureau'. In private enterprise, 'the bureau' is often called 'the office'.

In principle, the modern organization of the civil service separates the bureau from the private domicile of the official, and, in general, bureaucracy segregates official activity as something distinct from the sphere of private life. Public monies and equipment are divorced from the private property of the official. This condition is everywhere the product of a long development. Nowadays, it is found in public as well as in private enterprises; in the latter, the principle extends even to the leading entrepreneur. In principle, the executive office is separated from the household, business from private correspondence, and business assets from private fortunes. The more consistently the modern type of business management has been carried through the more are these separations the case. The beginnings of this process are to be found as early as the Middle Ages.

It is the peculiarity of the modern entrepreneur that he conducts himself as the 'first official' of his enterprise, in the very same way in which the ruler of a specifically modern bureaucratic state spoke of himself as 'the first servant' of the state.[1] The idea that the bureau activities of the state are intrinsically different in character from the management of private economic offices is a continental European notion and, by way of contrast, is totally foreign to the American way.

IV. Office management, at least all specialized office management – and such management is distinctly modern – usually presupposes thorough and expert training. This increasingly holds for the modern executive and employee of private enterprises, in the same manner as it holds for the state official.

V. When the office is fully developed, official activity demands the full working capacity of the official, irrespective of the fact that his obligatory time in the bureau may be firmly delimited. In the normal case, this is only the product of a long development, in the public as well as in the private office. Formerly, in all cases, the normal state of affairs was reversed: official business was discharged as a secondary activity.

VI. The management of the office follows general rules, which are more or less stable, more or less exhaustive, and which can be learned. Knowledge of these rules represents a special technical learning which the officials possess. It involves jurisprudence, or administrative or business management.

The reduction of modern office management to rules is deeply embedded in its very nature. The theory of modern public administration, for instance, assumes that the authority to order certain matters by decree – which has been legally granted to public authorities – does not entitle the bureau to regulate the matter by commands given for each case, but only to regulate the matter abstractly. This stands in extreme contrast to the regulation of all relationships through individual privileges and bestowals of favor, which is absolutely dominant in patrimonialism, at least in so far as such relationships are not fixed by sacred tradition.

II. The Position of the Official

All this results in the following for the internal and external position of the official:

I. Office holding is a 'vocation'. This is shown, first, in the requirement of a firmly prescribed course of training, which demands the entire capacity for work for a long period of time, and in the generally prescribed and special examinations which are prerequisites of employment. Furthermore, the position of the official is in the nature of a duty. This determines the internal structure of his relations, in the following manner: Legally and actually, office holding is not considered a source to be exploited for rents or emoluments, as was normally the case during the Middle Ages and frequently up to the threshold of recent times. Nor is office holding considered a usual exchange of services for equivalents, as is the case with free labor contracts. Entrance into an office, including one in the private economy, is considered an acceptance of a specific obligation of faithful management in return for a secure existence. It is decisive for the specific nature of modern loyalty to an office that, in the pure type, it does not establish a relationship to a *person*, like the vassal's or disciple's faith in feudal or in patrimonial relations of authority. Modern loyalty is devoted to impersonal and functional purposes. Behind the functional purposes, of course, 'ideas of culture-values' usually stand. These are *ersatz* for the earthly or supra-mundane personal master: ideas such as 'state', 'church', 'community', 'party', or 'enterprise' are thought of as being realized in a community; they provide an ideological halo for the master.

The political official – at least in the fully developed modern state – is not considered the personal servant of a ruler. Today, the bishop, the priest, and the preacher are in fact no longer, as in early Christian times, holders of purely personal charisma. The supra-mundane and sacred values which they offer are given to everybody who seems to be worthy of them and who asks for them. In former times, such leaders acted upon the personal command of their master; in principle, they were responsible only to him. Nowadays, in spite of the partial survival of the old theory, such religious leaders are officials in the service of a functional purpose, which in the present-day 'church' has become routinized and, in turn, ideologically hallowed.

II. The personal position of the official is patterned in the following way:

1. Whether he is in a private office or a public bureau, the modern official always strives and usually enjoys a distinct *social esteem* as compared with the governed. His social position is guaranteed by the prescriptive rules of rank order and, for the political official, by special definitions of the criminal code against 'insults of officials' and 'contempt' of state and church authorities.

The actual social position of the official is normally highest where, as in old civilized countries, the following conditions prevail: a strong demand for administration by trained experts; a strong and stable social differentiation, where the official predominantly derives from socially and economically privileged strata because of the social distribution of power; or where the costliness of the required training and status conventions are binding upon him. The possession of educational certificates – to be discussed elsewhere[2] – are usually linked with qualification for office. Naturally, such certificates or patents enhance the 'status element' in the social position of the official. For the rest this status factor in individual cases is explicitly and impassively acknowledged; for example, in the prescription that the acceptance or rejection of an aspirant to an official career depends upon the consent ('election') of the members of the official body. This is the case in the German army with the officer corps. Similar phenomena, which promote this guild-like closure of officialdom, are typically found in patrimonial and, particularly, in prebendal officialdoms of the past. The desire to resurrect such phenomena in changed forms is by no means infrequent among modern bureaucrats. For instance, they have played a role among the demands of the quite proletarian and expert officials (the *tretyj* element) during the Russian revolution.

Usually the social esteem of the officials as such is especially low where the demand for expert administration and the dominance of status conventions are weak. This is especially the case in the United States; it is often the case in new settlements by virtue of their wide fields for profit-making and the great instability of their social stratification.

2. The pure type of bureaucratic official is *appointed* by a superior authority. An official elected by the governed is not a purely bureaucratic figure. Of course, the formal existence of an election does not by itself mean that no appointment hides behind the election – in the state, especially, appointment by party chiefs. Whether or not this is the case does not depend upon legal statutes but upon the way in which the party mechanism functions. Once firmly organized, the parties can turn a formally free election into the mere acclamation of a candidate designated by the party chief. As a rule, however, a formally free election is turned into a fight, conducted according to definite rules, for votes in favor of one of two designated candidates.

In all circumstances, the designation of officials by means of an election among the governed modifies the strictness of hierarchical subordination. In principle, an official who is so elected has an autonomous position opposite the superordinate official. The elected official does not derive his position 'from above' but 'from below', or at least not from a superior authority of the official hierarchy but from powerful party men ('bosses'), who also determine his further career. The career of the elected official is not, or at least not primarily, dependent upon his chief in the administration. The official who is not elected but appointed by a chief normally functions more exactly, from a technical point of view, because, all other circumstances being equal, it is more likely that purely functional points of consideration and qualities will determine his selection and career. As laymen, the governed can become acquainted with the extent to which a candidate is expertly qualified for office only in terms of experience, and hence only after his service. Moreover, in every sort of selection of officials by election, parties quite naturally give decisive weight not to expert considerations but to the services a follower renders to the party boss. This holds for all kinds of procurement of officials by elections, for the designation of formally free, elected officials by party bosses when they determine the slate of candidates, or the free appointment by a chief who has himself been elected. The contrast, however, is relative: substantially similar conditions hold where legitimate monarchs and their subordinates appoint officials, except that the influence of the followings are then less controllable.

[...]

3. Normally, the position of the official is held for life, at least in public bureaucracies; and this is increasingly the case for all similar structures. As

a factual rule; *tenure for life* is presupposed, even where the giving of notice or periodic reappointment occurs. In contrast to the worker in a private enterprise, the official normally holds tenure. Legal or actual life-tenure, however, is not recognized as the official's right to the possession of office, as was the case with many structures of authority in the past. Where legal guarantees against arbitrary dismissal or transfer are developed, they merely serve to guarantee a strictly objective discharge of specific office duties free from all personal considerations. In Germany, this is the case for all juridical and, increasingly, for all administrative officials.

[. . .]

4. The official receives the regular *pecuniary* compensation of a normally fixed *salary* and the old age security provided by a pension. The salary is not measured like a wage in terms of work done, but according to 'status,' that is, according to the kind of function (the 'rank') and, in addition, possibly, according to the length of service. The relatively great security of the official's income, as well as the rewards of social esteem, make the office a sought-after position, especially in countries which no longer provide opportunities for colonial profits. In such countries, this situation permits relatively low salaries for officials.

5. The official is set for a *'career'* within the hierarchical order of the public service. He moves from the lower, less important, and lower paid to the higher positions. The average official naturally desires a mechanical fixing of the conditions of promotion: if not of the offices, at least of the salary levels. He wants these conditions fixed in terms of 'seniority', or possibly according to grades achieved in a developed system of expert examinations. Here and there, such examinations actually form a character *indelebilis* of the official and have lifelong effects on his career. To this is joined the desire to qualify the right to office and the increasing tendency toward status group closure and economic security. All of this makes for a tendency to consider the offices as 'prebends' of those who are qualified by educational certificates. The necessity of taking general personal and intellectual qualifications into consideration, irrespective of the often subaltern character of the educational certificate, has led to a condition in which the highest political offices, especially the positions of 'ministers', are principally filled without reference to such certificates.

III. The Presuppositions and Causes of Bureaucracy

The social and economic presuppositions of the modern structure of the office are as follows:

The development of the *money economy*, in so far as a pecuniary compensation of the officials is concerned, is a presupposition of bureaucracy. Today it not only prevails but is predominant. This fact is of very great importance for the whole bearing of bureaucracy, yet by itself it is by no means decisive for the existence of bureaucracy.

Historical examples of rather distinctly developed and quantitatively large bureaucracies are: (a) Egypt, during the period of the new Empire which, however, contained strong patrimonial elements; (b) the later Roman Principate, and especially the Diocletian monarchy and the Byzantine polity which developed out of it and yet retained strong feudal and patrimonial elements; (c) the Roman Catholic Church, increasingly so since the end of the thirteenth century; (d) China, from the time of Shi Hwangti until the present, but with strong patrimonial and prebendal elements; (e) in ever purer forms, the modern European states and, increasingly, all public corporations since the time of princely absolutism; (f) the large modern capitalist enterprise, the more so as it becomes greater and more complicated.

To a very great extent, partly even predominantly, cases (a) to (d) have rested upon compensation of the officials in kind. Yet they have displayed many other traits and effects characteristic of bureaucracy. The historical model of all later bureaucracies – the new Empire of Egypt – is at the same time one of the most grandiose examples of an organized subsistence economy. Yet this coincidence of bureaucracy and subsistence economy is understandable in view of the quite unique conditions that existed in Egypt. And the reservations – and they are quite considerable – which one must make in classifying this Egyptian structure as a bureaucracy are conditioned by the subsistence economy. A certain measure of a developed money economy is the normal precondition for the unchanged and continued existence, if not for the establishment, of pure bureaucratic administrations.

[...]

Even though the full development of a money economy is not an indispensable precondition for bureaucratization, bureaucracy as a permanent structure is knit to the one presupposition of a constant income for maintaining it. Where such an income cannot be derived from private profits, as is the case with the bureaucratic organization of large modern enterprises, or from fixed land rents, as with the manor, a stable system of *taxation* is the precondition for the permanent existence of bureaucratic administration. For well-known and general reasons, only a fully developed money economy offers a secure basis for such a taxation system. The degree of administrative bureaucratization in urban communities with fully developed money economies has not infrequently been relatively greater in the contemporary far larger states of plains. Yet as soon as these plain states have been able to develop orderly systems of tribute, bureaucracy has developed more comprehensively than in city states. Whenever the size of the city states has remained confined to moderate limits, the tendency for a plutocratic and collegial administration by notables has corresponded most adequately to their structure.

IV. The Quantitative Development of Administrative Tasks

The proper soil for the bureaucratization of an administration has always been the specific developments of administrative tasks. We shall first discuss the quantitative extension of such tasks. In the field of politics, the great state and the mass party are the classic soil for bureaucratization.

[. . .]

At the beginning of the modern period, all the prerogatives of the continental states accumulated in the hands of those princes who most relentlessly took the course of administrative bureaucratization. It is obvious that technically the great modern state is absolutely dependent upon a bureaucratic basis. The larger the state, and the more it is or the more it becomes a great power state, the more unconditionally is this the case.

The United States still bears the character of a polity which, at least in the technical sense, is not fully bureaucratized. But the greater the zones of friction with the outside and the more urgent the needs for administrative unity at home become, the more this character is inevitably and gradually giving way formally to the bureaucratic structure. Moreover, the partly unbureaucratic form of the state structure of the United States is materially balanced by the more strictly bureaucratic structures of those formations which, in truth, dominate politically, namely, the parties under the leadership of professionals or experts in organization and election tactics. The increasingly bureaucratic organization of all genuine mass parties offers the most striking example of the role of sheer quantity as a leverage for the bureaucratization of a social structure. In Germany, above all, the Social Democratic party, and abroad both of the 'historical' American parties are bureaucratic in the greatest possible degree.

[. . .]

V. Technical Advantages of Bureaucratic Organization

The decisive reason for the advance of bureaucratic organization has always been its purely technical superiority over any other form of organization. The fully developed bureaucratic mechanism compares with other organizations exactly as does the machine with the non-mechanical modes of production.

Precision, speed, unambiguity, knowledge of the files, continuity, discretion, unity, strict subordination, reduction of friction and of material and personal costs – these are raised to the optimum point in the strictly bureaucratic administration, and especially in its monocratic form. As compared with all collegiate, honorific, and avocational forms of administration, trained bureaucracy is superior on all these points. And as far as complicated tasks are concerned, paid bureaucratic work is not only more precise but, in the last analysis, it is often cheaper than, even formally unremunerated honorific service.

Honorific arrangements make administrative work an avocation and, for this reason alone, honorific service normally functions more slowly; being less bound to schemata and being more formless. Hence it is less precise and less unified than bureaucratic work because it is less dependent upon superiors and because the establishment and exploitation of the apparatus of subordinate officials and filing services are almost unavoidably less economical. Honorific service is less continuous than bureaucratic and frequently quite expensive. This is especially the case if one thinks not only of the money costs to the public treasury – costs which bureaucratic administration, in comparison with administration by notables, usually substantially increases – but also of the frequent economic losses of the governed caused by delays and lack of precision. The possibility of administration by, notables normally and permanently exists only where official management can be satisfactorily discharged as an avocation. With the qualitative increase of tasks the administration has to face, administration by notables reaches its limits – today, even in England. Work organized by collegiate bodies causes friction and delay and requires compromises between colliding interests and views. The administration, therefore, runs less precisely and is more independent of superiors; hence, it is less unified and slower. All advances of the Prussian administrative organization have been and will in the future be advances of the bureaucratic, and especially of the monocratic, principle.

Today, it is primarily the capitalist market economy which demands that the official business of the administration be discharged precisely, unambiguously, continuously, and with as much speed as possible. Normally, the very large, modern capitalist enterprises are themselves unequalled models of strict bureaucratic organization. Business management throughout rests on increasing precision, steadiness, and, above all, the speed of operations. This, in turn, is determined by the peculiar nature of the modern means of communication, including, among other things, the news service of the press. The extraordinary increase in the speed by which public announcements, as well as economic and political facts, are transmitted exerts a steady and sharp pressure in the direction of speeding up the tempo of administrative reaction towards various situations. The optimum of such reaction time is normally attained only by a strictly bureaucratic organization.*

Bureaucratization offers above all the optimum possibility for carrying through the principle of specializing administrative functions according to purely objective considerations. Individual performances are allocated to functionaries who have specialized training and who by constant practice

* Here we cannot discuss in detail how the bureaucratic apparatus may, and actually does, produce definite obstacles to the discharge of business in a manner suitable for the single case.

learn more and more. The 'objective' discharge of business primarily means a discharge of business according to *calculable rules* and 'without regard for persons'.

'Without regard for persons' is also the watchword of the 'market' and, in general, of all pursuits of naked economic interests. A consistent execution of bureaucratic domination means the leveling of status 'honor'. Hence, if the principle of the free-market is not at the same time restricted, it means the universal domination of the 'class situation'. That this consequence of bureaucratic domination has not set in everywhere, parallel to the extent of bureaucratization, is due to the differences among possible principles by which polities may meet their demands.

The second element mentioned, 'calculable rules', also is of paramount importance for modern bureaucracy. The peculiarity of modern culture, and specifically of its technical and economic basis, demands this very 'calculability' of results. When fully developed, bureaucracy also stands, in a specific sense, under the principle of *sine ira ac studio*. Its specific nature, which is welcomed by capitalism, develops the more perfectly the more the bureaucracy is 'dehumanized', the more completely it succeeds in eliminating from official business love, hatred, and all purely personal, irrational, and emotional elements which escape calculation. This is the specific nature of bureaucracy and it is appraised as its special virtue.

The more complicated and specialized modern culture becomes, the more its external supporting apparatus demands the personally detached and strictly 'objective' *expert*, in lieu of the master of older social structures, who was moved by personal sympathy and favor, by grace and gratitude. Bureaucracy offers the attitudes demanded by the external apparatus of modern culture in the most favorable combination. As a rule, only bureaucracy has established the foundation for the administration of a rational law conceptually systematized on the basis of such enactments as the latter Roman imperial period first created with a high degree of technical perfection. During the Middle Ages, this law was received along with the bureaucratization of legal administration, that is to say, with the displacement of the old trial procedure which was bound to tradition or to irrational presuppositions, by the rationally trained and specialized expert.

[...]

VI. THE CONCENTRATION OF THE MEANS OF ADMINISTRATION

The bureaucratic structure goes hand in hand with the concentration of the material means of management in the hands of the master. This concentration occurs, for instance, in a well-known and typical fashion, in the development of big capitalist enterprises, which find their essential characteristics in this process. A corresponding process occurs in public organizations.

The bureaucratically led army of the Pharaohs, the army during the later period of the Roman republic and the principate, and, above all, the army of the modern military state are characterized by the fact that their equipment and provisions are supplied from the magazines of the war lord. This is in contrast to the folk armies of agricultural tribes, the armed citizenry of ancient cities, the militias of early medieval cities, and all feudal armies; for these, the self-equipment and the self-provisioning of those obliged to fight was normal.

War in our time is a war of machines. And this makes magazines technically necessary, just as the dominance of the machine in industry promotes the concentration of the means of production and management. In the main, however, the bureaucratic armies of the past, equipped and provisioned by the lord, have risen when social and economic development has absolutely or relatively diminished the stratum of citizens who were economically able to equip themselves, so that their number was no longer sufficient for putting the required armies in the field. They were reduced at least relatively, that is, in relation to the range of power claimed for the polity. Only the bureaucratic army structure allowed for the development of the professional standing armies which are necessary for the constant pacification of large states of the plains, as well as for warfare against far-distant enemies, especially enemies overseas. Specifically, military discipline and technical training can be normally and fully developed, at least to its modern high level, only in the bureaucratic army.

[. . .]

VII. The Leveling of Social Differences

Bureaucratic organization has usually come into power on the basis of a leveling of economic and social differences. This leveling has been at least relative, and has concerned the significance of social and economic differences for the assumption of administrative functions.

Bureaucracy inevitably accompanies modern *mass democracy* in contrast to the democratic self-government of small homogeneous units. This results from the characteristic principle of bureaucracy: the abstract regularity of the execution of authority, which is a result of the demand for 'equality before the law' in the personal and functional sense – hence, of the horror of 'privilege', and the principled rejection of doing business 'from case to case'. Such regularity also follows from the social preconditions of the origin of bureaucracies. The non-bureaucratic administration of any large social structure rests in some way upon the fact that existing social, material, or honorific preferences and ranks are connected with administrative functions and duties. This usually means that a direct or indirect economic exploitation or a 'social' exploitation of position, which every sort of administrative activity gives to its bearers, is equivalent to the assumption of administrative functions.

[...]

VIII. THE PERMANENT CHARACTER OF THE BUREAUCRATIC MACHINE

Once it is fully established, bureaucracy is among those social structures which are the hardest to destroy. Bureaucracy is *the* means of carrying 'community action' over into rationally ordered 'societal action'. Therefore, as an instrument for 'societalizing' relations of power, bureaucracy has been and is a power instrument of the first order – for the one who controls the bureaucratic apparatus.

Under otherwise equal conditions, a 'societal action', which is methodically ordered and led, is superior to every resistance of 'mass' or even of 'communal action'. And where the bureaucratization of administration has been completely carried through, a form of power relation is established that is practically unshatterable.

The individual bureaucrat cannot squirm out of the apparatus in which he is harnessed. In contrast to the honorific or avocational 'notable', the professional bureaucrat is chained to his activity by his entire material and ideal existence. In the great majority of cases, he is only a single cog in an ever-moving mechanism which prescribes to him an essentially fixed route of march. The official is entrusted with specialized tasks and normally the mechanism cannot be put into motion or arrested by him, but only from the very top. The individual bureaucrat is thus forged to the community of all the functionaries who are integrated into the mechanism. They have a common interest in seeing that the mechanism continues its functions and that the societally exercised authority carries on.

The ruled, for their part, cannot dispense with or replace the bureaucratic apparatus of authority once it exists. For this bureaucracy rests upon expert training, a functional specialization of work, and an attitude set for habitual and virtuoso-like mastery of single yet methodically integrated functions. If the official stops working, or if his work is forcefully interrupted, chaos results, and it is difficult to improvise replacements from among the governed who are fit to master such chaos. This holds for public administration as well as for private economic management. More and more the material fate of the masses depends upon the steady and correct functioning of the increasingly bureaucratic organizations of private capitalism. The idea of eliminating these organizations becomes more and more utopian.

The discipline of officialdom refers to the attitude-set of the official for precise obedience within his *habitual* activity, in public as well as in private organizations. This discipline increasingly becomes the basis of all order, however great the practical importance of administration on the basis of the filed documents may be. The naive idea of Bakuninism of destroying the basis of 'acquired rights' and 'domination' by destroying public documents overlooks the settled orientation of *man* for keeping to the habitual rules and regulations that continue to exist independently of the documents. Every reorganization of beaten or dissolved troops, as well as the restoration of administrative orders destroyed by revolt, panic, or other catastrophes, is realized by appealing to the trained orientation of obedient compliance to such orders. Such compliance has been conditioned into the officials, on the one hand, and, on the other hand, into the governed. If such an appeal is successful it brings, as it were, the disturbed mechanism into gear again.

The objective indispensability of the once-existing apparatus, with its peculiar, 'impersonal' character, means that the mechanism – in contrast to feudal orders based upon personal piety – is easily made to work for anybody who knows how to gain control over it. A rationally ordered system of officials continues to function smoothly after the enemy has occupied the area; he merely needs to change the top officials. This body of officials continues to operate because it is to the vital interest of everyone concerned, including above all the enemy.

NOTES

1. Frederick II of Prussia.
2. Cf. *Wirtschaft und Gesellschaft*, pp. 73ff. and part II. (German Editor.)

CLASS, STATUS, PARTY

Max Weber

I. Economically Determined Power and the Social Order

Law exists when there is a probability that an order will be upheld by a specific staff of men who will use physical or psychical compulsion with the intention of obtaining conformity with the order, or of inflicting sanctions for infringement of it. The structure of every legal order directly influences the distribution of power, economic or otherwise, within its respective community. This is true of all legal orders and not only that of the state. In general, we understand by 'power' the chance of a man or of a number of men to realize their own will in a communal action even against the resistance of others who are participating in the action.

'Economically conditioned' power is not, of course, identical with 'power' as such. On the contrary, the emergence of economic power may be the consequence of power existing on other grounds. Man does not strive for power only in order to enrich himself economically. Power, including economic power, may be valued 'for its own sake'. Very frequently the striving for power is also conditioned by the social 'honor' it entails. Not all power, however, entails social honor: the typical American Boss, as well as the typical big speculator, deliberately relinquishes social honor. Quite generally, 'mere economic' power, and especially 'naked' money power, is by no means a recognized basis of social honor. Nor is power the only basis of

Max Weber (1948), 'Class, status, party', in H. H. Gerth and C. Wright Mills (eds), *From Max Weber*, London and Boston: Routledge and Kegan Paul.

social honor. Indeed, social honor, or prestige, may even be the basis of political or economic power, and very frequently has been. Power, as well as honor, may be guaranteed by the legal order, but, at least normally, it is not their primary source. The legal order is rather an additional factor that enhances the chance to hold power or honor; but it cannot always secure them.

The way in which social honor is distributed in a community between typical groups participating in this distribution we may call the 'social order'. The social order and the economic order are, of course, similarly related to the 'legal order'. However, the social and the economic order are not identical. The economic order is for us merely the way in which economic goods and services are distributed and used. The social order is of course conditioned by the economic order to a high degree, and in its turn reacts upon it.

Now: 'classes', 'status groups', and 'parties' are phenomena of the distribution of power within a community.

II. Determination of Class-Situation by Market-Situation

In our terminology, 'classes' are not communities; they merely represent possible, and frequent, bases for communal action. We may speak of a 'class' when (1) a number of people have in common a specific causal component of their life chances, in so far as (2) this component is represented exclusively by economic interests in the possession of goods and opportunities for income, and (3) is represented under the conditions of the commodity or labor markets. These points refer to 'class situation', which we may express more briefly as the typical chance for a supply of goods, external living conditions, and personal life experiences, in so far as this chance is determined by the amount and kind of power, or lack of such, to dispose of goods or skills for the sake of income in a given economic order. The term 'class' refers to any group of people that is found in the same class situation.

It is the most elemental economic fact that the way in which the disposition over material property is distributed among a plurality of people, meeting competitively in the market for the purpose of exchange, in itself creates specific life chances. According to the law of marginal utility this mode of distribution excludes the non-owners from competing for highly valued goods; it favors the owners and, in fact, gives to them a monopoly to acquire such goods. Other things being equal, this mode of distribution monopolizes the opportunities for profitable deals for all those who, provided with goods, do not necessarily have to exchange them. It increases, at least generally, their power in price wars with those who, being propertyless, have nothing to offer but their services in native form or goods in a form constituted through their own labor, and who above all are compelled to get rid of these products in order barely to subsist. This mode of distribution gives to the propertied a monopoly on the possibility of transferring property from the sphere of use as a 'fortune', to the sphere of 'capital goods'; that is, it gives them the entrepreneurial function and all chances to share directly or indirectly in returns on capital. All this holds true within the area in which pure market conditions prevail. 'Property' and 'lack of property' are, therefore, the basic categories of all class situations. It does not matter whether these two categories become effective in price wars or in competitive struggles.

Within these categories, however, class situations are further differentiated: on the one hand, according to the kind of property that is usable for returns; and, on the other hand, according to the kind of services that can be offered in the market. Ownership of domestic buildings; productive establishments; warehouses; stores; agriculturally usable land, large and small holdings – quantitative differences with possibly qualitative consequences; ownership of mines; cattle; men (slaves); disposition over mobile instruments of production, or capital goods of all sorts, especially money or objects that can be exchanged for money easily and at any time; disposition over products of one's own labor or of others' labor differing according to their various distances from consumability; disposition over transferable monopolies of any kind – all these distinctions differentiate the class situations of the propertied just as does the 'meaning' which they can and do give to the utilization of property, especially to property which has money equivalence. Accordingly, the propertied, for instance, may belong to the class of rentiers or to the class of entrepreneurs.

Those who have no property but who offer services are differentiated just as much according to their kinds of services as according to the way in which they make use of these services, in a continuous or discontinuous relation to a recipient. But always this is the generic connotation of the concept of class: that the kind of chance in the *market* is the decisive moment which presents a common condition for the individual's fate. 'Class situation' is, in this sense, ultimately 'market situation'. The effect of naked possession *per se*, which among cattle breeders gives the non-owning slave or serf into the power of the cattle owner, is only a forerunner of real 'class' formation. However, in the cattle loan and in the naked severity of the law of debts in such communities, for the first time mere 'possession' as such emerges as decisive for the fate of the individual. This is very much in contrast to the agricultural communities based on labor. The creditor–debtor relation becomes the basis of 'class situations' only in those cities where a 'credit market', however primitive, with rates of interest increasing according to the extent of dearth and a factual monopolization of credits, is developed by a plutocracy. Therewith 'class struggles' begin.

Those men whose fate is not determined by the chance of using goods or services for themselves on the market, e.g. slaves, are not, however, a 'class' in the technical sense of the term. They are, rather, a 'status group'.

III. COMMUNAL ACTION FLOWING FROM CLASS INTEREST

According to our terminology, the factor that creates 'class' is unambiguously economic interest, and indeed, only those interests involved in the existence of the 'market'. Nevertheless, the concept of 'class-interest' is an ambiguous one: even as an empirical concept it is ambiguous as soon as one understands by it something other than the factual direction of interests following with a certain probability from the class situation for a certain 'average' of those people subjected to the class situation. The class situation and other circumstances remaining the same, the direction in which the individual worker, for instance, is likely to pursue his interests may vary widely, according to whether he is constitutionally qualified for the task at hand to a high, to an average, or to a low degree. In the same way, the direction of interests may vary according to whether or not a *communal* action of a larger or smaller portion of those commonly affected by the 'class situation', or even an association among them, e.g. a 'trade union', has grown out of the class situation from which the individual may or may not expect promising results. Communal action refers to that action which is oriented to the feeling of the actors that they belong together. Societal action, on the other hand, is oriented to a rationally motivated adjustment of interests. The rise of societal or even of communal action from a common class situation is by no means universal phenomenon.

The class situation may be restricted in its effects to the generation of essentially *similar* reactions, that is to say, within our terminology, of 'mass actions'. However, it may not have even this result. Furthermore, often merely an amorphous communal action emerges. For example, the 'murmuring' of the workers known in ancient oriental ethics: the moral disapproval of the work-master's conduct, which in its practical significance was probably equivalent to an increasingly typical phenomenon of precisely the latest industrial development, namely, the 'slow down' (the deliberate limiting of work effort) of laborers by virtue of tacit agreement. The degree in which 'communal action' and possibly 'societal action', emerges from the 'mass actions' of the members of a class is linked to general cultural conditions, especially to those of an intellectual sort. It is also linked to the extent of the contrasts that have already evolved, and is especially linked to the *transparency* of the connections between the causes and the consequences of the 'class situation'. For however different life chances may be, this fact in itself, according to all experience, by no means gives birth to 'class action' (communal action by the members of a class). The fact of being conditioned and the results of the class situation must be distinctly recognizable. For only then the contrast of life chances can be felt not as an absolutely given fact to be accepted, but as a resultant from either (1) the given distribution of property, or (2) the structure of the concrete economic order. It is only then that people may react against the class structure not only through acts of an intermittent and irrational protest, but in the form of rational association. There have been 'class situations' of the first category (1), of a specifically naked and transparent sort, in the urban centers of Antiquity and during the Middle Ages; especially then, when great fortunes were accumulated by factually monopolized trading in industrial products of these localities or in foodstuffs. Furthermore, under certain circumstances, in the rural economy of the most diverse periods, when agriculture was increasingly exploited in a profit-making manner. The most important historical example of the second category (2) is the class situation of the modern 'proletariat.'

IV. TYPES OF 'CLASS STRUGGLE'

Thus every class may be the carrier of any one of the possibly innumerable forms of 'class action', but this is not necessarily so. In any case, a class does not in itself constitute a community. To treat 'class' conceptually as having the same value as 'community' leads to distortion. That men in the same class situation regularly react in mass actions to such tangible situations as economic ones in the direction of those interests that are most adequate to their average number is an important and after all simple fact for the understanding of historical events. Above all, this fact must not lead to that kind of pseudo-scientific operation with the concepts of 'class' and 'class interests' so frequently found these days, and which has found its most classic expression in the statement of a talented author, that the individual may be in error concerning his interests but that the 'class' is 'infallible' about its interests. Yet, if classes as such are not communities, nevertheless class situations emerge only on the basis of communalization. The communal action that brings forth class situations, however, is not basically action between members of the identical class; it is an action between members of different classes. Communal actions that directly determine the class situation of the worker and the entrepreneur are: the labor market, the commodities market, and the capitalistic enterprise. But, in its turn, the existence of a capitalistic enterprise presupposes that a very specific communal action exists and that it is specifically structured to protect the possession of goods *per se*, and especially the power of individuals to dispose, in principle freely, over the means of production. The existence of a capitalistic enterprise is preconditioned by a specific kind of 'legal order'. Each kind of class situation, and above all when it rests upon the power of property *per se*, will become most clearly efficacious when all other determinants of reciprocal relations are, as far as possible, eliminated in their significance. It is in this way that the utilization of the power of property in the market obtains its most sovereign importance.

[. . .]

V. STATUS HONOR

In contrast to classes, *status groups* are normally communities. They are, however, often of an amorphous kind. In contrast to the purely economically determined 'class situation' we wish to designate as 'status situation' every typical component of the life fate of men that is determined by a specific, positive or negative, social estimation of *honor*. This honor may be connected with any quality shared by a plurality, and, of course, it can be knit to a class situation: class distinctions are linked in the most varied ways with status distinctions. Property as such is not always recognized as a status qualification, but in the long run it is, and with extraordinary regularity. In the subsistence economy of the organized neighborhood, very often the richest man is simply the chieftain. However, this often means only an honorific preference. For example, in the so-called pure modern 'democracy', that is, one devoid of any expressly ordered status privileges for individuals, it may be that only the families coming under approximately the same tax class dance with one another. This example is reported of certain smaller Swiss cities. But status honor need not necessarily be linked with a 'class situation'. On the contrary, it normally stands in sharp opposition to the pretensions of sheer property.

Both propertied and propertyless people can belong to the same status group, and frequently they do with very tangible consequences. This 'equality' of social esteem may, however, in the long run become quite precarious. The 'equality' of status among the American 'gentlemen', for instance, is expressed by the fact that outside the subordination determined by the different functions of 'business', it would be considered strictly repugnant – wherever the old tradition still prevails – if even the richest 'chief', while playing billiards or cards in his club in the evening, would not treat his 'clerk' as in every sense fully his equal in birthright. It would be repugnant if the American 'chief' would bestow upon his 'clerk' the condescending 'benevolence' marking a distinction of 'position', which the German chief can never dissever from his attitude. This is one of the most important reasons why in America the German 'clubby-ness' has never been able to attain the attraction that the American clubs have.

VI. GUARANTEES OF STATUS STRATIFICATION

In content, status honor is normally expressed by the fact that above all else a specific *style of life* can be expected from all those who wish to belong to the circle. Linked with this expectation are restrictions on 'social' intercourse (that is, intercourse which is not subservient to economic or any other of business's 'functional' purposes). These restrictions may confine normal marriages to within the status circle and may lead to complete endogamous closure. As soon as there is not a mere individual and socially irrelevant imitation of another style of life, but an agreed-upon communal action of this closing character, the 'status' development is under way.

In its characteristic form, stratification by 'status groups' on the basis of conventional styles of life evolves at the present time in the United States out of the traditional democracy. For example, only the resident of a certain street ('the street') is considered as belonging to 'society', is qualified for social intercourse, and is visited and invited. Above all, this differentiation evolves in such a way as to make for strict submission to the fashion that is dominant at a given time in society. This submission to fashion also exists among men in America to a degree unknown in Germany. Such submission is considered to be an indication of the fact that a given man *pretends* to qualify as a gentleman. This submission decides, at least *prima facie*, that he will be treated as such. And this recognition becomes just as important for his employment chances in 'swank' establishments, and above all, for social intercourse and marriage with 'esteemed' families, as the qualification for dueling among Germans in the Kaiser's day. As for the rest: certain families resident for a long time, and, of course, correspondingly wealthy, e.g. 'F.F.V., i.e. First Families of Virginia', or the actual or alleged descendants of the 'Indian Princess' Pocahontas, of the Pilgrim fathers, or of the Knickerbockers, the members of almost inaccessible sects and all sorts of circles setting themselves apart by means of any other characteristics and badges . . . all these elements usurp 'status' honor. The development of status is essentially a question of stratification resting upon usurpation. Such usurpation is the normal origin of almost all status honor. But the road from this purely conventional situation to legal privilege, positive or negative, is easily traveled as soon as a certain stratification of the social order has in fact been 'lived in' and has achieved stability by virtue of a stable distribution of economic power.

VII. 'Ethnic' Segregation and 'Caste'

Where the consequences have been realized to their full extent, the status group evolves into a closed 'caste'. Status distinctions are then guaranteed not merely by conventions and laws, but also by *rituals*. This occurs in such a way that every physical contact with a member of any caste that is considered to be 'lower' by the members of a 'higher' caste is considered as making for a ritualistic impurity and to be a stigma which must be expiated by a religious act. Individual castes develop quite distinct cults and gods.

In general, however, the status structure reaches such extreme consequences only where there are underlying differences which are held to be 'ethnic'. The 'caste' is, indeed, the normal form in which ethnic communities usually live side by side in a 'societalized' manner. These ethnic communities believe in blood relationship and exclude exogamous marriage and social intercourse. Such a caste situation is part of the phenomenon of 'pariah' peoples and is found all over the world. These people form communities, acquire specific occupational traditions of handicrafts or of other arts, and cultivate a belief in their ethnic community. They live in a 'diaspora' strictly segregated from all personal intercourse, except that of an unavoidable sort, and their situation is legally precarious. Yet, by virtue of their economic indispensability, they are tolerated, indeed, frequently privileged, and they live in interspersed political communities. The Jews are the most impressive historical example.

A 'status' segregation grown into a 'caste' differs in its structure from a mere 'ethnic' segregation: the caste structure transforms the horizontal and unconnected coexistences of ethnically segregated groups into a vertical social system of super- and subordination. Correctly formulated: a comprehensive societalization integrates the ethnically divided communities into specific political and communal action. In their consequences they differ precisely in this way: ethnic coexistences condition a mutual repulsion and disdain but allow each ethnic community to consider its own honor as the highest one; the caste structure brings about a social subordination and an acknowledgment of 'more honor' in favor of the privileged caste and status groups. This is due to the fact that in the caste structure ethnic distinctions as such have become 'functional' distinctions within the political societalization (warriors, priests, artisans that are politically important for war and for building, and so on). But even pariah people who are most despised are usually apt to continue cultivating in some manner that which is equally peculiar to ethnic and to status communities: the belief in their own specific 'honor'. This is the case with the Jews.

Only with the negatively privileged status groups does the 'sense of dignity' take a specific deviation. A sense of dignity is the precipitation in individuals of social honor and of conventional demands which a positively privileged status group raises for the deportment of its members. The sense of dignity that characterizes positively privileged status groups is naturally related to their 'being' which does not transcend itself, that is, it is to their 'beauty and excellence' (ϰαλο-ἀγαϑια). Their kingdom is 'of this world'. They live for the present and by exploiting their great past. The sense of dignity of the negatively privileged strata naturally refers to a future lying beyond the present, whether it is of this life or of another. In other words, it must be nurtured by the belief in a providential 'mission' and by a belief in a specific honor before God, The 'chosen people's' dignity is nurtured by a belief either that in the beyond 'the last will be the first', or that in this life a Messiah will appear to bring forth into the light of the world which has cast them out the hidden honor of the pariah people. This simple state of affairs, and not the 'resentment' which is so strongly emphasized in Nietzsche's much admired construction in the *Genealogy of Morals*, is the source of the religiosity cultivated by pariah status groups. In passing, we may note that resentment may be accurately applied only to a limited extent; for one of Nietzsche's main examples, Buddhism, it is not at all applicable.

Incidentally, the development of status groups from ethnic segregations is by no means the normal phenomenon. On the contrary, since objective 'racial differences' are by no means basic to every subjective sentiment of an ethnic community, the ultimately racial foundation of status structure is rightly and absolutely a question of the concrete individual case. Very frequently a status group is instrumental in the production of a thoroughbred anthropological type. Certainly a status group is to a high degree effective in producing extreme types, for they select personally qualified individuals (e.g. the Knighthood selects those who are fit for warfare, physically and psychically). But selection is far from being the only, or the predominant, way in which status groups are formed: political membership or class situation has at all times been at least as frequently decisive. And today the class situation is by far the predominant factor, for of course the possibility of a style of life expected for members of a status group is usually conditioned economically.

VIII. Status Privileges

For all practical purposes, stratification by status goes hand in hand with a monopolization of ideal and material goods or opportunities, in a manner we have come to know as typical. Besides the specific status honor, which always rests upon distance and exclusiveness, we find all sorts of material monopolies. Such honorific preferences may consist of the privilege of wearing special costumes, of eating special dishes taboo to others, of carrying arms – which is most obvious in its consequences – the right to pursue certain non-professional dilettante artistic practices, e.g. to play certain musical instruments. Of course, material monopolies provide the most effective motives for the exclusiveness of a status group; although, in themselves, they are rarely sufficient, almost always they come into play to some extent. Within a status circle there is the question of intermarriage: the interest of the families in the monopolization of potential bridegrooms is at least of equal importance and is parallel to the interest in the monopolization of daughters. The daughters of the circle must be provided for. With an increased inclosure of the status group, the conventional preferential opportunities for special employment grow into a legal monopoly of special offices for the members. Certain goods become objects for monopolization by status groups. In the typical fashion these include 'entailed estates' and frequently also the possessions of serfs or bondsmen and, finally, special trades. This monopolization occurs positively when the status group is exclusively entitled to own and to manage them; and negatively when, in order to maintain its specific way of life, the status group must *not* own and manage them.

The decisive role of a 'style of life' in status 'honor' means that status groups are the specific bearers of all 'conventions'. In whatever way it may be manifest, all 'stylization' of life either originates in status groups or is at least conserved by them. Even if the principles of status conventions differ greatly, they reveal certain typical traits, especially among those strata which are most privileged. Quite generally, among privileged status groups there is a status disqualification that operates against the performance of common physical labor. This disqualification is now 'setting in' in America against the old tradition of esteem for labor. Very frequently every rational economic pursuit, and especially 'entrepreneurial activity', is looked upon as a disqualification of status. Artistic and literary activity is also considered as degrading work as soon as it is exploited for income, or at least when it is connected with hard physical exertion. An example is the sculptor working like a mason in his dusty smock as over against the painter in his salon-like 'studio' and those forms of musical practice that are acceptable to the status group.

IX. ECONOMIC CONDITIONS AND EFFECTS OF STATUS STRATIFICATION

The frequent disqualification of the gainfully employed as such is a direct result of the principle of status stratification peculiar to the social order, and of course, of this principle's opposition to a distribution of power which is regulated exclusively through the market. These two factors operate along with various individual ones, which will be touched upon below.

We have seen above that the market and its processes 'knows no personal distinctions': 'functional' interests dominate it. It knows nothing of 'honor'. The status order means precisely the reverse, viz.: stratification in terms of 'honor' and of styles of life peculiar to status groups as such. If mere economic acquisition and naked economic power still bearing the stigma of its extra-status origin could bestow upon anyone who has won it the same honor as those who are interested in status by virtue of style of life claim for themselves, the status order would be threatened at its very root. This is the more so as, given equality of status honor, property *per se* represents an addition even if it is not overtly acknowledged to be such. Yet if such economic acquisition and power gave the agent any honor at all, his wealth would result in his attaining more honor than those who successfully claim honor by virtue of style of life. Therefore all groups having interests in the status order react with special sharpness precisely against the pretensions of purely economic acquisition. In most cases they react the more vigorously the more they feel themselves threatened. Calderon's respectful treatment of the peasant, for instance, as opposed to Shakespeare's simultaneous and ostensible disdain of the *canaille* illustrates the different way in which a firmly structured status order reacts as compared with a status order that has become economically precarious. This is an example of a state of affairs that recurs everywhere. Precisely because of the rigorous reactions against the claims of property *per se*, the 'parvenu' is never accepted, personally and without reservation, by the privileged status groups, no matter how completely his style of life has been adjusted to theirs. They will only accept his descendants who have been educated in the conventions of their status group and who have never besmirched its honor by their own economic labor.

As to the general *effect* of the status order, only one consequence can be stated, but it is a very important one: the hindrance of the free development of the market occurs first for those goods which status groups directly withheld from free exchange by monopolization. This monopolization may be effected either legally or conventionally. For example, in many Hellenic cities during the epoch of status groups, and also originally in Rome, the inherited estate (as is shown by the old formula for indiction against spendthrifts) was monopolized just as were the estates of knights, peasants, priests, and especially the clientele of the craft and merchant guilds. The market is restricted, and the power of naked property *per se*, which gives its stamp to 'class formation,' is pushed into the background. The results of this process can be most varied. Of course, they do not necessarily weaken the contrasts in the economic situation. Frequently they strengthen these contrasts, and in any case, where stratification by status permeates a community as strongly as was the case in all political communities of antiquity and of the Middle Ages, one can never speak of a genuinely free market competition as we understand it today. There are wider effects than this direct exclusion of special goods from the market. From the contrariety between the status order and the purely economic order mentioned above, it follows that in most instances the notion of honor peculiar to status absolutely abhors that which is essential to the market: higgling. Honor abhors higgling among peers and occasionally it taboos higgling for the members of a status group in general. Therefore, everywhere some status groups, and usually the most influential, consider almost any kind of overt participation in economic acquisition as absolutely stigmatizing.

With some over-simplification, one might thus say that 'classes' are stratified according to their relations to the production and acquisition of goods; whereas 'status groups' are stratified according to the principles of their *consumption* of goods as represented by special 'styles of life'.

An '*occupational group*' is also a status group. For normally, it successfully claims social honor only by virtue of the special style of life which may be determined by it. The differences between classes and status groups frequently overlap. It is precisely those status communities most strictly segregated in terms of honor (viz. the Indian castes) who today show, although within very rigid limits, a relatively high degree of indifference to pecuniary income. However, the Brahmins seek such income in many different ways.

As to the general economic conditions making for the predominance of stratification by 'status,' only very little can be said. When the bases of the acquisition and distribution of goods are relatively stable, stratification by status is favored. Every technological repercussion and economic transformation threatens stratification by status and pushes the class situation into the foreground. Epochs and countries in which the naked class situation is of predominant significance are regularly the periods of technical and economic transformations. And every slowing down of the shifting of economic stratifications leads, in due course, to the growth of status structures and makes for a resuscitation of the important role of social honor.

X. PARTIES

Whereas the genuine place of 'classes' is within the economic order, the place of 'status groups' is within the social order, that is, within the sphere of the distribution of 'honor.' From within these spheres, classes and status groups influence one another and they influence the legal order and are in turn influenced by it. But 'parties' live in a house of 'power'.

Their action is oriented toward the acquisition of social 'power', that is to say, toward influencing a communal action no matter what its content may be. In principle, parties may exist in a social 'club' as well as in a 'state'. As over against the actions of classes and status groups, for which this is not necessarily the case, the communal actions of 'parties' always mean a societalization. For party actions are always directed toward a goal which is striven for in planned manner. This goal may be a 'cause' (the party may aim at realizing a program for ideal or material purposes), or the goal may be 'personal' (sinecures, power, and from these, honor for the leader and the followers of the party). Usually the party action aims at all these simultaneously. Parties are, therefore, only possible within communities that are societalized, that is, which have some rational order and a staff of persons available who are ready to enforce it. For parties aim precisely at influencing this staff, and if possible, to recruit it from party followers.

In any individual case, parties may represent interests determined through 'class situation' or 'status situation', and they may recruit their following respectively from one or the other. But they need be neither purely 'class' nor purely 'status' parties. In most cases they are partly class parties and partly status parties, but sometimes they are neither. They may represent ephemeral or enduring structures. Their means of attaining power may be quite varied, ranging from naked violence of any sort to canvassing for votes with coarse or subtle means: money, social influence, the force of speech, suggestion, clumsy hoax, and so on to the rougher or more artful tactics of obstruction in parliamentary bodies.

The sociological structure of parties differs in a basic way according to the kind of communal action which they struggle to influence. Parties also differ according to whether or not the community is stratified by status or by classes. Above all else, they vary according to the structure of domination within the community. For their leaders normally deal with the conquest of a community. They are, in the general concept which is maintained here, not only products of specially modern forms of domination. We shall also designate as parties the ancient and medieval 'parties', despite the fact that their structure differs basically from the structure of modern parties. By virtue of these structural differences of domination it is impossible to say anything about the structure of parties without discussing the structural forms of social domination *per se*. Parties, which are always structures struggling for domination, are very frequently organized in a very strict 'authoritarian' fashion . . .

Concerning 'classes', 'status groups', and 'parties', it must be said in general that they necessarily presuppose a comprehensive societalization, and especially a political framework of communal action, within which they operate. This does not mean that parties would be confined by the frontiers of any individual political community. On the contrary, at all times it has been the order of the day that the societalization (even when it aims at the use of military force in common) reaches beyond the frontiers of politics. This has been the case in the solidarity of interests among the Oligarchs and among the democrats in Hellas, among the Guelfs and among Ghibellines in the Middle Ages, and within the Calvinist party during the period of religious struggles. It has been the case up to the solidarity of the landlords (international congress of agrarian landlords), and has continued among princes (holy alliance, Karlsbad decrees), socialist workers, conservatives (the longing of Prussian conservatives for Russian intervention in 1850). But their aim is not necessarily the establishment of new international political, i.e. *territorial*, dominion. In the main they aim to influence the existing dominion.

WITHOUT REGARD FOR PERSONS

Derek Sayer

The world, which seems,
To lie before us like a land of dreams,
So various, so beautiful, so new,
Hath really neither joy, nor love, nor light,
Nor certitude, nor peace, nor help for pain;
And we are here as on a darkling plain
Swept with confused alarms of struggle and flight,
Where ignorant armies clash by night.

Matthew Arnold, 'Dover Beach'

I.

It is rationalization, then, not capitalism *per se*, which for Weber lies at the root of the modern world order, and the reasons for this are to be found in various peculiarities of 'the West'. Capitalism is but one theatre among others in which the drama of rationality is played out; and all the leading motifs of modern capitalism have their exact counterparts in many other arenas of social life. But if, for Weber, capitalism is no longer Marx's demiurge of modern society, it continues to furnish him with the paradigms through which modernity is analysed. Not only is it the major agency of global rationalization, capitalism is also the template in terms of which

Derek Sayer (1990), 'Without regard for persons', in *Capitalism and Modernity: An Excursus on Marx and Weber*, London: Routledge.

the overall social consequences of rationalization are comprehended. In this sense it remains the keystone of his general sociology of the modern world.

Thus, as we saw above, Weber draws a parallel between the separation of the worker from the means of production and the separation of the soldier from 'the paraphernalia of war'. Marx said that this 'severance of the conditions of production, on the one hand, from the producers, on the other, forms the *conception* of capital' (Marx 1971: 246). For Weber, such severance is a feature of modern social organization across *all* spheres of life: 'this whole process of rationalization, in the factory as elsewhere, and especially in the bureaucratic state machine, parallels the centralization of the material implements of organization in the discretionary power of the overlord' (Weber 1968: 39). The beginnings of the modern state lie in 'the expropriation of the autonomous and "private" bearers of executive power ... who in their own right possess the means of administration, warfare, and financial organization'. 'The whole process' of state-making, Weber says, 'is a complete parallel to the development of the capitalist enterprise through gradual expropriation of the independent producers' (Weber 1970: 82). In effect he generalizes Marx's model of alienation, with the result that capitalism becomes a special case – if a uniquely 'fateful' one – of a more encompassing 'expropriation' which is the foundation of the discipline which sinews the modern subject into the 'machines' of modern society. Severance of the material means of a given human activity from its agents (which, just as for Marx, implies their isolation as solitary individuals) is the generic basis for all institutional rationalization. This is the key principle of that bureaucracy which for Weber pervades most arenas of modern life, capitalism included, and in bureaucracy we have discipline's 'most rational offspring', its perfected social form (Weber 1968: 29).

In 'modern officialdom', says Weber, there are 'fixed and official jurisdictional areas, which are generally ordered by rules, that is, by laws or administrative regulations'. Regular activities of the bureaucratic structure are 'distributed in a fixed way as official duties', as is the authority to command the discharge of these duties; and the exercise of this authority is 'strictly delimited by rules' concerning the sanctions officials may employ to secure compliance with their orders. This pattern is typical of 'bureaucratic authority' in the public domain and of 'bureaucratic management' in the private, and is respectively 'fully developed ... only in the modern state and ... only in the most advanced institutions of capitalism. Permanent and public office authority, with fixed jurisdiction, is not the historical rule but rather the exception'. Pre-modern rulers worked through 'personal trustees, table-companions, or court servants', and commissions of authority were 'not precisely delimited' in their scope, and *ad hoc* rather than permanent. Within this new unified jurisdictional space there is a clear, and hierarchical, division of labour and responsibility, 'a firmly ordered system of super- and subordination in which there is supervision of the lower offices by the higher ones' (Weber 1970: 196–7).

The essence of all such bureaucratic discipline is 'the consistently rationalized, methodically trained and exact execution of the received order, in which all personal criticism is unconditionally suspended and the actor is unswervingly and exclusively set for carrying out the command' (Weber 1968: 28). Specifically, Weber emphasizes, 'the discipline of officialdom refers to the attitude-set of the official for precise obedience within his *habitual* activity, in public as well as private organizations', and 'this discipline increasingly becomes the basis of all order, however great the practical importance of administration on the basis of the filed documents may be'. It is 'the settled orientation of *man*' – that is, of *modern* 'man' – 'for keeping to the habitual rules and regulations' that is the foundation of this *neue Ordnung* (Weber 1970: 229). Bureaucracy rests on the reorganization of *habitus*. Weber argues that such 'mechanization' is facilitated by a guaranteed salary and the opportunity of 'a career that is not dependent upon mere accident and arbitrariness'; working in the same direction are 'status sentiment among officials', and 'the purely impersonal character of office work' (Weber 1970: 208). The individual bureaucrat, unable to 'squirm out of the apparatus in which he is harnessed', is thus 'forged to the community of all the functionaries who are integrated into the mechanism' (Weber 1970: 228).

Officials, whether employees of private businesses or state servants, undergo 'thorough and expert training'. 'Educational certificates' are 'linked with qualifications for office', which enhances the 'status element' in the position of the official (Weber 1970: 198, 200); 'more and more the specialized knowledge of the expert became the foundation for the power position of the officeholder' (Weber 1970: 235). 'The system of rational, specialized, and expert examinations', Weber maintains, 'is increasingly indispensable for modern bureaucracy', and 'capitalism, with its demand for expertly trained technicians, clerks, et cetera, carries such examinations all over the world' (Weber 1970: 240–1). This valuation of technical expertise is radically different from the ideal of the 'cultivated man' which 'formed the basis of social esteem in such various systems as the feudal, theocratic, and patrimonial structures of domination' (Weber 1970: 243) – an esteem which rested on the gentleman precisely not being tied to a career but being an 'amateur', one whose means gave him the leisure to cultivate the self in ways that would enhance the public good. Weber clearly regrets the passing of this ideal; in the famous words of *The Protestant Ethic*, modernity turns the world over to 'specialists without spirit, sensualists without heart'; and 'this nullity', he scathingly writes, 'imagines that it has attained a level of civilization never before achieved' (Weber 1974: 182). Within the developed bureau, there is no room for gentlemanly amateurs: where previously 'official business was discharged as a secondary activity', nowadays 'official activity demands the full working capacity of the official'. Otherwise put, 'office holding is a "vocation"' and 'the position of the official is in the nature of a duty' (Weber 1970: 198–9).

In so far, Weber remarks, as this discipline appeals to any 'firm motives of an "ethical" character, it presupposes a "sense of duty" and "conscientiousness"' (which contrasts sharply with moralities of 'honour') (Weber 1968: 29). The functioning of the amoral 'machine' of bureaucracy thus rests, paradoxically, on a striking moralization of the individual's relation to it. The morality is one of subservience, of abnegation of individual responsibility; it is the morality demonstrated repeatedly at the Nürnberg trials. Weber summarized it well:

> The honor of the civil servant is vested in his ability to execute conscientiously the order of the superior authorities, exactly as if the order agreed with his own conviction. This holds even if the order appears wrong to him and if, despite the civil servants' remonstrances, the authority insists on the order.

He insists that 'without this moral discipline and self-denial, in the highest sense, the whole apparatus would fall to pieces' (Weber 1970: 95). This is exactly the same moral discipline and self-denial we encountered in the last chapter in the very different context of the Puritan sects, and reinforces the connection I drew there between this subjectivity and specifically modern forms of power.

Anticipating much subsequent writing on documentation as a critical modality of power, Weber highlights the fact that 'the management of the modern office is based upon written documents ("the files"), which are preserved', and associated with this is 'a staff of subaltern officials and scribes of all sorts' (Weber 1970: 197). More recent work has stressed the ways in which individual identities (as, for instance, a voter, taxpayer, driver, married person or schoolchild – all of them statuses 'licensed' by such recording practices) are comprehensively regulated thereby. Philippe Ariès has remarked a very material connection between modern subjectivity and state documentation: it is impossible, today, to survive in the world without knowing one's exact date of birth, something, for most people, which was rare before the eighteenth century (Ariès 1962: 15–16). Our date of birth has become part of our civic identity (and what used to be called the 'ages of man' are marked by institutional *rites de passage*, from kindergarten graduation to mandatory retirement). Weber himself places more emphasis, as we might expect, on the purely technical advantages that rationalized documentation brings to the exercise of power.

He also emphasizes another, for him equally novel facet of bureaucracy, which is that the 'bureau' is 'in principle . . . separate from the private domicile of the official, and, in general, bureaucracy segregates official activity as something distinct from the sphere of private life'. Marx also regarded the public/private division as fundamental to modernity, as we have seen. For Weber there is a symmetrical distinction of the 'personal' and the 'official' in both the 'public' and 'private' spheres, as Marx distinguished these. If within the modern state all 'public monies and equipment are divorced from the private property of the official', then within the modern corporation too 'the executive office is separated from the household, business from private correspondence, and business assets from private fortunes' (Weber 1970: 197). This 'separation of business from the household, which completely dominates modern economic life', he maintains elsewhere, is one of two key factors (the other being rational bookkeeping) in whose absence 'the modern rational organization of the capitalistic enterprise would not have been possible' (Weber 1974: 21–2). This separation is once again a mainly occidental phenomenon, whose 'beginnings . . . are to be found as early as the Middle Ages' (Weber 1970: 197).

[. . .]

II.

There are obvious affinities between Max Weber's conception of bureaucracy (and in particular of the modern bureaucratic state) and Marx's, discussed earlier. Weber sees 'a developed money economy' as being the 'normal precondition for the unchanged and continued existence . . . of pure bureaucratic administrations' – if only because bureaucrats are salaried – and inversely views the rational-bureaucratic state as a *sine qua non* for rational capitalism (Weber 1970: 204–5). Like Marx, he argues that it is only in 'the complete depersonalization of administrative management by bureaucracy' that 'the separation of public and private' spheres fundamental to capitalism is realized 'fully and in principle' (Weber 1970: 239). Marx would doubtless have approved his observations on the tensions between democracy and bureaucracy. 'Bureaucracy inevitably accompanies modern *mass democracy* in contrast to the democratic self-government of small homogeneous units', and 'the democratization of society in its totality, and in the *modern* sense of the term, whether actual or perhaps merely formal, is an especially favourable basis for bureaucratization'. But, Weber warns, '"democratization", in the sense here intended, does not necessarily mean an increasingly active share of the governed in the authority of the social structure'; 'the most decisive thing here – indeed it is rather exclusively so – is the *levelling of the governed* in opposition to the ruling and bureaucratically articulated group, which in turn may occupy a quite autocratic position, both in fact and in form' (Weber 1970: 224–6, 231). As with Marx, the political subjectivity of the governed is illusory, the reality that they are objects of policy and administration. Like Marx too, Weber notes the association of bureaucracy and control of knowledge: 'the official secret', he argues, is 'the specific invention of bureaucracy', and for it 'nothing is so fanatically defended' (Weber 1970: 233).

Weber's is, in fact, a severely realistic, if not a cynical, conception of the state: 'a relation of men dominating men, a relation supported by means of legitimate (i.e. considered to be legitimate) violence'. He cites Trotsky's words at Brest-Litovsk – 'every state is founded on force' – in his support. The 'inner justification' of the modern state, differentiating it from its precursors, is 'the belief in the validity of legal statute and functional 'competence' based on rationally created *rules*' (Weber 1970: 78–9). But it remains the case that 'the modern state is a compulsory association which organizes domination' (Weber 1970: 82). To my mind, however, the most significant of Weber's echoes of Marx lie in the contrast both draw between personalized and impersonal modes of administration and forms of power, and the bases of their legitimacy (in Weber's terms, 'traditional' or 'patrimonial' vs. 'rational-legal'). This threads each of their accounts of both capitalism and the modern state (and for both it connects the two).

[...]

III.

Rational bureaucracy, in the famous image (earlier used in *The Protestant Ethic* of 'victorious capitalism'), is an 'iron cage' from which escape is ever more improbable. 'Iron cage' is in fact an unfortunate translation (Kent 1983). *The Protestant Ethic* speaks of 'the care for external goods', which Baxter says should 'lie on the shoulders of the "saint like a light cloak, which can be thrown aside at any moment"', turning into *ein stahlhartes Gehäuse*: a casing, or housing, as hard as steel (Weber 1974: 181). If we are to translate metaphorically, a better choice of analogy than Bunyan's man in the iron cage (which inspired Talcott Parsons's rendition) might be the shell (also *Gehäuse*) on a snail's back: a burden perhaps, but something impossible to live without, in either sense of the word. A cage remains an external restraint: unlock the door, and one walks out free. This *Gehäuse* is a prison altogether stronger, the armour of modern subjectivity itself. Dependency on 'mechanized petrification' has become an integral part of who we are.

Weber observes that the 'objective indispensability' and '"impersonal"' character of bureaucracy mean that 'the mechanism – in contrast to feudal orders based upon personal piety – is easily made to work for anybody who knows how to gain control over it'. As in Marx, power has become divorced from persons and objectified – intellectualized and disembodied. One example of 'indispensability' Weber gives is interesting, because Marx used it too: 'with all the changes in France since the time of the First Empire, the power machine has remained essentially the same [...] In classic fashion, France has demonstrated how this process [bureaucratization] has substituted *coups d'état* for "revolutions"' (Weber 1970: 229–30). In 1871 Marx wrote, of the Paris Commune, that 'all [previous] revolutions perfected the state machinery instead of throwing off this deadening incubus', while the Commune was 'a revolution against the *State* itself (Marx 1987: 484–6). He drew the moral that 'the working class cannot simply lay hold on the ready-made state machinery and wield it for their own purpose' (Marx 1987: 548), and repudiated the *Communist Manifesto*'s 'revolutionary measures' for centralization in the hands of the state accordingly (Marx and Engels 1967). The 'machine' as such needed to be smashed. Weber was more pessimistic. As the 'objective indispensability' of modernity's bureaucratic forms of social organization – including those of private capital – grows, 'the idea of eliminating these organizations becomes more and more utopian'. Quite simply, for him 'such a machine makes "revolution", in the sense of the forcible creation of entirely new formations of authority, technically more and more impossible, especially when the apparatus controls the modern means of communication... and also by virtue of its internal rationalized structure' (Weber 1970: 230).

Weber's hostility to socialism must be understood in this context. In the political sphere 'the great state and the mass party are the classic soil for bureaucratization' (Weber 1970: 209), and socialism elevates both, just as, in the economic realm, the socialization of the means of production would, he believed, merely increase the power of bureaucratized management. 'In any rationally organized socialistic economy', he wrote in *Economy and Society*, 'the expropriation of all the workers would be retained and merely brought to completion by the expropriation of private owners' (Weber 1964: 248). His essay on socialism of 1916 takes the view that 'it is the dictatorship of the official, not that of the worker, which... is on the advance', and ends with the question: 'Who would then take control of and direct this new economy?'

[...]

IV.

More is at stake here than simply a critique of modern socialism. Weber's antipathy is rooted in a much deeper disenchantment with rationalization itself. Though an acute observer of modernity, he was, as David Frisby puts it, 'a determined anti-modernist' (Frisby 1985: 2). It is no accident that in his wrenching *cri de coeur* 'Science as a vocation' – perhaps the most profound reflection on the modern condition to be found anywhere in his work – Weber recalls both Nietzsche and Baudelaire. This was an address that he delivered at Munich University in the year 1918, when the savagery which lurks at the heart of civilization was in full flood. It cannot have much comforted his audience. 'Since Nietzsche', he says, 'we realize that something can be beautiful, not only in spite of the aspect in which it is not good, but rather in that very aspect. You will find this expressed earlier in the *Fleurs du mal*' (Weber 1970: 148). It is not a question here of either/or, but rather of both/and; of intractable paradoxes, not contradictions resolvable by Hegelian sleight of hand. Modern life has this quality. It is like the well-known drawing which can be seen at once as a beautiful young woman and as an old and ugly crone. Rational, scientific, intellectual 'disenchantment of the world' implies not only an emancipation from magic and superstition, but also an irretrievable loss. In Weber's hands, this realization amounts to very much more than a conventional conservative nostalgia for an idealized past.

Let me for a last time contrast Weber and Marx. Writing in Paris, the 'capital of the nineteenth century', at the start of 1844 – in the same essay in which he 'discovered' the proletariat as the 'material weapon' of philosophy – Marx asserted that 'criticism of religion is the beginning of all criticism'. Religion, as his famous cadences have it, is 'the sigh of the oppressed creature, the heart of a heartless world... the spirit of spiritless conditions. It is the *opium of the people*'; and 'to abolish religion as the *illusory* happiness of the people is to demand their *real* happiness'. Disillusionment – and reason – are here unambiguously positive, 'progressive', 'Criticism has torn up the imaginary flowers from the chain not so that man shall wear the unadorned, bleak chain but so that he will shake off the chain and pluck the living flower.' The criticism of religion 'disillusions man to make him think and act and shape his reality like a man who has been disillusioned and has come to reason, so that he will revolve around himself' (Marx 1975f: 175–6). Weber had a darker view of the matter. Disillusion meant disenchantment, in both senses of the word; and 'reason' lay at the very root of the problem.

For Weber, to espouse religion, in a world overwhelmed by the rationality of science, was no more possible than for Marx. He voiced compassion for those who, unable 'to bear the fate of the times', fled into the arms of the church; but he regarded this as involving an 'intellectual sacrifice' (Weber 1970: 155). As he bluntly put it, 'redemption from the rationalism and intellectualism of science is the fundamental presupposition of living in unity with the divine' (Weber 1970: 142). Science – and a world built on the principles of scientific rationality – must inexorably corrode religion, except as a vehicle of mystical escape from rationalism itself. Weber was not prepared to sacrifice his intellect. He declares a vocation for science, and affirms its value (for those *few* who dare to pursue it). But he does so in a way that totally lacks Marx's rationalist (and modernist) stridency, and is itself paradoxical. Weber affirms science, he says, 'from precisely the standpoint that hates intellectualism as the worst devil'. It is in order 'to settle with this devil... to see the devil's ways to the end in order to realize his power and his limitations' and 'not take to flight before him as so many do nowadays' (Weber 1970: 152) that he endorses the value of science, and, furthermore, of a science which is 'ethically neutral'. The latter prescription is often misunderstood, not to say turned on its head. Far from being a demand for technocratic neutrality, it was an attempt to protect the sphere of free value judgement from the pretensions of scientific imperialism. 'An *attitude of moral indifference*', he is adamant, 'has no connection with *scientific* "objectivity"' (Weber 1949: 60). Weber regards scientific rationality as the most efficient technical means of understanding the world, including the 'devil' of rationalization itself – but that is all. He is very well aware of the ironies of this position.

Science has *no* meaning that transcends 'the purely practical and technical'. The 'former illusions' that it might be the 'way to true being' (the Greeks), the 'way to true art' and thereby the 'way to true nature' (the Renaissance), the 'way to true God' (Protestantism) or – a modernist fallacy, nowadays believed in only by 'a few big children in university chairs' – the 'way to true happiness', have been dispelled (Weber 1970: 139–43). Science is a means of establishing the facts of the case, no more and no less. And between the realm of facts and the realm of values there is a 'logical gulf' (Weber 1949; 51–63). Science (Weber quotes Tolstoy) 'is meaningless because it gives no answer to our question, the only question important for us: "What shall we do and how shall we live?"' (Weber 1970: 143). At best science may provide empirical knowledge individuals might take into account in determining the practical means of attaining or consequences of striving for particular ends; and it may thereby serve those who choose to live by an 'ethic of responsibility' rather than an 'absolute ethic' of ultimate ends (Weber 1970: 118f.). It need not: the trains to Treblinka doubtless ran on time. But science cannot provide or evaluate ends themselves. We cannot '"refute scientifically" the ethic of the Sermon on the Mount' (Weber 1970: 148). Science, in short, has *nothing* to say on questions of value, or in other words, so far as Weber is concerned, is silent on exactly that which gives all human life and action their meaning.

Worse still, science, in its very rationality, undermines exactly those standpoints from which value is capable of being derived: above all religious ethics. Empirically, science and technology demonstrate that 'there are no mysterious incalculable forces that come into play . . . one can, in principle, master all things by calculation' (Weber 1970: 139). Logically, reason shows the foundations of all values – including those of science itself – to be arbitrary. It is the lone individual who 'has to decide which is God for him and which is the devil' (Weber 1970: 148). This predicament is not an easy one; for not only are transcendental bases of decision no longer available, there can be no rational criteria for choosing between ultimate ends either. That which alone gives to human lives their point and purpose thus becomes, in a thoroughly rationalized world, irremediably contingent – and transitory, and fugitive. In fine, rational disenchantment not only destroys the possibility of that kind of religious framework which can bestow transcendental meaning on everyday actions, but it is incapable in principle of furnishing any kind of substitute for it. This is what I mean by irretrievable loss. There can be no going back – such contingency is the modern condition. To be disillusioned, *pace* Marx, is to 'wear the bleak, unadorned chain'. There are no living flowers waiting to be plucked, unless it be Baudelaire's *fleurs du mal*.

Yet still we must live, as did the ancients: and the stark question, 'Which of the warring gods shall we serve?' (Weber 1970: 155), far from going away, takes on new urgency. 'Our civilization destines us to realize more clearly these struggles again, after our eyes have been blinded for a thousand years' by 'the grandiose moral fervour of Christian ethics'. And today 'many old gods ascend from their graves; they are disenchanted and hence take the form of impersonal forces. They strive to gain power over our lives and again they resume their eternal struggle with one another'. It is, Weber says, 'how to measure up to *workaday* existence' in this disenchanted world that is so 'hard for modern man' (Weber 1970: 149). His personal answer is the ethic of responsibility, which he explains with eloquence in 'Politics as a vocation'. Its essence is that 'one has to give an account of the foreseeable results of one's action' (Weber 1970: 120). His social prognosis is not a cheerful one. 'Not summer's bloom lies ahead of us, but rather a polar night of icy darkness and hardness, no matter which group may triumph externally now. Where there is nothing, not only the Kaiser but the proletarian has lost his rights' (Weber 1970: 128).

Humanity, and humaneness, are everywhere in retreat before these impersonal deities of modernity. Though Weber does not say so, *L'Être Suprême* – Reason – who presided over the guillotine in the Year One of the modern age heralded much. For him, 'the ultimate and most sublime values have retreated from public life either into the transcendental realm of mystic life or into the brotherliness of direct and personal human relations'. 'Today', it is 'only within the smallest and intimate circles, in personal human situations, in *pianissimo*, that something is pulsating that corresponds to the prophetic *pneuma*, which in former times swept though the great communities like a firebrand, welding them together'. Humane values are hemmed into that little world of Penn's letters. The wider society is a mechanism without a soul, and the individuals within it become prey to *ersatz* religion and 'academic prophecies' of a sort capable of producing 'fanatical sects but never a genuine community' (Weber 1970: 155). These words were written in the land of Goethe, Schiller and Beethoven, just fifteen years before Hitler took power. What modernity leaves us with is the unprecedented loneliness of the single individual, in the face, now, of no god at all, and the passing consolation of personal integrity. It is 'a godless and prophetless time' – and a perilous one (Weber 1970: 153).

[. . .]

V.

An elective affinity, then, for the modern age: between those qualities we most prize in scientific discourse – objectivity, universality, logic, consistency, simplicity, systematicity, quantifiability, precision, unambiguity and a certain aesthetic elegance – and the principles upon which Weber's (and Marx's) machines of modernity operate. In neither is there room for the concrete, the particular, and the personal. These are banished to the 'irrational' realm of 'private life'. The modern era, as Marx said, is ruled by abstractions. It may be that capitalism is the foundation upon which this rule is first erected; Marx and Weber provide compelling reason for thinking it is. But it may also be that today, this abstraction has gone very far beyond capitalism itself, and we will not be rid of it just by changing the title deeds on property (or still less by 'capturing' 'state power'). This is the enduring importance of Weber's analysis of rationalization and the bureaucratization which is its ubiquitous concomitant. Disembodied, the very forms of our sociality turn against us, and within them there is no place for humane values. The soulful corporation or the compassionate state are, by virtue of the very constitution of these social forms, contradictions in terms. This was also, of course, the message of Marx's critique of alienation. But Weber, I think, quite legitimately extends Marx's argument, to a point where capitalism, because of the selfsame 'anarchy' that grounds this alienation, appears now as the ironic guarantor that the 'iron casing' of a new Ptolemaic order does not imprison all. Insubstantial as modern bourgeois liberties may be – and Weber had few illusions on the matter – they are preferable to none at all. The 'private life' of the 'abstract individual' becomes the pathetic sanctuary of humanity.

This makes any notion of an emancipatory politics deeply problematic, in so far as the very forms in which modern politics are conducted – states, parties, ideologies – partake of the same nexus of estrangement. The history of socialism, in this century, has confirmed Weber's worst forebodings; its proponents have proved all too willing to strike Faustian bargains with his modern devils, notably the machines of industry and state. I do not draw the conclusion that improvement of the human condition is impossible; but I would insist that it is no longer capitalism alone, but the monstrously abstracted progeny it has engendered, that is our problem. The modern world is in one respect at least different from all of its predecessors. Only now is the survival of the human race itself in jeopardy. What earlier century had even a presentiment that such destructive forces slumbered in the lap of social labour?

The ultimate measure of the awesome power, and the fundamental violence, of unfettered abstraction is to be found in the millions upon millions of nameless corpses which this most vicious of centuries has left as its memorial, human sacrifices to one or another of Weber's renascent modern gods. War itself is not new, modernity's contribution is to have waged it, with characteristic efficiency, under the sign of various totalizing abstractions which name and claim the lives of all. Here the 'lightness' of the modern subject becomes all too evident, and the truth of the real living individual as Marx's 'plaything of alien forces' is written in blood. These abstractions, I should perhaps add, have by no means only been socialist: there were killing fields in Cambodia before what the Khmer Rouge, following Robespierre's precedent, proclaimed as Year One. But nor can they plausibly all be laid at the door of capitalism. The nineteenth century, when things might reasonably have appeared so, is long over. We are at another *fin de siècle*.

In *The German Ideology* of 1845–6, Marx asked himself a question:

> Individuals always proceeded, and always proceed, from themselves. Their relations are the relations of their real life-process. How does it happen that their relations assume an independent existence over against them? and that the forces of their own life become superior to them? (Marx and Engels 1976: 93)

Capitalism is a vital part of the answer, for reasons explored in this book. It is the ground upon which other modern forms of estrangement arose, and furnishes the template for the 'severance' which gives modernity's machines their terrible force. But it is this wider mechanization of human social life itself which is the problem, and this is no longer, if it ever was, confined to those theatres within which capital rules. Mechanization is of course but a metaphor. What we are actually talking of are our own forms of sociality and subjectivity, as Karl Marx was among the first to make clear. Weber's devils stare out of Baudelaire's mirror.

I do not wholly share Weber's pessimism: it may be that out of this 'mechanical petrification . . . new prophets will arise, or there will be a great rebirth of old ideas and ideals' (Weber 1974: 182). But I believe it should be taken seriously; and most of all by those who do aspire not merely to interpret the world, but to change it.

Part 5

CULTURE AND COMMUNICATION IN THE FRANKFURT SCHOOL

INTRODUCTION

I. The Origins of Critical Theory

The selections from Weber indicate his concern with the rationalisation of society and forms of reasoning. His work on bureaucracy highlights the development of ever more efficient forms of social control. We have come some way from the Marxist notion of historical progress, which perhaps suggests why, during the dark days of the early twentieth century, Weber's work carried great influence over the next generation of Marxist theorists, particularly the critical theorists of the Frankfurt school.

The Institute of Social Research at Frankfurt University was established in 1923 and soon came under the directorship of Max Horkheimer. Along with Theodor Adorno, he gave the school a more philosophical orientation as is reflected in their joint work *The Dialectic of Enlightenment* (Adorno and Horkheimer 1986), from which extracts are reproduced below. Nazi rule forced the members of the school into exile. However, the time spent in the United States tended to deepen the pessimism of the writings, with comparisons drawn between the methods of fascist dictatorship and the methods of consumer culture in the United States. Members of the school developed an interest in psychoanalysis to explain how social cohesion develops through mass psychology, the manipulation of desire and the suppression of the pleasure principle. They examined how social cohesion developed through the production of conformity – a process aided by a developing political and cultural apparatus.

The fascist state, the product of a particular historical period of social crisis, is taken by the Frankfurt theorists as representative of late capitalist society. Fascism and war are the inevitable products of a monopoly form of capitalism. With monopoly in the economic sphere comes totalitarianism in the political domain while both are underwritten by the spread of bureaucracy and technology. The Frankfurt theorists combine Weber's arguments about the rationalisation and disenchantment of society with Marx's theories of alienation and commodity fetishism. Commodities – both material and cultural products – take over people's lives, prevent them from thinking deeply, and create a sense of stupefied contentment. Adorno and Horkheimer develop the idea of the culture industry to show how culture combines with monopoly production to produce standardised entertainment that pacifies the masses. Needless to say, this results in a very bleak and pessimistic outlook. Social cohesion is almost total, rebellion almost impossible. Despite claiming allegiance to Marxism, the Frankfurt theorists radically depart from the main emancipatory ideas of Marx, and would seem instead to accept Weber's notion of the 'iron cage'.

The notion of 'late capitalism' incorporates Weber's ideas on modernity, the role of the state, the growth of bureaucracy and the prevalence of instrumental reason. Along with mass production and consumption and the development of the culture industry, society is very different to the world described by Marx, but nevertheless follows the same logic of commodity production. By extending their critique to cover all industrial and bureaucratic societies, including the Soviet Union, it would seem that the social critique offered by the Frankfurt school is directed more at modern societies in general, rather than specifically at capitalist ones. Indeed, Adorno and Horkheimer pitch their critique not so much at the economic level, but in terms of the logic of modernity and modern forms of reasoning. The first extract explores their idea of how Enlightenment reasoning turns against itself.

II. Dialectic of Enlightenment

Whereas for Marx alienation is a product of capitalist production, Adorno and Horkheimer see our estrangement as something deeper than this, located in the relation between society and nature itself. The more people come to dominate nature, the more they become alienated from themselves. As Horkheimer puts it: 'The history of man's efforts to subjugate nature is also the history of man's subjugation by man' (Horkheimer 1987: 105). As society tries to free itself from nature by bringing it under control, so, at the same time it degrades humanity and destroys its own basis. In *Dialectic of Enlightenment* Adorno and Horkheimer write:

> As soon as man discards his awareness that he himself is nature, all the aims for which he keeps himself alive – social progress, the

> intensification of all his material and spiritual powers, even consciousness itself – are nullified... Man's domination over himself, which grounds his selfhood, is almost always the destruction of the subject in whose service it is undertaken. (Adorno and Horkheimer 1986: 54)

Our attitude towards nature and towards each other and ourselves becomes merely instrumental. This affects our ways of thinking and Enlightenment reason becomes uncritical and unquestioning. The rise of scientific rationality and instrumental reason leads to cultural decline and to the types of bureaucratic and totalitarian forms of domination and control mentioned above. Thus

> on the one hand the growth of economic productivity furnishes the conditions for a world of greater justice; on the other hand it allows the technical apparatus and the social groups which administer it a disproportionate superiority to the rest of the population. The individual is wholly devalued in relation to the economic powers, which at the same time press the control of society over nature to hitherto unsuspected heights. (Adorno and Horkheimer 1979: xiv)

The extracts selected show how Adorno and Horkheimer trace the development of late capitalism to the logic of the Enlightenment project which turns against itself and subordinates reason to commerce and industry. Justice, equality, happiness and tolerance, all of which are supposed to be inherent in or sanctioned by reason, have lost their intellectual roots. Yet somehow this is willingly given up in the name of progress. Thus the immiseration of the masses takes place, not as Marx and Engels had suggested, but in intellectual and cultural rather than material terms. The stability of society is based on the masses being confined to a state of insecurity, unable to control their own lives or develop a critical consciousness. The next selection, from the essay 'The Culture Industry', looks at how this condition is institutionalised.

III. The Culture Industry

The culture industry is a consequence of late capitalism, commodity fetishism and instrumental rationality. It monopolises public opinion and minimises critical awareness. In this sense it might be compared to ideology in that it secures consensus through preventing us from seeing things as they really are. It engineers a social consensus that is deep and underlying in that it goes right down to the foundations of social life, yet at the same time it is a rather shallow and complacent industry. It makes no real attempt to disguise its false or manipulative aspect, and indeed celebrates its commodified and commercialised form. It is not deep or profound, it simply claims that things are the way that they are. The ideology of late capitalism is transparent.

Through the concept of the culture industry, Adorno and Horkheimer show how commodity production and fetishism are extended into the cultural sphere. As opposed to the high art of the classical bourgeois age, cultural products are now standardised, marketable and interchangeable just like any other product. The term 'industry' connotes the churning out of mass-produced goods. Of course, this standardisation and conformity in production affects those who consume it and hence contributes to the maintenance of social cohesion. The cultural product loses its innovativeness and uniqueness although small differences of features create the illusion of choice. General formulas reinforce certain images and types of behaviour and encourage stereotyping, and this satisfies our pathological disposition for that which is familiar. Hence the culture industry contributes to social cohesion through the encouragement of pathological forms of collectivity. This explains why Adorno and Horkheimer compare the psychological affects of the culture industry and advertising to totalitarian government and the mass psychology of the Führer. Like fascist ideology, the culture industry appeals to the emotions and impulses. We submit ourselves to its products because of our psychological needs.

IV. MARCUSE

Cohesion and consent seem overpowering; late capitalism seems irreversible. The working class seems entirely pacified and assimilated into the economic and cultural order. We are left wondering: which way out? Adorno turns his focus to the bourgeois individual and the educated middle classes. He comes to the view that political action should not be about overthrowing the bourgeois order, but about protecting freedoms and preserving individual liberty. Herbert Marcuse argues a similar line to Adorno and Horkheimer when he claims that the working class has been so integrated into capitalist society that it no longer has a revolutionary potential. However, Marcuse does maintain hope of revolutionary change, only he turns from the working class to the outcasts, outsiders, rebels and intellectuals, who, he believes, have not been integrated and who represent the most radical consciousness. This led to Marcuse becoming a darling of the radical student movement, a strange position indeed considering the accusations of intellectual elitism and passivity levelled against the other members of the school.

Marcuse echoes the theme of *Dialectic of Enlightenment* when he writes of the 'totalitarian universe of technological rationality as the latest transmutation of the idea of Reason' (Marcuse 1964: 123). Advanced industrial civilisation contains a 'terrifying harmony of freedom and oppression, productivity and destruction, growth and regression' (Marcuse 1964: 124). Society sustains itself because alongside this domination it offers continued material development and progress, but this is achieved at a high political and personal price: 'The productivity and growth potential of this system stabilise the society and contain technical progress within the framework of domination' (Marcuse 1964: xvi).

Marcuse makes an interesting contribution to the arguments of critical theory by examining how the domination of the system becomes internalised and how these processes shape the development of the individual. The development of modern society has obliterated our metal faculties by providing abundant material goods while shaping our desires and needs. As a result 'the ideology of today lies in that production and consumption reproduce and justify domination. . . . The individual pays by sacrificing his time, his consciousness, his dreams; civilisation pays by sacrificing its own promises of liberty, justice and peace for all' (Marcuse 1969: 80).

In his social-psychoanalytic work *Eros and Civilisation* Marcuse writes: 'Even at the beginning of Western civilisation, long before this principle was institutionalised, reason was defined as an instrument of constraint, of instinctual suppression; the domain of the instincts, sensuousness, was considered eternally hostile and detrimental to reason' (Marcuse 1969: 132). Whereas Marxism emphasises the alienation of labour, Marcuse is now concerned with how social cohesion is maintained through the repression of erotic and aesthetic needs and impulses. Following Freud, it is argued that human history is the history of repression. Culture constrains our societal and biological existence and controls our instincts. History becomes that of the denial of pleasure and civilised morality is the morality of repressed instincts. Marcuse sees this in terms of the transformation of the pleasure principle into the reality principle, which is based on renunciation and restraint. The individual realises that the gratification of their needs is impossible and that unrestrained pleasure comes into conflict with our natural and human environment. The reality principle modifies our behaviour: immediate satisfaction becomes delayed satisfaction; pleasure is restrained; joy, play, receptiveness and the absence of repression are replaced with work, productiveness and security (Marcuse 1969: 30).

V. Habermas and Communication

Jürgen Habermas tries to overcome the pessimism of the earlier Frankfurt school by retrieving the project of modernity and moving away from the instrumental view of reason to examine the intersubjective foundations of social consensus. These are to be found in the public sphere, the lifeworld and the structures of communication and discourse. Whereas Marx sees history and society in terms of the mode of production, Habermas shifts attention to forms of language and communication as the main basis for social cohesion, integration and emancipation.

In his early work, Habermas sees the public sphere as a mediation between civil society and the state. It concerns matters of public interest or social concern. Consensus is grounded in the intersubjective understanding of interests and needs. However, although this develops with the rise of the bourgeoisie in eighteenth-century Europe, the development of capitalism ultimately undermines the classical liberal public sphere and its institutions. The "progressive 'societalisation' of the state simultaneously with an increasing 'statification' of society gradually destroyed the basis of the bourgeois public sphere – the separation of state and society" (Habermas 1989: 142). Returning to the themes of earlier critical theorists – the impact of the culture industry, the manipulation of public opinion, the role of the mass media, the bureaucratisation of social and private life, and the instrumental actions of the state – Habermas argues that the public sphere undergoes a structural transformation.

Habermas's discussion of the consequences of increased state intervention and the undermining of the public sphere leads to his work on legitimation crisis. Like the early Frankfurt theorists Habermas sees how capitalism has developed a state-regulated market in an effort to overcome crisis tendencies while also using cultural means to manipulate mass consciousness. The state intervenes in the public sphere and the economic system in order to prevent economic crisis. However, this involves the danger that any crisis of the economy may be transferred to other spheres of social and political life:

> The political system requires an input of mass loyalty that is as diffuse as possible. The output consists in sovereignly executed administrative decisions. Output crises have the form of a *rationality crisis* in which the administrative system does not succeed in reconciling and fulfilling the imperatives received from the economic system. Input crises have the form of a *legitimation crisis*; the legitimising system does not succeed in maintaining the requisite level of mass loyalty while the steering imperatives taken over from the economic system are carried through. (Habermas 1988: 46)

Rationalisation and the overextension of the instrumentalism of economic life leads to the impoverishment of culture and the depoliticisation of the public sphere. However, Weber and the Marxists one-sidedly focus on instrumental reason, ignoring the processes of communicative interaction. It is in this latter sphere that Habermas believes we can retrieve more progressive and emancipatory theories of modernity and rationality. Habermas grounds his idea of reason in the universal structures of communicative understanding. These structures are dialogical and mutual, they are where we integrate the contents of the symbolic world through communicative action, discussion, negotiation and agreement. 'As soon as we conceive of knowledge as communicatively mediated, rationality is assessed in terms of the capacity of responsible participants in interaction to orientate themselves in relation to validity claims geared to intersubjective recognition' (Habermas 1987b: 314).

In order for communication to be possible at all, these communicative forms of reason are necessarily prior to any instrumental or strategic ones.

Communicative rationality is therefore a necessary condition for meaningful social life. It is universal and transcendental in the sense that it is necessarily presupposed by forms of social activity. Habermas invokes the notion of an ideal speech situation in which a rationally motivated consensus or agreement is achieved. As the extract from *Theory of Communicative Action* (1987a) argues, as well as providing the basis for mutual understanding, communicative action is also responsible for social integration and socialisation. Social integration is concerned with mutual obligations and legitimately ordered interpersonal relations. The process of socialisation secures personal identity and social competence.

Habermas distinguishes between system and lifeworld to show how the erosion of the communicative sphere by the market and administrative system leads to the kinds of problems identified in the earlier works. The lifeworld provides a set of background understandings that give coherence to our social actions and forms the horizon within which communicative actions are always already moving. The lifeworld is concerned with cultural reproduction, social integration, the stabilisation of group identity, solidarity, socialisation and the development of competences.

The system–lifeworld distinction replaces the Marxist notion of base and superstructure so that instead of a model of economic base and cultural, political and ideological superstructure, we have a model based on systemic functioning and communicative interaction. Societies reproduce themselves both materially and symbolically. The system requires the integration of diverse activities in accordance with adaptive goals of the market economy and the political–administrative system. The problem is that systemic integration needs to be institutionalised and anchored in the lifeworld, requiring laws and institutions. The danger here is that of the system overextending itself so that the lifeworld is subject to colonisation by economy and state, power and bureaucracy. The dominance of instrumental reason is indicative of this process of colonisation.

If the lifeworld represents the general set of background conditions, then worldviews represent a more conscious and historical framework, bringing together the personal, the cultural and the political, shaping group identity and interests and also legitimating political systems. If the modern worldview is one of rationalisation, it has a positive aspect in that it rids society of dogma, mysticism and religion and opens up the possibility of critical debate and discussion. It also requires political power to be legitimated and provides the basis for rational consensus.

Habermas optimistically believes that there is an inherent human interest in emancipation. This he defines as communication without distortion or domination. Through this focus politics shifts from the sphere of production to the lifeworld. He looks to such activities as democratic debate, protest, civil rights campaigning, identity politics, lifestyle politics and any activities that show resistance to the colonisation of the lifeworld. His aim is not to overthrow the system but to safeguard it and to protect the public spheres of communication and identity. In keeping with this perspective, Habermas, like other critical theorists, looks not to any one privileged agent but to many diverse actors. His focus is not on the economy but on culture, the aesthetic, the psychological and the lifeworld. Marx's ideal of a free society of producers is replaced with the idea of a fully rationalised lifeworld.

FROM 'THE CONCEPT OF ENLIGHTENMENT'

Theodor Adorno and Max Horkheimer

In the most general sense of progressive thought, the Enlightenment has always aimed at liberating men from fear and establishing their sovereignty. Yet the fully enlightened earth radiates disaster triumphant. The program of the Enlightenment was the disenchantment of the world; the dissolution of myths and the substitution of knowledge for fancy. Bacon, the 'father of experimental philosophy',[1] had defined its motives. He looked down on the masters of tradition, the 'great reputed authors' who first

> believe that others know that which they know not; and after themselves know that which they know not. But indeed facility to believe, impatience to doubt, temerity to answer, glory to know, doubt to contradict, end to gain, sloth to search, seeking things in words, resting in part of nature; these and the like have been the things which have forbidden the happy match between the mind of man and the nature of things; and in place thereof have married it to vain notions and blind experiments: and what the posterity and issue of so honorable a match may be, it is not hard to consider. Printing, a gross invention; artillery, a thing that lay not far out of the way; the needle, a thing partly known before: what a change have these three things made in the world in these times; the one in state of learning, the other in the state of war, the third in the state of treasure, commodities, and

Theodor Adorno and Max Horkheimer (1986), 'The concept of enlightenment', in *Dialectic of Enlightenment*, tr. John Cumming, 2nd ed., London: Verso.

> navigation! And those, I say, were but stumbled upon and lighted upon by chance. Therefore, no doubt, the sovereignty of man lieth hid in knowledge; wherein many things are reserved, which kings with their treasure cannot buy, nor with their force command; their spials and intelligencers can give no news of them, their seamen and discoverers cannot sail where they grow: now we govern nature in opinions, but we are thrall unto her in necessity: but if we would be led by her in invention, we should command her by action.[2]

Despite his lack of mathematics, Bacon's view was appropriate to the scientific attitude that prevailed after him. The concordance between the mind of man and the nature of things that he had in mind is patriarchal: the human mind, which overcomes superstition, is to hold sway over a disenchanted nature. Knowledge, which is power, knows no obstacles: neither in the enslavement of men nor in compliance with the world's rulers. As with all the ends of bourgeois economy in the factory and on the battlefield, origin is no bar to the dictates of the entrepreneurs: kings, no less directly than businessmen, control technology; it is as democratic as the economic system with which it is bound up. Technology is the essence of this knowledge. It does not work by concepts and images, by the fortunate insight, but refers to method, the exploitation of others' work, and capital. The 'many things' which, according to Bacon, 'are reserved', are themselves no more than instrumental: the radio as a sublimated printing press, the dive bomber as a more effective form of artillery, radio control as a more reliable compass. What men want to learn from nature is how to use it in order wholly to dominate it and other men. That is the only aim. Ruthlessly, in despite of itself, the Enlightenment has extinguished any trace of its own self-consciousness. The only kind of thinking that is sufficiently hard to shatter myths is ultimately self-destructive. In face of the present triumph of the factual mentality, even Bacon's nominalist credo would be suspected of a metaphysical bias and come under the same verdict of vanity that he pronounced on scholastic philosophy. Power and knowledge are synonymous.[3] For Bacon as for Luther, 'knowledge that tendeth but to satisfaction, is but as a courtesan, which is for pleasure, and not for fruit or generation'. Not 'satisfaction, which men call truth', but 'operation', 'to do the business', is the 'right mark': for '... what is the true end, scope, or office of knowledge, which I have set down to consist not in any plausible, delectable, reverend or admired discourse, or any satisfactory arguments, but in effecting and working, and in discovery of particulars not revealed before, for the better endowment and help of man's life'.[4] There is to be no mystery – which means, too, no wish to reveal mystery.

[...]

For the scientific mind, the separation of thought from business for the purpose of adjusting actuality, departure from the privileged area of real existence, is as insane and self-destructive as the primitive magician would consider stepping out of the magic circle he has prepared for his invocation; in both cases the offense against the taboo will actually result in the malefactor's ruin. The mastery of nature draws the circle into which the criticism of pure reason banished thought. Kant joined the theory of its unceasingly laborious advance into infinity with an insistence on its deficiency and everlasting limitation. His judgment is an oracle. There is no form of being in the world that science could not penetrate, but what can be penetrated by science is not being. According to Kant, philosophic judgment aims at the new; and yet it recognizes nothing new, since it always merely recalls what reason has always deposited in the object. But there is a reckoning for this form of thinking that considers itself secure in the various departments of science – secure from the dreams of a ghost-seer: world domination over nature turns against the thinking subject himself; nothing is left of him but that eternally same *I think* that must accompany all my ideas. Subject and object are both rendered ineffectual. The abstract self, which justifies record-making and systematization, has nothing set over against it but the abstract material which possesses no other quality than to be a substrate of such possession. The equation of spirit and world arises eventually, but only with a mutual restriction of both sides. The reduction of thought to a mathematical apparatus conceals the sanction of the world as its own yardstick. What appears to be the triumph of subjective rationality, the subjection of all reality to logical formalism, is paid for by the obedient subjection of reason to what is directly given. What is abandoned is the whole claim and approach of knowledge: to comprehend the given as such; not merely to determine the abstract spatio-temporal relations of the facts which allow them just to be grasped, but on the contrary to conceive them as the superficies, as mediated conceptual moments which come to fulfillment only in the development of their social, historical, and human significance. The task of cognition does not consist in mere apprehension, classification, and calculation, but in the determinate negation of each immediacy. Mathematical formalism, however, whose medium is number, the most abstract form of the immediate, instead holds thinking firmly to mere immediacy. Factuality wins the day; cognition is restricted to its repetition; and thought becomes mere tautology. The more the machinery of thought subjects existence to itself, the more blind its resignation in reproducing existence. Hence enlightenment returns to mythology, which it never really knew how to elude. For in its figures mythology had the essence of the *status quo*: cycle, fate, and domination of the world reflected as the truth and deprived of hope.

[...]

In the enlightened world, mythology has entered into the profane. In its blank purity, the reality which has been cleansed of demons and their conceptual descendants assumes the numinous character which the ancient world attributed to demons. Under the title of brute facts, the social injustice from which they proceed is now as assuredly sacred a preserve as the medicine man was sacrosanct by reason of the protection of his gods. It is not merely that domination is paid for by the alienation of men from the objects dominated: with the objectification of spirit, the very relations of men – even those of the individual to himself – were bewitched. The individual is reduced to the nodal point of the conventional responses and modes of operation expected of him. Animism spiritualized the object, whereas industrialism objectifies the spirits of men. Automatically, the economic apparatus, even before total planning, equips commodities with the values which decide human behavior. Since, with the end of free exchange, commodities lost all their economic qualities except for fetishism, the latter has extended its arthritic influence over all aspects of social life. Through the countless agencies of mass production and its culture the conventionalized modes of behavior are impressed on the individual as the only natural, respectable, and rational ones. He defines himself only as a thing, as a static element, as success or failure. His yardstick is self-preservation, successful or unsuccessful approximation to the objectivity of his function and the models established for it. Everything else, idea and crime, suffers the force of the collective, which monitors it from the classroom to the trade union. But even the threatening collective belongs only to the deceptive surface, beneath which are concealed the powers which manipulate it as the instrument of power. Its brutality, which keeps the individual up to scratch, represents the true quality of men as little as value represents the things which he consumes. The demonically distorted form which things and men have assumed in the light of unprejudiced cognition, indicates domination, the principle which effected the specification of *mana* in spirits and gods and occurred in the jugglery of magicians and medicine men. The fatality by means of which prehistory sanctioned the incomprehensibility of death is transferred to wholly comprehensible real existence. The noontide panic fear in which men suddenly became aware of nature as totality has found its like in the panic which nowadays is ready to break out at every moment: men expect that the world, which is without any issue, will be set on fire by a totality which they themselves are and over which they have no control.

The mythic terror feared by the Enlightenment accords with myth. Enlightenment discerns it not merely in unclarified concepts and words, as demonstrated by semantic language-criticism, but in any human assertion that has no place in the ultimate context of self-preservation. Spinoza's '*Conatus sese conservandi primum et unicum virtutis est fundamentum*'[5] contains the true maxim of all Western civilization, in which the religious and philosophical differences of the middle class are reconciled. The self (which, according to the methodical extirpation of all natural residues because they are mythological, must no longer be either body or blood, or soul, or even the natural I), once sublimated into the transcendental or logical subject, would form the reference point of reason, of the determinative instance of action. Whoever resigns himself to life without any rational reference to self-preservation would, according to the Enlightenment – and Protestantism – regress to prehistory. Impulse as such is as mythic as superstition; to serve the god not postulated by the self is as idiotic as drunkenness. Progress has prepared the same fate for both adoration and descent into a state of directly natural being, and has anathematized both the self-abandonment of thought and that of pleasure. The social work of every individual in bourgeois society is mediated through the principle of self; for one, labor will bring an increased return on capital; for others, the energy for extra labor. But the more the process of self-preservation is effected by the bourgeois division of labor, the more it requires the self-alienation of the individuals who must model their body and soul according to the technical apparatus. This again is taken into account by enlightened thought: in the end the transcendental subject of cognition is apparently abandoned as the last reminiscence of subjectivity and replaced by the much smoother work of automatic control mechanisms. Subjectivity has given way to the logic of the allegedly indifferent rules of the game, in order to dictate all the more unrestrainedly. Positivism, which finally did not spare thought itself, the chimera in a cerebral form, has removed the very last insulating instance between individual behavior and the social norm. The technical process, into which the subject has objectified itself after being removed from the consciousness, is free of the ambiguity of mythic thought as of all meaning altogether, because reason itself has become the mere instrument of the all-inclusive economic apparatus. It serves as a general tool, useful for the manufacture of all other tools, firmly directed toward its end, as fateful as the precisely calculated movement of material production, whose result for mankind is beyond all calculation. At last its old ambition, to be a pure organ of ends, has been realized. The exclusiveness of logical laws originates in this unique functional significance, and ultimately in the compulsive nature of self-preservation. And self-preservation repeatedly culminates in the choice between survival and destruction, apparent again in the principle that of two contradictory propositions only one can be true and only one false. The formalism of this principle, and of the entire logic in which form it is established, derives from the opacity and complexity of interests in a society in which the maintenance of forms and the preservation of individuals coincide only by chance. The derivation of thought from logic ratifies in the lecture room the reification of man in the factory and the office. In this way the taboo encroaches upon the anathematizing power, and enlightenment upon the spirit which it itself comprises. Then, however, nature as true self-preservation is released by the very process which promised to extirpate it, in the individual as in the collective destiny of crisis and armed conflict. If the only norm that remains for theory is the ideal of unified science, practice must be subjected to the irrepressible process of world history. The self that is wholly comprehended by civilization resolves itself in an element of the inhumanity which from the beginning has aspired to evade civilization. The primordial fear of losing one's own name is realized. For civilization, pure natural existence, animal and vegetative, was the absolute danger. One after the other, mimetic, mythic and metaphysical modes of behavior were taken as superseded eras, any reversion to which was to be feared as implying a reversion of the self to that mere state of nature from which it had estranged itself with so huge an effort, and which therefore struck such terror into the self. In every century, any living reminiscence of olden times, not only of nomadic antiquity but all the more of the pre-patriarchal stages, was most rigorously punished and extirpated from human consciousness. The spirit of enlightenment replaced the fire and the rack by the stigma it attached to all irrationality, because it led to corruption. Hedonism was moderate, finding the extreme no less odious than did Aristotle. The bourgeois ideal of naturalness intends not amorphous nature, but the virtuous mean. Promiscuity and asceticism, excess and hunger, are directly identical, despite the antagonism, as powers of disintegration. By subjecting the whole of life to the demands of its maintenance, the dictatorial minority guarantees, together with its own security, the persistence of the whole. From Homer to modern times, the dominant spirit wishes to steer between the Scylla of a return to mere reproduction and the Charybdis of unfettered fulfillment; it has always mistrusted any star other than that of the lesser evil. The new German pagans and warmongers want to set pleasure free once more. But under the pressure of labor, through the centuries, pleasure has learned self-hatred, and therefore in the state of totalitarian emancipation remains mean and disabled by self-contempt. It remains in the grip of the self-preservation to which it once trained reason – deposed in the meantime. At the turning points of Western civilization, from the transition to Olympian religion up to the Renaissance, Reformation, and bourgeois atheism, whenever new nations and classes more firmly repressed myth, the fear of uncomprehended, threatening nature, the consequence of its very materialization and objectification, was reduced to animistic superstition, and the subjugation of nature was made the absolute purpose of life within and without. If in the end self-preservation has been automated, so reason has been abandoned by those who, as administrators of production, entered upon its inheritance and now fear it in the persons of the disinherited. The essence of enlightenment is the alternative whose ineradicability is that of domination. Men have always had to choose between their subjection to nature or the subjection of nature to the Self. With the extension of the bourgeois commodity economy, the dark horizon of myth is illumined by the sun of calculating reason, beneath whose cold rays the seed of the new barbarism grows to fruition. Under the pressure of domination human labor has always led away from myth – but under domination always returns to the jurisdiction of myth.

[. . .]

The restriction of thought to organization and administration, practiced by rulers from the cunning Odysseus to the naïve managing directors of today, necessarily implies the restriction which comes upon the great as soon as it is no longer merely a question of manipulating the small. Hence the spirit becomes the very apparatus of domination and self-domination which bourgeois thought has always mistakenly supposed it to be. The stopped ears which the pliable proletarians have retained ever since the time of myth have no advantage over the immobility of the master. The over-maturity of society lives by the immaturity of the dominated. The more complicated and precise the social, economic, and scientific apparatus with whose service the production system has long harmonized the body, the more impoverished the experiences which it can offer. The elimination of qualities, their conversion into functions, is translated from science by means of rationalized modes of labor to the experiential world of nations, and tends to approximate it once more to that of the amphibians. The regression of the masses today is their inability to hear the unheard-of with their own ears, to touch the unapprehended with their own hands – the new form of delusion which deposes every conquered mythic form. Through the mediation of the total society which embraces all relations and emotions, men are once again made to be that against which the evolutionary law of society, the principle of self, had turned: mere species beings, exactly like one another through isolation in the forcibly united collectivity. The oarsmen, who cannot speak to one another, are each of them yoked in the same rhythm as the modern worker in the factory, movie theater, and collective. The actual working conditions in society compel conformism – not the conscious influences which also made the suppressed men dumb and separated them from truth. The impotence of the worker is not merely a stratagem of the rulers, but the logical consequence of the industrial society into which the ancient Fate – in the very course of the effort to escape it – has finally changed.

But this logical necessity is not conclusive. It remains tied to domination, as both its reflection and its tool. Therefore its truth is no less questionable than its evidence is irrefutable. Of course thought has always sufficed concretely to characterize its own equivocation. It is the servant that the master cannot check as he wishes. Domination, ever since men settled down, and later in the commodity society, has become objectified as law and organization and must therefore restrict itself. The instrument achieves independence: the mediating instance of the spirit, independently of the will of the master, modifies the directness of economic injustice. The instruments of domination, which would encompass all – language, weapons, and finally machines – must allow themselves to be encompassed by all. Hence in domination the aspect of rationality prevails as one that is also different from it. The 'objectivity' of the means, which makes it universally available, already implies the criticism of that domination as whose means thought arose. On the way from mythology to logistics, thought has lost the element of self-reflection, and today machinery disables men even as it nurtures them. But in the form of machines the alienated *ratio* moves toward a society which reconciles thought in its fixed form as a material and intellectual apparatus with free, live, thought, and refers to society itself as the real subject of thought. The specific origin of thought and its universal perspective have always been inseparable. Today, with the transformation of the world into industry, the perspective of universality, the social realization of thought, extends so far that in its behalf the rulers themselves disavow thought as mere ideology. The bad conscience of cliques which ultimately embody economic necessity is betrayed in that its revelations, from the intuitions of the Leader to the dynamic *Weltanschauung*, no longer recognize (in marked contrast to earlier bourgeois apologetics) their own misdeeds as necessary consequences of statutory contexts. The mythological lies of mission and destiny which they use as substitutes never declare the whole truth: gone are the objective laws of the market which ruled in the actions of the entrepreneurs and tended toward catastrophe. Instead the conscious decision of the managing directors executes as results (which are more obligatory than the blindest price-mechanisms) the old law of value and hence the destiny of capitalism. The rulers themselves do not believe in any objective necessity, even though they sometimes describe their concoctions thus. They declare themselves to be the engineers of world history. Only the ruled accept as unquestionable necessity the course of development that with every decreed rise in the standard of living makes them so much more powerless. When the standard of living of those who are still employed to service the machines can be assured with a minimal part of the working time available to the rulers of society, the superfluous reminder, the vast mass of the population, is drilled as yet another battalion – additional material to serve the present and future great plans of the system. The masses are fed and quartered as the army of the unemployed. In their eyes, their reduction to mere objects of the administered life, which preforms every sector of modern existence including language and perception, represents objective necessity, against which they believe there is nothing they can do. Misery as the antithesis of power and powerlessness grows immeasurably, together with the capacity to remove all misery permanently. Each individual is unable to penetrate the forest of cliques and institutions which, from the highest levels of command to the last professional rackets, ensure the boundless persistence of status. For the union boss, let alone the director, the proletarian (should he ever come face to face with him) is nothing but a supernumerary example of the mass, while the boss in his turn has to tremble at the thought of his own liquidation.

The absurdity of a state of affairs in which the enforced power of the system over men grows with every step that takes it out of the power of nature, denounces the rationality of the rational society as obsolete. Its necessity is illusive, no less than the freedom of the entrepreneurs who ultimately reveal their compulsive nature in their inevitable wars and contracts. This illusion, in which a wholly enlightened mankind has lost itself, cannot be dissolved by a philosophy which, as the organ of domination, has to choose between command and obedience. Without being able to escape the confusion which still ensnares it in prehistory, it is nevertheless able to recognize the logic of either-or, of consequence and antinomy, with which it radically emancipated itself from nature, as this very nature, unredeemed and self-alienated. Thinking, in whose mechanism of compulsion nature is reflected and persists, inescapably reflects its very own self as its own forgotten nature – as a mechanism of compulsion. Ideation is only an instrument. In thought, men distance themselves from nature in order thus imaginatively to present it to themselves – but only in order to determine how it is to be dominated. Like the thing, the material tool, which is held on to in different situations as the same thing, and hence divides the world as the chaotic, manysided, and disparate from the known, one, and identical, the concept is the ideal tool, fit to do service for everything, wherever it can be applied. And so thought becomes illusionary whenever it seeks to deny the divisive function, distancing and objectification. All mystic unification remains deception, the impotently inward trace of the absolved revolution. But while enlightenment maintains its justness against any hypostatization of utopia and unfailingly proclaims domination to be disunion, the dichotomy between subject and object that it will not allow to be obscured becomes the index of the untruth of that dichotomy and of truth. The proscription of superstition has always signified not only the progress of domination but its compromise. Enlightenment is more than enlightenment – the distinct representation of nature in its alienation. In the self-cognition of the spirit as nature in disunion with itself, as in prehistory, nature calls itself to account; no longer directly, as *mana* – that is, with the alias that signifies omnipotence – but as blind and lame. The decline, the forfeiture, of nature consists in the subjugation of nature without which spirit does not exist. Through the decision in which spirit acknowledges itself to be domination and retreats into nature, it abandons the claim to domination which makes it a vassal of nature. Even though in the flight from necessity, in progress and civilization, mankind cannot hold the course without abandoning knowledge itself, at least it no longer mistakes the ramparts that it erects against necessity (the institutions and practices of subjection that have always redounded on society from the subjugation of nature) for guarantees of the freedom to come. Every progress made by civilization has renewed together with domination that prospect of its removal. Whereas, however, real history is woven out of a real suffering that is not lessened in proportion to the growth of means for its abrogation, the realization of the prospect is referred to the notion, the concept. For it does not merely, as science, distance men from nature, but, as the self-consideration of thought that in the form of science remains tied to blind economic tendency, allows the distance perpetuating injustice to be measured. By virtue of this remembrance of nature in the subject, in whose fulfillment the unacknowledged truth of all culture lies hidden, enlightenment is universally opposed to domination; and the call to check enlightenment resounded even in the time of Vanini[6] less out of fear of exact science than out of that hatred of undisciplined ideas which emerges from the jurisdiction of nature even as it acknowledges itself to be nature's very dread of its own self. The priests always avenged *mana* on the prophet of enlightenment, who propitiated *mana* by a terror-stricken attitude to what went by the name of terror, and the augurs of the Enlightenment were one with the priests in their hybris. In its bourgeois form, the Enlightenment had lost itself in its positivistic aspect long before Turgot and d'Alembert. It was never immune to the exchange of freedom for the pursuit of self-preservation. The suspension of the concept, whether in the name of progress or of culture – which had already long before tacitly leagued themselves against the truth – opened the way for falsehood. And this in a world that verified only evidential propositions, and preserved thought – degraded to the achievement of great thinkers – as a kind of stock of superannuated clichés, no longer to be distinguished from truth neutralized as a cultural commodity.

But to recognize domination, even in thought itself, as unreconciled nature, would mean a slackening of the necessity whose perpetuity socialism itself prematurely confirmed as a concession to reactionary common sense. By elevating necessity to the status of the basis for all time to come, and by idealistically degrading the spirit for ever to the very apex, socialism held on all too surely to the legacy of bourgeois philosophy. Hence the relation of necessity to the realm of freedom would remain merely quantitative and mechanical, and nature, posited as wholly alien – just as in the earliest mythology – would become totalitarian and absorb freedom together with socialism. With the abandonment of thought, which in its reified form of mathematics, machine, and organization avenges itself on the men who have forgotten it, enlightenment has relinquished its own realization. By taking everything unique and individual under its tutelage, it left the uncomprehended whole the freedom, as domination, to strike back at human existence and consciousness by way of things. But true revolutionary practice depends on the intransigence of theory in the face of the insensibility with which society allows thought to ossify. It is not the material prerequisites of fulfillment – liberated technology as such – which jeopardize fulfillment. That is asserted by those sociologists who are again searching for an antidote, and – should it be a collectivist measure – to master the antidote.[7] Guilt is a context of social delusion. The mythic scientific respect of the peoples of the earth for the *status quo* that they themselves unceasingly produce, itself finally becomes positive fact: the oppressor's fortress in regard to which even revolutionary imagination despises itself as utopism and decays to the condition of pliable trust in the objective tendency of history. As the organ of this kind of adaptation, as a mere construction of means, the Enlightenment is as destructive as its romantic enemies accuse it of being. It comes into its own only when it surrenders the last remaining concordance with the latter and dares to transcend the false absolute, the principle of blind domination. The spirit of this kind of unrelenting theory would turn even the mind of relentless progress to its end. Its herald Bacon dreamed of the many things 'which kings with their treasure cannot buy, nor with their force command', of which 'their spials and intelligencers can give no news'. As he wished, they fell to the burghers, the enlightened heirs of those kings. While bourgeois economy multiplied power through the mediation of the market, it also multiplied its objects and powers to such an extent that for their administration not just the kings, not even the middle classes are no longer necessary, but all men. They learn from the power of things to dispense at last with power. Enlightenment is realized and reaches its term when the nearest practical ends reveal themselves as the most distant goal now attained, and the lands of which 'their spials and intelligencers can give no news', that is, those of the nature despised by dominant science, are recognized as the lands of origin. Today, when Bacon's utopian vision that we should 'command nature by action' – that is, in practice – has been realized on a tellurian scale, the nature of the thralldom that he ascribed to unsubjected nature is clear. It was domination itself. And knowledge, in which Bacon was certain the 'sovereignty of man lieth hid', can now become the dissolution of domination. But in the face of such a possibility, and in the service of the present age, enlightenment becomes wholesale deception of the masses.

NOTES

1. Voltaire, *Lettres Philosophiques*, XII, *Œuvres Complètes* (Garnier: Paris, 1879), Vol. XXII, p. 118.
2. Bacon, 'In Praise of Human Knowledge' (*Miscellaneous Tracts upon Human Knowledge*), *The Works of Francis Bacon*, ed. Basil Montagu (London, 1825), Vol. I, pp. 254ff.
3. Cf. Bacon, *Novum Organum*, *Works*, Vol. XIV, p. 31.
4. Bacon, 'Valerius Terminus: Of the Interpretation of Nature' (*Miscellaneous Tracts upon Human Knowledge*), *Works*, Vol. I, p. 281.
5. *Ethica*, Pars. IV. Propos, XXII. Coroll.
6. Lucilio Vanini, a quasi-pantheistic Italian philosopher (1584–1619) sentenced and burned for blasphemy by the Inquisition. – Tr.
7. 'The supreme question which confronts our generation today – the question to which all other problems are merely corollaries – is whether technology can be brought under control... Nobody can be sure of the formula by which this end can be achieved... We must draw on all the resources to which access can be had...' (*The Rockefeller Foundation. A Review for 1943* [New York, 1944], pp. 33ff.).

FROM 'THE CULTURE INDUSTRY: ENLIGHTENMENT AS MASS DECEPTION'

Theodor Adorno and Max Horkheimer

The morality of mass culture is the cheap form of yesterday's children's books. In a first-class production, for example, the villainous character appears as a hysterical woman who (with presumed clinical accuracy) tries to ruin the happiness of her opposite number, who is truer to reality, and herself suffers a quite untheatrical death. So much learning is of course found only at the top. Lower down less trouble is taken. Tragedy is made harmless without recourse to social psychology. Just as every Viennese operetta worthy of the name had to have its tragic finale in the second act, which left nothing for the third except to clear up misunderstandings, the culture industry assigns tragedy a fixed place in the routine. The well-known existence of the recipe is enough to allay any fear that there is no restraint on tragedy. The description of the dramatic formula by the housewife as 'getting into trouble and out again' embraces the whole of mass culture from the idiotic women's serial to the top production. Even the worst ending which began with good intentions confirms the order of things and corrupts the tragic force, either because the woman whose love runs counter to the laws of the game plays with her death for a brief spell of happiness, or because the sad ending in the film all the more clearly stresses the indestructibility of actual life. The tragic film becomes an institution for moral improvement. The masses, demoralized by their life under the pressure of the system, and who show signs of civilization only in modes of behavior

Theodor Adorno and Max Horkheimer (1986), 'The culture industry: enlightenment as mass deception', in *Dialectic of Enlightenment*, tr. John Cumming, 2nd ed., London: Verso.

which have been forced on them and through which fury and recalcitrance show everywhere, are to be kept in order by the sight of an inexorable life and exemplary behavior. Culture has always played its part in taming revolutionary and barbaric instincts. Industrial culture adds its contribution. It shows the condition under which this merciless life can be lived at all. The individual who is thoroughly weary must use his weariness as energy for his surrender to the collective power which wears him out. In films, those permanently desperate situations which crush the spectator in ordinary life somehow become a promise that one can go on living. One has only to become aware of one's own nothingness, only to recognize defeat and one is one with it all. Society is full of desperate people and therefore a prey to rackets. In some of the most significant German novels of the pre-Fascist era such as Döblin's *Berlin Alexanderplatz* and Fallada's *Kleiner Mann, Was Nun*, this trend was as obvious as in the average film and in the devices of jazz. What all these things have in common is the self-derision of man. The possibility of becoming a subject in the economy, an entrepreneur or a proprietor, has been completely liquidated. Right down to the humblest shop, the independent enterprise, on the management and inheritance of which the bourgeois family and the position of its head had rested, became hopelessly dependent. Everybody became an employee; and in this civilization of employees the dignity of the father (questionable anyhow) vanishes. The attitude of the individual to the racket, business, profession or party, before or after admission, the Führer's gesticulations before the masses, or the suitor's before his sweetheart, assume specifically masochistic traits. The attitude into which everybody is forced in order to give repeated proof of his moral suitability for this society reminds one of the boys who, during tribal initiation, go round in a circle with a stereotyped smile on their faces while the priest strikes them. Life in the late capitalist era is a constant initiation rite. Everyone must show that he wholly identifies himself with the power which is belaboring him. This occurs in the principle of jazz syncopation, which simultaneously derides stumbling and makes it a rule. The eunuch-like voice of the crooner on the radio, the heiress's smooth suitor, who falls into the swimming pool in his dinner jacket, are models for those who must become whatever the system wants. Everyone can be like this omnipotent society; everyone can be happy, if only he will capitulate fully and sacrifice his claim to happiness. In his weakness society recognizes its strength, and gives him some of it. His defenselessness makes him reliable. Hence tragedy is discarded. Once the opposition of the individual to society was its substance. It glorified 'the bravery and freedom of emotion before a powerful enemy, an exalted affliction, a dreadful problem'.[1] Today tragedy has melted away into the nothingness of that false identity of society and individual, whose terror still shows for a moment in the empty semblance of the tragic. But the miracle of integration, the permanent act of grace by the authority who receives the defenseless person – once he has swallowed his rebelliousness – signifies Fascism. This can be seen in the humanitarianism which Döblin uses to let his Biberkopf find refuge, and again in socially-slanted films. The capacity to find refuge, to survive one's own ruin, by which tragedy is defeated, is found in the new generation; they can do any work because the work process does not let them become attached to any. This is reminiscent of the sad lack of conviction of the homecoming soldier with no interest in the war, or of the casual laborer who ends up by joining a paramilitary organization. This liquidation of tragedy confirms the abolition of the individual.

In the culture industry the individual is an illusion not merely because of the standardization of the means of production. He is tolerated only so long as his complete identification with the generality is unquestioned. Pseudo individuality is rife: from the standardized jazz improvization to the exceptional film star whose hair curls over her eye to demonstrate her originality. What is individual is no more than the generality's power to stamp the accidental detail so firmly that it is accepted as such. The defiant reserve or elegant appearance of the individual on show is mass-produced like Yale locks, whose only difference can be measured in fractions of millimeters. The peculiarity of the self is a monopoly commodity determined by society; it is falsely represented as natural. It is no more than the moustache, the French accent, the deep voice of the woman of the world, the Lubitsch touch: finger prints on identity cards which are otherwise exactly the same, and into which the lives and faces of every single person are transformed by the power of the generality. Pseudo individuality is the prerequisite for comprehending tragedy and removing its poison: only because individuals have ceased to be themselves and are now merely centers where the general tendencies meet, is it possible to receive them again, whole and entire, into the generality. In this way mass culture discloses the fictitious character of the 'individual' in the bourgeois era, and is merely unjust in boasting on account of this dreary harmony of general and particular. The principle of individuality was always full of contradiction. Individuation has never really been achieved. Self-preservation in the shape of class has kept everyone at the stage of a mere species being. Every bourgeois characteristic, in spite of its deviation and indeed because of it, expressed the same thing: the harshness of the competitive society. The individual who supported society bore its disfiguring mark: seemingly free, he was actually the product of its economic and social apparatus. Power based itself on the prevailing conditions of power when it sought the approval of persons affected by it. As it progressed, bourgeois society did also develop the individual. Against the will of its leaders, technology has changed human beings from children into persons. However, every advance in individuation of this kind took place at the expense of the individuality in whose name it occurred, so that nothing was left but the resolve to pursue one's own particular purpose. The bourgeois whose existence is split into a business and a private life, whose private life is split into keeping up his public image and intimacy, whose intimacy is split into the surly partnership of marriage and the bitter comfort of being quite alone, at odds with himself and everybody else, is already virtually a Nazi, replete both with enthusiasm and abuse; or a modern city-dweller who can now only imagine friendship as a 'social contact': that is, as being in social contact with others with whom he has no inward contact. The only reason why the culture industry can deal so successfully with individuality is that the latter has always reproduced the fragility of society. On the faces of private individuals and movie heroes put together according to the patterns on magazine covers vanishes a pretense in which no one now believes; the popularity of the hero models comes partly from a secret satisfaction that the effort to achieve individuation has at last been replaced by the effort to imitate, which is admittedly more breathless. It is idle to hope that this self-contradictory, disintegrating 'person' will not last for generations, that the system must collapse because of such a psychological split, or that the deceitful substitution of the stereotype for the individual will of itself become unbearable for mankind. Since Shakespeare's *Hamlet*, the unity of the personality has been seen through as a pretense. Synthetically produced physiognomies show that the people of today have already forgotten that there was ever a notion of what human life was. For centuries society has been preparing for Victor Mature and Mickey Rooney. By destroying they come to fulfill.

[...]

The work of art, by completely assimilating itself to need, deceitfully deprives men of precisely that liberation from the principle of utility which it should inaugurate. What might be called use value in the reception of cultural commodities is replaced by exchange value; in place of enjoyment there are gallery-visiting and factual knowledge: the prestige seeker replaces the connoisseur. The consumer becomes the ideology of the pleasure industry, whose institutions he cannot escape. One simply 'has to' have seen *Mrs. Miniver*, just as one 'has to' subscribe to *Life* and *Time*. Everything is looked at from only one aspect: that it can be used for something else, however vague the notion of this use may be. No object has an inherent value; it is valuable only to the extent that it can be exchanged. The use value of art, its mode of being, is treated as a fetish; and the fetish, the work's social rating (misinterpreted as its artistic status) becomes its use value – the only quality which is enjoyed. The commodity function of art disappears only to be wholly realized when art becomes a species of commodity instead, marketable and interchangeable like an industrial product. But art as a type of product which existed to be sold and yet to be unsaleable is wholly and hypocritically converted into 'unsaleability' as soon as the transaction ceases to be the mere intention and becomes its sole principle. No tickets could be bought when Toscanini conducted over the radio; he was heard without charge, and every sound of the symphony was accompanied, as it were, by the sublime puff that the symphony was not interrupted by any advertising: 'This concert is brought to you as a public service.' The illusion was made possible by the profits of the united automobile and soap manufacturers, whose payments keep the radio stations going – and, of course, by the increased sales of the electrical industry, which manufactures the radio sets. Radio, the progressive latecomer of mass culture, draws all the consequences at present denied the film by its pseudo-market. The technical structure of the commercial radio system makes it immune from liberal deviations such as those the movie industrialists can still permit themselves in their own sphere. It is a private enterprise which really does represent the sovereign whole and is therefore some distance ahead of the other individual combines. Chesterfield is merely the nation's cigarette, but the radio is the voice of the nation. In bringing cultural products wholly into the sphere of commodities, radio does not try to dispose of its culture goods themselves as commodities straight to the consumer. In America it collects no fees from the public, and so has acquired the illusory form of disinterested, unbiased authority which suits Fascism admirably. The radio becomes the universal mouthpiece of the Führer; his voice rises from street loud-speakers to resemble the howling of sirens announcing panic – from which modern propaganda can scarcely be distinguished anyway. The National Socialists knew that the wireless gave shape to their cause just as the printing press did to the Reformation. The metaphysical charisma of the Führer invented by the sociology of religion has finally turned out to be no more than the omnipresence of his speeches on the radio, which are a demoniacal parody of the omnipresence of the divine spirit. The gigantic fact that the speech penetrates everywhere replaces its content, just as the benefaction of the Toscanini broadcast takes the place of the symphony. No listener can grasp its true meaning any longer, while the Führer's speech is lies anyway. The inherent tendency of radio is to make the speaker's word, the false commandment, absolute. A recommendation becomes an order. The recommendation of the same commodities under different proprietary names, the scientifically based praise of the laxative in the announcer's smooth voice between the overture from *La Traviata* and that from *Rienzi* is the only thing that no longer works, because of its silliness. One day the edict of production, the actual advertisement (whose actuality is at present concealed by the pretense of a choice) can turn into the open command of the Führer. In a society of huge Fascist rackets which agree among themselves what part of the social product should be allotted to the nation's needs, it would eventually seem anachronistic to recommend the use of a particular soap powder. The Führer is more up-to-date in unceremoniously giving direct orders for both the holocaust and the supply of rubbish.

Even today the culture industry dresses works of art like political slogans and forces them upon a resistant public at reduced prices; they are as accessible for public enjoyment as a park. But the disappearance of their genuine commodity character does not mean that they have been abolished in the life of a free society, but that the last defense against their reduction to culture goods has fallen. The abolition of educational privilege by the device of clearance sales does not open for the masses the spheres from which they were formerly excluded, but, given existing social conditions, contributes directly to the decay of education and the progress of barbaric meaninglessness. Those who spent their money in the nineteenth or the early twentieth century to see a play or to go to a concert respected the performance as much as the money they spent. The bourgeois who wanted to get something out of it tried occasionally to establish some rapport with the work. Evidence for this is to be found in the literary 'introductions' to works, or in the commentaries on *Faust*. These were the first steps toward the biographical coating and other practices to which a work of art is subjected today. Even in the early, prosperous days of business, exchange-value did carry use value as a mere appendix but had developed it as a prerequisite for its own existence; this was socially helpful for works of art. Art exercised some restraint on the bourgeois as long as it cost money. That is now a thing of the past. Now that it has lost every restraint and there is no need to pay any money, the proximity of art to those who are exposed to it completes the alienation and assimilates one to the other under the banner of triumphant objectivity. Criticism and respect disappear in the culture industry; the former becomes a mechanical expertise, the latter is succeeded by a shallow cult of leading personalities. Consumers now find nothing expensive. Nevertheless, they suspect that the less anything costs, the less it is being given them. The double mistrust of traditional culture as ideology is combined with mistrust of industrialized culture as a swindle. When thrown in free, the now debased works of art, together with the rubbish to which the medium assimilates them, are secretly rejected by the fortunate recipients, who are supposed to be satisfied by the mere fact that there is so much to be seen and heard. Everything can be obtained. The screenos and vaudevilles in the movie theater, the competitions for guessing music, the free books, rewards and gifts offered on certain radio programs, are not mere accidents but a continuation of the practice obtaining with culture products. The symphony becomes a reward for listening to the radio, and – if technology had its way – the film would be delivered to people's homes as happens with the radio. It is moving toward the commercial system. Television points the way to a development which might easily enough force the Warner Brothers into what would certainly be the unwelcome position of serious musicians and cultural conservatives. But the gift system has already taken hold among consumers. As culture is represented as a bonus with undoubted private and social advantages, they have to seize the chance. They rush in lest they miss something. Exactly what, is not clear, but in any case the only ones with a chance are the participants. Fascism, however, hopes to use the training the culture industry has given these recipients of gifts, in order to organize them into its own forced battalions.

Culture is a paradoxical commodity. So completely is it subject to the law of exchange that it is no longer exchanged; it is so blindly consumed in use that it can no longer be used. Therefore it amalgamates with advertising. The more meaningless the latter seems to be under a monopoly, the more omnipotent it becomes. The motives are markedly economic. One could certainly live without the culture industry, therefore it necessarily creates too much satiation and apathy. In itself, it has few resources itself to correct this. Advertising is its elixir of life. But as its product never fails to reduce to a mere promise the enjoyment which it promises as a commodity, it eventually coincides with publicity, which it needs because it cannot be enjoyed. In a competitive society, advertising performed the social service of informing the buyer about the market; it made choice easier and helped the unknown but more efficient supplier to dispose of his goods. Far from costing time, it saved it. Today, when the free market is coming to an end, those who control the system are entrenching themselves in it. It strengthens the firm bond between the consumers and the big combines. Only those who can pay the exorbitant rates charged by the advertising agencies, chief of which are the radio networks themselves; that is, only those who are already in a position to do so, or are co-opted by the decision of the banks and industrial capital, can enter the pseudo-market as sellers. The costs of advertising, which finally flow back into the pockets of the combines, make it unnecessary to defeat unwelcome outsiders by laborious competition. They guarantee that power will remain in the same hands – not unlike those economic decisions by which the establishment and running of undertakings is controlled in a totalitarian state. Advertising today is a negative principle, a blocking device: everything that does not bear its stamp is economically suspect. Universal publicity is in no way necessary for people to get to know the kinds of goods – whose supply is restricted anyway. It helps sales only indirectly. For a particular firm, to phase out a current advertising practice constitutes a loss of prestige, and a breach of the discipline imposed by the influential clique on its members. In wartime, goods which are unobtainable are still advertised, merely to keep industrial power in view. Subsidizing ideological media is more important than the repetition of the name. Because the system obliges every product to use advertising, it has permeated the idiom – the 'style' – of the culture industry. Its victory is so complete that it is no longer evident in the key positions: the huge buildings of the top men, floodlit stone advertisements, are free of advertising; at most they exhibit on the rooftops, in monumental brilliance and without any self-glorification, the firm's initials. But, in contrast, the nineteenth-century houses, whose architecture still shamefully indicates that they can be used as a consumption commodity and are intended to be lived in, are covered with posters and inscriptions from the ground right up to and beyond the roof: until they become no more than backgrounds for bills and sign-boards. Advertising becomes art and nothing else, just as Goebbels – with foresight – combines them: *l'art pour l'art*, advertising for its own sake, a pure representation of social power. In the most influential American magazines, *Life* and *Fortune*, a quick glance can now scarcely distinguish advertising from editorial picture and text. The latter features an enthusiastic and gratuitous account of the great man (with illustrations of his life and grooming habits) which will bring him new fans, while the advertisement pages use so many factual photographs and details that they represent the ideal of information which the editorial part has only begun to try to achieve. The assembly-line character of the culture industry, the synthetic, planned method of turning out its products (factory-like not only in the studio but, more or less, in the compilation of cheap biographies, pseudodocumentary novels, and hit songs) is very suited to advertising: the important individual points, by becoming detachable, interchangeable, and even technically alienated from any connected meaning, lend themselves to ends external to the work. The effect, the trick, the isolated repeatable device, have always been used to exhibit goods for advertising purposes, and today every monster close-up of a star is an advertisement for her name, and every hit song a plug for its tune. Advertising and the culture industry merge technically as well as economically. In both cases the same thing can be seen in innumerable places, and the mechanical repetition of the same culture product has come to be the same as that of the propaganda slogan. In both cases the insistent demand for effectiveness makes technology into psycho-technology, into a procedure for manipulating men. In both cases the standards are the striking yet familiar, the easy yet catchy, the skillful yet simple; the object is to overpower the customer, who is conceived as absent-minded or resistant.

NOTE

1. Nietzsche, *Götzendämmerung, Werke*, Vol. VIII, p. 136.

FROM 'THE NEW FORMS OF CONTROL'

Herbert Marcuse

A comfortable, smooth, reasonable, democratic unfreedom prevails in advanced industrial civilization, a token of technical progress. Indeed, what could be more rational than the suppression of individuality in the mechanization of socially necessary but painful performances; the concentration of individual enterprises in more effective, more productive corporations; the regulation of free competition among unequally equipped economic subjects; the curtailment of prerogatives and national sovereignties which impede the international organization of resources. That this technological order also involves a political and intellectual coordination may be a regrettable and yet promising development.

The rights and liberties which were such vital factors in the origins and earlier stages of industrial society yield to a higher stage of this society: they are losing their traditional rationale and content. Freedom of thought, speech, and conscience were – just as free enterprise, which they served to promote and protect – essentially *critical* ideas, designed to replace an obsolescent material and intellectual culture by a more productive and rational one. Once institutionalized, these rights and liberties shared the fate of the society of which they had become an integral part. The achievement cancels the premises.

To the degree to which freedom from want, the concrete substance of all freedom, is becoming a real possibility, the liberties which pertain to a

Herbert Marcuse (1964), 'The new forms of control', in *One-Dimensional Man*, Boston: Beacon Press.

state of lower productivity are losing their former content. Independence of thought, autonomy, and the right to political opposition are being deprived of their basic critical function in a society which seems increasingly capable of satisfying the needs of the individuals through the way in which it is organized. Such a society may justly demand acceptance of its principles and institutions, and reduce the opposition to the discussion and promotion of alternative policies *within* the status quo. In this respect, it seems to make little difference whether the increasing satisfaction of needs is accomplished by an authoritarian or a non-authoritarian system. Under the conditions of a rising standard of living, non-conformity with the system itself appears to be socially useless, and the more so when it entails tangible economic and political disadvantages and threatens the smooth operation of the whole. Indeed, at least in so far as the necessities of life are involved, there seems to be no reason why the production and distribution of goods and services should proceed through the competitive concurrence of individual liberties.

Freedom of enterprise was from the beginning not altogether a blessing. As the liberty to work or to starve, it spelled toil, insecurity, and fear for the vast majority of the population. If the individual were no longer compelled to prove himself on the market, as a free economic subject, the disappearance of this kind of freedom would be one of the greatest achievements of civilization. The technological processes of mechanization and standardization might release individual energy into a yet uncharted realm of freedom beyond necessity. The very structure of human existence would be altered; the individual would be liberated from the work world's imposing upon him alien needs and alien possibilities. The individual would be free to exert autonomy over a life that would be his own. If the productive apparatus could be organized and directed toward the satisfaction of the vital needs, its control might well be centralized; such control would not prevent individual autonomy, but render it possible.

This is a goal within the capabilities of advanced industrial civilization, the 'end' of technological rationality. In actual fact, however, the contrary trend operates: the apparatus imposes its economic and political requirements for defense and expansion on labor time and free time, on the material and intellectual culture. By virtue of the way it has organized its technological base, contemporary industrial society tends to be totalitarian. For 'totalitarian' is not only a terroristic political coordination of society, but also a non-terroristic economic-technical coordination which operates through the manipulation of needs by vested interests. It thus precludes the emergence of an effective opposition against the whole. Not only a specific form of government or party rule makes for totalitarianism, but also a specific system of production and distribution which may well be compatible with a 'pluralism' of parties, newspapers, 'countervailing powers', etc.

Today political power asserts itself through its power over the machine process and over the technical organization of the apparatus. The government of advanced and advancing industrial societies can maintain and secure itself only when it succeeds in mobilizing, organizing, and exploiting the technical, scientific, and mechanical productivity available to industrial civilization. And this productivity mobilizes society as a whole, above and beyond any particular individual or group interests. The brute fact that the machine's physical (only physical?) power surpasses that of the individual, and of any particular group of individuals, makes the machine the most effective political instrument in any society whose basic organization is that of the machine process. But the political trend may be reversed; essentially the power of the machine is only the stored-up and projected power of man. To the extent to which the work world is conceived of as a machine and mechanized accordingly, it becomes the *potential* basis of a new freedom for man.

Contemporary industrial civilization demonstrates that it has reached the stage at which 'the free society' can no longer be adequately defined in the traditional terms of economic, political, and intellectual liberties, not because these liberties have become insignificant, but because they are too significant to be confined within the traditional forms. New modes of realization are needed, corresponding to the new capabilities of society.

Such new modes can be indicated only in negative terms because they would amount to the negation of the prevailing modes. Thus economic freedom would mean freedom *from* the economy – from being controlled by economic forces and relationships; freedom from the daily struggle for existence, from earning a living. Political freedom would mean liberation of the individuals *from* politics over which they have no effective control. Similarly, intellectual freedom would mean the restoration of individual thought now absorbed by mass communication and indoctrination, abolition of 'public opinion' together with its makers. The unrealistic sound of these propositions is indicative, not of their utopian character, but of the strength of the forces which prevent their realization. The most effective and enduring form of warfare against liberation is the implanting of material and intellectual needs that perpetuate obsolete forms of the struggle for existence.

The intensity, the satisfaction and even the character of human needs, beyond the biological level, have always been preconditioned. Whether or not the possibility of doing or leaving, enjoying or destroying, possessing or rejecting something is seized as a *need* depends on whether or not it can be seen as desirable and necessary for the prevailing societal institutions and interests. In this sense, human needs are historical needs and, to the extent to which the society demands the repressive development of the individual, his needs themselves and their claim for satisfaction are subject to overriding critical standards.

We may distinguish both true and false needs. 'False' are those which are superimposed upon the individual by particular social interests in his repression: the needs which perpetuate toil, aggressiveness, misery, and injustice. Their satisfaction might be most gratifying to the individual, but this happiness is not a condition which has to be maintained and protected if it serves to arrest the development of the ability (his own and others) to recognize the disease of the whole and grasp the chances of curing the disease. The result then is euphoria in unhappiness. Most of the prevailing needs to relax, to have fun, to behave and consume in accordance with the advertisements, to love and hate what others love and hate, belong to this category of false needs.

Such needs have a societal content and function which are determined by external powers over which the individual has no control; the development and satisfaction of these needs is heteronomous. No matter how much such needs may have become the individual's own, reproduced and fortified by the conditions of his existence; no matter how much he identifies himself with them and finds himself in their satisfaction, they continue to be what they were from the beginning – products of a society whose dominant interest demands repression.

The prevalence of repressive needs is an accomplished fact, accepted in ignorance and defeat, but a fact that must be undone in the interest of the happy individual as well as all those whose misery is the price of his satisfaction. The only needs that have an unqualified claim for satisfaction are the vital ones – nourishment, clothing, lodging at the attainable level of culture. The satisfaction of these needs is the prerequisite for the realization of *all* needs, of the unsublimated as well as the sublimated ones.

For any consciousness and conscience, for any experience which does not accept the prevailing societal interest as the supreme law of thought and behavior, the established universe of needs and satisfactions is a fact to be questioned – questioned in terms of truth and falsehood. These terms are historical throughout, and their objectivity is historical. The judgment of needs and their satisfaction, under the given conditions, involves standards of *priority* – standards which refer to the optimal development of the individual, of all individuals, under the optimal utilization of the material and intellectual resources available to man. The resources are calculable. 'Truth' and 'falsehood' of needs designate objective conditions to the extent to which the universal satisfaction of vital needs and, beyond it, the progressive alleviation of toil and poverty, are universally valid standards. But as historical standards, they do not only vary according to area and stage of development, they also can be defined only in (greater or lesser) *contradiction* to the prevailing ones. What tribunal can possibly claim the authority of decision?

In the last analysis, the question of what are true and false needs must be answered by the individuals themselves, but only in the last analysis; that is, if and when they are free to give their own answer. As long as they are kept incapable of being autonomous, as long as they are indoctrinated and manipulated (down to their very instincts), their answer to this question cannot be taken as their own. By the same token, however, no tribunal can justly arrogate to itself the right to decide which needs should be developed and satisfied. Any such tribunal is reprehensible, although our revulsion does not do away with the question: how can the people who have been the object of effective and productive domination by themselves create the conditions of freedom?

The more rational, productive, technical, and total the repressive administration of society becomes, the more unimaginable the means and ways by which the administered individuals might break their servitude and seize their own liberation. To be sure, to impose Reason upon an entire society is a paradoxical and scandalous idea – although one might dispute the righteousness of a society which ridicules this idea while making its own population into objects of total administration. All liberation depends on the consciousness of servitude, and the emergence of this consciousness is always hampered by the predominance of needs and satisfactions which, to a great extent, have become the individual's own. The process always replaces one system of preconditioning by another; the optimal goal is the replacement of false needs by true ones, the abandonment of repressive satisfaction.

The distinguishing feature of advanced industrial society is its effective suffocation of those needs which demand liberation – liberation also from that which is tolerable and rewarding and comfortable – while it sustains and absolves the destructive power and repressive function of the affluent society. Here, the social controls exact the overwhelming need for the production and consumption of waste; the need for stupefying work where it is no longer a real necessity; the need for modes of relaxation which soothe and prolong this stupefication; the need for maintaining such deceptive liberties as free competition at administered prices, a free press which censors itself, free choice between brands and gadgets.

Under the rule of a repressive whole, liberty can be made into a powerful instrument of domination. The range of choice open to the individual is not the decisive factor in determining the degree of human freedom, but *what* can be chosen and what *is* chosen by the individual. The criterion for free choice can never be an absolute one, but neither is it entirely relative. Free election of masters does not abolish the masters or the slaves. Free choice among a wide variety of goods and services does not signify freedom if these goods and services sustain social controls over a life of toil and fear – that is, if they sustain alienation. And the spontaneous reproduction of superimposed needs by the individual does not establish autonomy; it only testifies to the efficacy of the controls.

Our insistence on the depth and efficacy of these controls is open to the objection that we overrate greatly the indoctrinating power of the 'media', and that by themselves the people would feel and satisfy the needs which are now imposed upon them. The objection misses the point. The preconditioning does not start with the mass production of radio and television and with the centralization of their control. The people enter this stage as preconditioned receptacles of long standing; the decisive difference is in the flattening out of the contrast (or conflict) between the given and the possible, between the satisfied and the unsatisfied needs. Here, the so-called equalization of class distinctions reveals its ideological function. If the worker and his boss enjoy the same television program and visit the same resort places, if the typist is as attractively made up as the daughter of her employer, if the Negro owns a Cadillac, if they all read the same newspaper, then this assimilation indicates not the disappearance of classes, but the extent to which the needs and satisfactions that serve the preservation of the Establishment are shared by the underlying population.

Indeed, in the most highly developed areas of contemporary society, the transplantation of social into individual needs is so effective that the difference between them seems to be purely theoretical. Can one really distinguish between the mass media as instruments of information and entertainment, and as agents of manipulation and indoctrination? Between the automobile as nuisance and as convenience? Between the horrors and the comforts of functional architecture? Between the work for national defense and the work for corporate gain? Between the private pleasure and the commercial and political utility involved in increasing the birth rate?

We are again confronted with one of the most vexing aspects of advanced industrial civilization: the rational character of its irrationality. Its productivity and efficiency, its capacity to increase and spread comforts, to turn waste into need, and destruction into construction, the extent to which this civilization transforms the object world into an extension of man's mind and body makes the very notion of alienation questionable. The people recognize themselves in their commodities; they find their soul in their automobile, hi-fi set, split-level home, kitchen equipment. The very mechanism which ties the individual to his society has changed, and social control is anchored in the new needs which it has produced.

The prevailing forms of social control are technological in a new sense. To be sure, the technical structure and efficacy of the productive and destructive apparatus has been a major instrumentality for subjecting the population to the established social division of labor throughout the modern period. Moreover, such integration has always been accompanied by more obvious forms of compulsion: loss of livelihood, the administration of justice, the police, the armed forces. It still is. But in the contemporary period, the technological controls appear to be the very embodiment of Reason for the benefit of all social groups and interests – to such an extent that all contradiction seems irrational and all counteraction impossible.

No wonder then that, in the most advanced areas of this civilization, the social controls have been introjected to the point where even individual protest is affected at its roots. The intellectual and emotional refusal 'to go along' appears neurotic and impotent. This is the socio-psychological aspect of the political event that marks the contemporary period: the passing of the historical forces which, at the preceding stage of industrial society, seemed to represent the possibility of new forms of existence.

But the term 'introjection' perhaps no longer describes the way in which the individual by himself reproduces and perpetuates the external controls exercised by his society. Introjection suggests a variety of relatively spontaneous processes by which a Self (Ego) transposes the 'outer' into the 'inner'. Thus introjection implies the existence of an inner dimension distinguished from and even antagonistic to the external exigencies – an individual consciousness and an individual unconscious *apart from* public opinion and behavior.[1] The idea of 'inner freedom' here has its reality: it designates the private space in which man may become and remain 'himself'.

Today this private space has been invaded and whittled down by technological reality. Mass production and mass distribution claim the *entire* individual, and industrial psychology has long since ceased to be confined to the factory. The manifold processes of introjection seem to be ossified in almost mechanical reactions. The result is, not adjustment but *mimesis*: an immediate identification of the individual with *his* society and, through it, with the society as a whole.

This immediate, automatic identification (which may have been characteristic of primitive forms of association) reappears in high industrial civilization; its new 'immediacy', however, is the product of a sophisticated, scientific management and organization. In this process, the 'inner' dimension of the mind in which opposition to the status quo can take root is whittled down. The loss of this dimension, in which the power of negative thinking – the critical power of Reason – is at home, is the ideological counterpart to the very material process in which advanced industrial society silences and reconciles the opposition. The impact of progress turns Reason into submission to the facts of life, and to the dynamic capability of producing more and bigger facts of the same sort of life. The efficiency of the system blunts the individuals' recognition that it contains no facts which do not communicate the repressive power of the whole. If the individuals find themselves in the things which shape their life, they do so, not by giving, but by accepting the law of things – not the law of physics but the law of their society.

I have just suggested that the concept of alienation seems to become questionable when the individuals identify themselves with the existence which is imposed upon them and have in it their own development and satisfaction. This identification is not illusion but reality. However, the reality constitutes a more progressive stage of alienation. The latter has become entirely objective; the subject which is alienated is swallowed up by its alienated existence. There is only one dimension, and it is everywhere and in all forms. The achievements of progress defy ideological indictment as well as justification; before their tribunal, the 'false consciousness' of their rationality becomes the true consciousness.

This absorption of ideology into reality does not, however, signify the 'end of ideology'. On the contrary, in a specific sense advanced industrial culture is *more* ideological than its predecessor, inasmuch as today the ideology is in the process of production itself.[2] In a provocative form, this proposition reveals the political aspects of the prevailing technological rationality. The productive apparatus and the goods and services which it produces 'sell' or impose the social system as a whole. The means of mass transportation and communication, the commodities of lodging, food, and clothing, the irresistible output of the entertainment and information industry carry with them prescribed attitudes and habits, certain intellectual and emotional reactions which bind the consumers more or less pleasantly to the producers and, through the latter, to the whole. The products indoctrinate and manipulate; they promote a false consciousness which is immune against its falsehood. And as these beneficial products become available to more individuals in more social classes, the indoctrination they carry ceases to be publicity; it becomes a way of life. It is a good way of life – much better than before – and as a good way of life, it militates against qualitative change. Thus emerges a pattern of *one-dimensional thought and behavior* in which ideas, aspirations, and objectives that, by their content, transcend the established universe of discourse and action are either repelled or reduced to terms of this universe. They are redefined by the rationality of the given system and of its quantitative extension.

NOTES

1. The change in the function of the family here plays a decisive role: its 'socializing' functions are increasingly taken over by outside groups and media. See [Marcuse's] *Eros and Civilization* (Boston: Beacon Press, 1955), p. 96 ff.
2. Theodor W. Adorno, *Prismen. Kulturkritik und Gesellschaft* (Frankfurt: Suhrkamp, 1955), p. 24 f.

EXTACTS FROM *THE THEORY OF COMMUNICATIVE ACTION, VOL. 2*

Jürgen Habermas

From 'The Authority of the Sacred'

In societies that have attained the level of civilizations, worldviews have the function, among others, of legitimating political leadership. They offer a potential for grounding that can be used to justify a political order or the institutional framework of a society in general. Thus they lend support to the moral authority or validity of basic norms. As Weber emphasized, the legitimating power of worldviews is to be explained primarily by the fact that cultural knowledge can meet with rationally motivated approval. The situation is different with the not yet intellectually elaborated worldviews common in tribal societies; they do make available a potential for narrative explanations, but they are still so tightly interwoven with the system of institutions that they explicate it rather than subsequently legitimate it. These worldviews establish an analogical nexus between man, nature, and society which is represented as a totality in the basic concepts of mythical powers. Because these worldviews project a totality in which everything corresponds with everything else, they subjectively attach the collective identity of the group or the tribe to the cosmic order and integrate it with the system of social institutions. In the limit case, worldviews function as a kind of drive belt that transforms the basic religious consensus into the energy of social solidarity and passes it on to social institutions, thus giving them a moral authority.

Jürgen Habermas (1987), *The Theory of Communicative Action, vol. 2: Lifeworld and System – a Critique of Functionalist Reason*, tr. Thomas McCarthy, Cambridge: Polity Press.

What is of primary interest in analyzing the interrelation between normative consensus, worldview, and institutional system, however, is that the connection is established through channels of linguistic communication. Whereas ritual actions take place at a pregrammatical level, religious worldviews are connected with full-fledged communicative actions. The situational interpretations entering into everyday communication are fed by worldviews, however archaic; worldviews can, in turn, reproduce themselves only by way of these processes of reaching understanding. In virtue of this feedback relation they have the form of cultural knowledge, a knowledge that is based on both cognitive and socially integrative experiences. In the epistemological parts of his sociology of religion, Durkheim did not entirely neglect the role of language: 'The system of concepts with which we think in everyday life is that expressed by the vocabulary of our mother tongues; for every word translates a concept.' But he rashly subsumes both the communality of normative consensus accomplished through ritual and the intersubjectivity of knowledge established through speech acts under the same concept of collective consciousness. For this reason it remains unclear how institutions draw their validity from the religious springs of social solidarity. We can resolve this problem only if we bear in mind that profane everyday practice proceeds by way of linguistically differentiated processes of reaching understanding and forces us to specify validity claims for actions appropriate to situations in the normative context of roles and institutions.[1] Communicative action is a switching station for the energies of social solidarity; Durkheim did not pay it sufficient heed.

FROM 'THE CONCEPT OF THE LIFEWORLD'

Only the limited segments of the lifeworld brought into the horizon of a situation constitute a thematizable context of action oriented to mutual understanding; only they appear under the category of *knowledge*. From a perspective turned toward the situation, the lifeworld appears as a reservoir of taken-for-granteds, of unshaken convictions that participants in communication draw upon in cooperative processes of interpretation. Single elements, specific taken-for-granteds, are, however, mobilized in the form of consensual and yet problematizable knowledge only when they become relevant to a situation.

If we now relinquish the basic concepts of the philosophy of consciousness in which Husserl dealt with the problem of the lifeworld, we can think of the lifeworld as represented by a culturally transmitted and linguistically organized stock of interpretive patterns. Then the idea of a 'context of relevance' that connects the elements of the situation with one another, and the situation with the lifeworld, need no longer be explained in the framework of a phenomenology and psychology of perception.[2] Relevance structures can be conceived instead as interconnections of meaning holding between a given communicative utterance, the immediate context, and its connotative horizon of meanings. Contexts of relevance are based on *grammatically regulated* relations among the elements of a *linguistically organized* stock of knowledge.

If, as usual in the tradition stemming from Humboldt,[3] we assume that there is an internal connection between structures of lifeworlds and structures of linguistic worldviews, language and cultural tradition take on a certain transcendental status in relation to everything that can become an element of a situation. Language and culture neither coincide with the formal world concepts by means of which participants in communication together define their situations, nor do they appear as something innerworldly. Language and culture are constitutive for the lifeworld itself. They are neither one of the formal frames, that is, the worlds to which participants assign elements of situations, nor do they appear as something in the objective, social, or subjective worlds. In performing or understanding a speech act, participants are very much moving within their language, so that they cannot bring a present utterance *before themselves* as 'something intersubjective', in the way they experience an event as something objective, encounter a pattern of behavior as something normative, experience or ascribe a desire or feeling as something subjective. The very medium of mutual understanding abides in a peculiar *half-transcendence*. So long as participants maintain their performative attitudes, the language actually in use remains *at their backs*. Speakers cannot take up an extramundane position in relation to it. The same is true of culture – of those patterns of interpretation transmitted in language. From a semantic point of view, language does have a peculiar affinity to linguistically articulated worldviews. Natural languages conserve the contents of tradition, which persist only in symbolic forms, for the most part in linguistic embodiment. For the semantic capacity of a language has to be adequate to the complexity of the stored-up cultural contents, the patterns of interpretation, valuation, and expression.

This stock of knowledge supplies members with unproblematic, common, background convictions that are assumed to be guaranteed; it is from these that contexts for processes of reaching understanding get shaped, processes in which those involved use tried and true situation definitions or negotiate new ones. Participants find the relations between the objective, social, and subjective worlds already preinterpreted. When they go beyond the horizon of a given situation, they cannot step into a void; they find themselves right away in another, now actualized, yet *preinterpreted* domain of what is culturally taken for granted. In everyday communicative practice there are no completely unfamiliar situations. Every new situation appears in a lifeworld composed of a cultural stock of knowledge that is 'always already' familiar. Communicative actors can no more take up an extramundane position in relation to their lifeworld than they can in relation to language as the medium for the processes of reaching understanding through which their lifeworld maintains itself. In drawing upon a cultural tradition, they also continue it.

The category of the lifeworld has, then, a different status than the normal world-concepts dealt with above. Together with criticizable validity claims, these latter concepts form the frame or categorial scaffolding that serves to order problematic situations – that is, situations that need to be agreed upon – in a lifeworld that is already substantively interpreted. With the formal world-concepts, speakers and hearers can qualify the possible referents of their speech acts so that they can relate to something objective, normative, or subjective. The lifeworld, by contrast, does not allow for analogous assignments; speakers and hearers cannot refer by means of it to something as 'something intersubjective'. Communicative actors are always moving *within* the horizon of their lifeworld; they cannot step outside of it. As interpreters, they themselves belong to the lifeworld, along with their speech acts, but they cannot refer to 'something in the lifeworld' in the same way as they can to facts, norms, or experiences. The structures of the lifeworld lay down the forms of the intersubjectivity of possible understanding. It is to them that participants in communication owe their extramundane positions vis-à-vis the innerworldly items about which they can come to an understanding. The lifeworld is, so to speak, the transcendental site where speaker and hearer meet, where they can reciprocally raise claims that their utterances fit the world (objective, social, or subjective), and where they can criticize and confirm those validity claims, settle their disagreements, and arrive at agreements. In a sentence: participants cannot assume *in actu* the same distance in relation to language and culture as in relation to the totality of facts, norms, or experiences concerning which mutual understanding is possible.

[...]

Communicative actors locate and date their utterances in social spaces and historical times. In the communicative practice of everyday life, persons do not only encounter one another in the attitude of participants; they also give narrative presentations of events that take place in the context of their lifeworld. *Narration* is a specialized form of constative speech that serves to describe sociocultural events and objects. Actors base their narrative presentations on a lay concept of the 'world', in the sense of the everyday world or lifeworld, which defines the totality of states of affairs that can be reported in true stories.

This everyday concept carves out of the objective world the region of narratable events or historical facts. Narrative practice not only serves trivial needs for mutual understanding among members trying to coordinate their common tasks; it also has a function in the self-understanding of persons. They have to objectivate their belonging to the lifeworld to which, in their actual roles as participants in communication, they do belong. For they can develop personal identities only if they recognize that the sequences of their own actions form narratively presentable life histories; they can develop social identities only if they recognize that they maintain their membership in social groups by way of participating in interactions, and thus that they are caught up in the narratively presentable histories of collectivities. Collectivities maintain their identities only to the extent that the ideas members have of their lifeworld overlap sufficiently and condense into unproblematic background convictions.

The lay concept of the lifeworld refers to the totality of sociocultural facts and thus provides a jumping-off point for social theory. In my view, one methodologically promising way to clarify this concept would be to analyze the form of narrative statements, as Arthur Danto was one of the first to do,[4] and to analyze the form of narrative texts. In the grammar of narratives we can see how we identify and *describe* states and events that appear in a lifeworld; how we *interlink* and *sequentially organize* into complex unities members' interactions in social spaces and historical times; how we explain the actions of individuals and the events that befall them, the acts of collectivities and the fates they meet with, from the perspective of managing situations. In adopting the narrative form, we are choosing a perspective that 'grammatically' forces us to base our descriptions on an everyday concept of the lifeworld as a *cognitive reference system*.

This intuitively accessible *concept of the sociocultural lifeworld* can be rendered theoretically fruitful if we can develop from it a reference system for descriptions and explanations relevant to the lifeworld as a whole and not merely to occurrences within it. Whereas narrative presentation refers to what is innerworldly, theoretical presentation is intended to explain the reproduction of the lifeworld itself. Individuals and groups maintain themselves by mastering situations; but how is the lifeworld, of which each situation forms only a segment, maintained? A narrator is already constrained grammatically, through the form of narrative presentation, to take an interest in the identity of the persons acting as well as in the integrity of their life-context. When we tell stories, we cannot avoid also saying indirectly how the subjects involved in them are faring, and what fate the collectivity they belong to is experiencing. Nevertheless, we can make harm to personal identity or threats to social integration visible only indirectly in narratives. While narrative presentations do point to higher-level reproduction processes – to the maintenance imperatives of lifeworlds – they cannot take as their theme the structures of a lifeworld the way they do with what happens in it. The everyday concept of the lifeworld that we bring to narrative presentation as a reference system has to be worked up for theoretical purposes in such a way as to make possible statements about the reproduction or self-maintenance of communicatively structured lifeworlds.

Whereas the lifeworld is given from the *perspective of participants* only as the horizon-forming context of an action situation, the everyday concept of the lifeworld presupposed in the *perspective of narrators* is already being used for cognitive purposes. To make it theoretically fruitful we have to start from those basic functions that, as we learned from Mead, the medium of language fulfills for the reproduction of the lifeworld. In coming to an understanding with one another about their situation, participants in interaction stand in a cultural tradition that they at once use and renew; in coordinating their actions by way of intersubjectively recognizing criticizable validity claims, they are at once relying on membership in social groups and strengthening the integration of those same groups; through participating in interactions with competently acting reference persons, the growing child internalizes the value orientations of his social group and acquires generalized capacities for action.

Under the functional aspect of *mutual understanding*, communicative action serves to transmit and renew cultural knowledge; under the aspect of *coordinating action*, it serves social integration and the establishment of solidarity; finally, under the aspect of *socialization*, communicative action serves the formation of personal identities. The symbolic structures of the lifeworld are reproduced by way of the continuation of valid knowledge, stabilization of group solidarity, and socialization of responsible actors. The process of reproduction connects up new situations with the existing conditions of the lifeworld; it does this in the *semantic* dimension of meanings or contents (of the cultural tradition), as well as in the dimensions of *social space* (of socially integrated groups), and *historical time* (of successive generations). Corresponding to these processes of *cultural reproduction, social integration*, and *socialization* are the structural components of the lifeworld; culture, society, person.

I use the term *culture* for the stock of knowledge from which participants in communication supply themselves with interpretations as they come to an understanding about something in the world. I use the term *society* for the legitimate orders through which participants regulate their memberships in social groups and thereby secure solidarity. By *personality* I understand the competences that make a subject capable of speaking and acting, that put him in a position to take part in processes of reaching understanding and thereby to assert his own identity. The dimensions in which communicative action extends comprise the semantic field of symbolic contents, social space, and historical time. The interactions woven into the fabric of every communicative practice constitute the medium through which culture, society, and person get reproduced. These reproduction processes cover the symbolic structures of the lifeworld. We have to distinguish from this the maintenance of the material substratum of the lifeworld.

Material reproduction takes place through the medium of the purposive activity with which sociated individuals intervene in the world to realize their aims. As Weber pointed out, the problems that actors have to deal with in a given situation can be divided into problems of 'inner need' and problems of 'outer need'. To these categories of tasks as viewed from the perspective of action, there correspond, when the matter is viewed from the perspective of lifeworld maintenance, processes of symbolic and material reproduction.

FROM 'THE TASKS OF A CRITICAL THEORY'

On our assumption, a considerably rationalized lifeworld is one of the initial conditions for modernization processes. It must be possible to anchor money and power in the lifeworld as media, that is, to institutionalize them by means of positive law. If these conditions are met, economic and administrative systems can be differentiated out, systems that have a complementary relation to one another and enter into interchanges with their environments via steering media. At this level of system differentiation modern societies arise, first capitalist societies, and later – setting themselves off from those – bureaucratic-socialist societies. A capitalist path of modernization opens up as soon as the economic system develops its own intrinsic dynamic of growth and, with its endogenously produced problems, takes the lead, that is, the evolutionary primacy, for society as a whole. The path of modernization runs in another direction when, on the basis of state ownership of most of the means of production and an institutionalized one-party rule, the administrative action system gains a like autonomy in relation to the economic system.

To the extent that these organizational principles are established, there arise interchange relations between the two functionally interlocked subsystems and the societal components of the lifeworld in which the media are anchored. The lifeworld, more or less relieved of tasks of material reproduction, can in turn become more differentiated in its symbolic structures and can set free the inner logic of development of cultural modernity. At the same time, the private and public spheres are now set off as the environments of the system. According to whether the economic system or the state apparatus attains evolutionary primacy, either private households or politically relevant memberships are the points of entry for crises that are shifted from the subsystems to the lifeworld. In modernized societies disturbances in the material reproduction of the lifeworld take the form of stubborn systemic disequilibria; the latter either take effect directly as *crises* or they call forth *pathologies* in the lifeworld.

Steering crises were first studied in connection with the business cycle of market economies. In bureaucratic socialism, crisis tendencies spring from self-blocking mechanisms in planning administrations, as they do on the other side from endogenous interruptions of accumulation processes. Like the paradoxes of exchange rationality, the paradoxes of planning rationality can be explained by the fact that rational action orientations come into contradiction with themselves through unintended systemic effects.

These crisis tendencies are worked through not only in the subsystem in which they arise, but also in the complementary action system into which they can be shifted. Just as the capitalist economy relies on organizational performances of the state, the socialist planning bureaucracy has to rely on self-steering performances of the economy. Developed capitalism swings between the contrary policies of 'the market's self-healing powers' and state interventionism.[5] The structural dilemma is even clearer on the other side, where policy oscillates hopelessly between increased central planning and decentralization, between orienting economic programs toward investment and toward consumption.

These *systemic disequilibria* become *crises* only when the performances of economy and state remain manifestly below an established level of aspiration and harm the symbolic reproduction of the lifeworld by calling forth conflicts and reactions of resistance there. It is the societal components of the lifeworld that are directly affected by this. Before such conflicts threaten core domains of social integration, they are pushed to the periphery – before anomic conditions arise there are appearances of withdrawal of legitimation or motivation (see Figure 5.2). But when steering crises – that is, perceived disturbances of material reproduction – are successfully intercepted by having recourse to lifeworld resources, pathologies arise in the lifeworld. These resources appear in Figure 5.1 as contributions to cultural reproduction, social integration, and socialization. For the continued existence of the economy and the state, it is the resources listed in the middle column as contributing to the maintenance of society that are relevant, for it is here, in the institutional orders of the lifeworld, that subsystems are anchored.

We can represent the replacement of steering crises with lifeworld pathologies as follows: anomic conditions are avoided, and legitimations and motivations important for maintaining institutional orders are secured, at the expense of, and through the ruthless exploitation of, other resources. Culture and personality come under attack for the sake of warding off crises and stabilizing society (first and third columns versus middle column in Figure 5.1). The consequences of this substitution can be seen in Figure 5.2. instead of manifestations of anomie (and instead of the withdrawal of legitimation and motivation in place of anomie), phenomena of alienation and the unsettling of collective identity emerge. I have traced such phenomena back to a colonization of the lifeworld and characterized them as a reification of the communicative practice of everyday life.

However, deformations of the lifeworld take the form of a reification of communicative relations only in capitalist societies, that is, only where the private household is the point of incursion for the displacement of crises into the lifeworld. This is not a question of the overextension of a single medium but of the monetarization and bureaucratization of the spheres of action of employees and of consumers, of citizens and of clients of state bureaucracies.

Structural components / Reproduction processes	Culture	Society	Personality
Cultural reproduction	Interpretive schemes fit for consensus ("valid knowledge")	Legitimations	Socialization patterns Educational goals
Social integration	Obligations	Legitimately ordered interpersonal relations	Social memberships
Socialization	Interpretive accomplishments	Motivations for actions that conform to norms	Interactive capabilities ("personal identity")

Figure 5.1. Contributions of reproduction processes to maintaining the structural components of the lifeworld.

Deformations of the lifeworld take a different form in societies in which the points of incursion for the penetration of crises into the lifeworld are politically relevant memberships. There too, in bureaucratic-socialist societies, domains of action that are dependent on social integration are switched over to mechanisms of system integration. But instead of the reification of communicative relations we find the shamming of communicative relations in bureaucratically desiccated, forcibly 'humanized' domains of pseudopolitical intercourse in an overextended and administered public sphere. This pseudopoliticization is symmetrical to reifying privatization in certain respects. The lifeworld is not directly assimilated to the system, that is, to legally regulated, formally organized domains of action; rather, systemically self-sufficient organizations are fictively put back into a simulated horizon of the lifeworld. While the system is draped out as the lifeworld, the lifeworld is absorbed by the system.[6]

Disturbances in the domain of \ Structural components	Culture	Society	Person	Dimension of evaluation
Cultural reproduction	Loss of meaning	Withdrawal of legitimation	Crisis in orientation and education	Rationality of knowledge
Social integration	Unsettling of collective identity	Anomie	Alienation	Solidarity of members
Socialization	Rupture of tradition	Withdrawal of motivation	Psychopathologies	Personal responsibility

Figure 5.2. Manifestations of crisis when reproduction processes are disturbed (pathologies).

[...]

I distinguished two sorts of media that can ease the burden of the (risky and demanding) coordinating mechanism of reaching understanding: on the one hand, steering media, via which subsystems are differentiated out of the lifeworld; on the other hand, generalized forms of communication, which do not replace reaching agreement in language but merely condense it, and thus remain tied to lifeworld contexts. Steering media uncouple the coordination of action from building consensus in language altogether and neutralize it in regard to the alternative of coming to an agreement or failing to do so. In the other case we are dealing with a specialization of linguistic processes of consensus formation that remains dependent on recourse to the resources of the lifeworld background. The mass media belong to these generalized forms of communication. They free communication processes from the provinciality of spatiotemporally restricted contexts and permit public spheres to emerge, through establishing the abstract simultaneity of a virtually present network of communication contents far removed in space and time and through keeping messages available for manifold contexts.

These media publics hierarchize and at the same time remove restrictions on the horizon of possible communication. The one aspect cannot be separated from the other – and therein lies their ambivalent potential. Insofar as mass media one-sidedly channel communication flows in a centralized network – from the center to the periphery or from above to below – they considerably strengthen the efficacy of social controls. But tapping this authoritarian potential is always precarious because there is a counterweight of emancipatory potential built into communication structures themselves. Mass media can simultaneously contextualize and concentrate processes of reaching understanding, but it is only in the first instance that they relieve interaction from yes/no responses to criticizable validity claims. Abstracted and clustered though they are, these communications cannot be reliably shielded from the possibility of opposition by responsible actors.

When communications research is not abridged in an empiricist manner and allows for dimensions of reification in communicative everyday practice,[7] it confirms this ambivalence. Again and again reception research and program analysis have provided illustrations of the theses in culture criticism that Adorno, above all, developed with a certain overstatement. In the meantime, the same energy has been put into working out the contradictions resulting from the facts that

- the broadcasting networks are exposed to competing interests; they are not able to smoothly integrate economic, political and ideological, professional and aesthetic viewpoints;[8]
- normally the mass media cannot, without generating conflict, avoid the obligations that accrue to them from their journalistic mission and the professional code of journalism;[9]
- the programs do not only, or even for the most part, reflect the standards of mass culture;[10] even when they take the trivial forms of popular entertainment, they may contain critical messages – 'popular culture as popular revenge';[11]
- ideological messages miss their audience because the intended meaning is turned into its opposite under conditions of being received against a certain subcultural background;[12]
- the inner logic of everyday communicative practice sets up defenses against the direct manipulative intervention of the mass media;[13] and
- the technical development of electronic media does not necessarily move in the direction of centralizing networks, even though 'video pluralism' and 'television democracy' are at the moment not much more than anarchist visions.[14]

[...]

My thesis concerning the colonization of the lifeworld, for which Weber's theory of societal rationalization served as a point of departure, is based on a critique of functionalist reason, which agrees with the critique of instrumental reason only in its intention and in its ironic use of the word 'reason'. One major difference is that the theory of communicative action conceives of the lifeworld as a sphere in which processes of reification do not appear as mere reflexes – as manifestations of a repressive integration emanating from an oligopolistic economy and an authoritarian state. In this respect, the earlier critical theory merely repeated the errors of Marxist functionalism.[15] My references to the socializatory relevance of the uncoupling of system and lifeworld and my remarks on the ambivalent potentials of mass media and mass culture show the private and public spheres in the light of a rationalized lifeworld in which system imperatives *clash with* independent communication structures. The transposition of communicative action to media-steered interactions and the deformation of the structures of a damaged intersubjectivity are by no means predecided processes that might be distilled from a few global concepts. The analysis of lifeworld pathologies calls for an (unbiased) investigation of tendencies *and* contradictions. The fact that in welfare-state mass democracies class conflict has been institutionalized and thereby pacified does not mean that protest potential has been altogether laid to rest. But the potentials for protest emerge now along different lines of conflict – just where we would expect them to emerge if the thesis of the colonization of the lifeworld were correct.

In the past decade or two, conflicts have developed in advanced Western societies that deviate in various ways from the welfare-state pattern of institutionalized conflict over distribution. They no longer flare up in domains of material reproduction; they are no longer channeled through parties and associations; and they can no longer be allayed by compensations. Rather, these new conflicts arise in domains of cultural reproduction, social integration, and socialization; they are carried out in sub-institutional – or at least extraparliamentary – forms of protest; and the underlying deficits reflect a reification of communicatively structured domains of action that will not respond to the media of money and power. The issue is not primarily one of compensations that the welfare state can provide, but of defending and restoring endangered ways of life. In short, the new conflicts are not ignited by distribution problems but by questions having to do with the grammar of forms of life.

This new type of conflict is an expression of the 'silent revolution' in values and attitudes that R. Inglehart has observed in entire populations.[16] Studies by Hildebrandt and Dalton, and by Barnes and Kaase, confirm the change in themes from the 'old politics' (which turns on questions of economic and social security, internal and military security) to a 'new politics'.[17]

The new problems have to do with quality of life, equal rights, individual self-realization, participation, and human rights. In terms of social statistics, the 'old politics' is more strongly supported by employers, workers, and middle-class tradesmen, whereas the new politics finds stronger support in the new middle classes, among the younger generation, and in groups with more formal education. These phenomena tally with my thesis regarding internal colonization.

If we take the view that the growth of the economic-administrative complex sets off processes of erosion in the lifeworld, then we would expect old conflicts to be overlaid with new ones. A line of conflict forms between, on the one hand, a center composed of strata *directly* involved in the production process and interested in maintaining capitalist growth as the basis of the welfare-state compromise, and, on the other hand, a periphery composed of a variegated array of groups that are lumped together. Among the latter are those groups that are further removed from the 'productivist core of performance' in late capitalist societies,[18] that have been more strongly sensitized to the self-destructive consequences of the growth in complexity or have been more strongly affected by them.[19] The bond that unites these heterogeneous groups is the critique of growth. Neither the bourgeois emancipation movements nor the struggles of the organized labor movement can serve as a model for this protest. Historical parallels are more likely to be found in the social-romantic movements of the early industrial period, which were supported by craftsmen, plebeians, and workers, in the defensive movements of the populist middle class, in the escapist movements (nourished by bourgeois critiques of civilization) undertaken by reformers, the *Wandervögel*, and the like.

NOTES

1. Parsons is critical of Durkheim on this pont. He finds no clear differentiation between the level of cultural values and the level of institutionalized values, that is, of norms related to situations via social roles. See 'Durkheim's Contribution'. See also G. Mulligan and B. Lederman, 'Social Facts and Rules of Practice'. *American Journal of Sociology* 83 (1977): 539ff.
2. E. Husserl, *Experience and Judgment* (Evanston, 1973). For a critique of the foundation in consciousness of Schutz's phenomenological ontology of the social, see Michael Theunissen, *The Other: Studies in the Social Ontology of Husserl, Heidegger, Sartre and Buber* (Cambridge, Mass., 1984), pp. 345–52.
3. L. Weisgerber, *Die Muttersprache im Aufbau unserer Kultur* (Düsseldorf, 1957); R. Hoberg, *Die Lehre vom sprachlichen Feld* (Düsseldorf, 1970); H. Gipper, *Gibt es ein sprachliches Relativitätsprinzip?* (Frankfurt, 1972).
4. Arthur Danto, *Analytical Philosophy of History* (Cambridge, 1968). See also P. Gardiner, ed., *The Philosophy of History* (Oxford, 1974). For the German discussion, see H. M. Baumgartner, *Kontinuität und Geschichte* (Frankfurt, 1972); R. Koselleck and W. Stempel, eds., *Geschichte, Ereignis und Erzählung* (Munich, 1973); K. Acham, *Analytische Geschichtsphilosophie* (Freiburg, 1974); J. Rüsen, *Für eine erneuerte Historik* (Stuttgart, 1976); H. Baumgartner and J. Rüsen, eds., *Geschichte und Theorie* (Frakfurt, 1976).

5. On the discussion of the breakdown of Keynesian economic policy in the West, see P. C. Roberts, 'The Breakdown of the Keynesian Model', *Public Interest* (1978): 20ff.; J. A. Kregel, 'From Post-Keynes to Pre-Keynes', *Social Research* 46 (1979): 212ff.; J. D. Wisman, 'Legitimation, Ideology-Critique and Economics', *Social Research* 46 (1979): 291ff.; P. Davidson, 'Post Keynesian Economics', *Public Interest* (1980): 151ff.
6. A. Arato, 'Critical Sociology and Authoritarian State Socialism', in D. Held and J. Thompson, eds., *Habermas: Critical Debates* (Cambridge, Mass., 1982), pp. 196–218.
7. C. W. Mills, *Politics, Power and People* (New York. 1963); B. Rosenberg and D. White, eds., *Mass Culture* (Glencoe, Ill., 1957); A. Gouldner, *The Dialectics of Ideology and Technology* (New York, 1976); E. Barnouw, *The Sponser* (New York, 1977); D. Smythe, 'Communications: Blind Spot of Western Marxism', *Canadian Journal of Political and Social Theory* 1 (1977); T. Gitlin, 'Media Sociology: The Dominant Paradigm', *Theory and Society* 6 (1978): 205ff.
8. D. Kellner, 'Network Television and American Society: Introduction to a Critical Theory of Television', *Theory and Society* 10 (1981); 31ff.
9. Ibid., pp. 38ff.
10. A. Singlewood, *The Myth of Mass Culture* (London, 1977).
11. D. Kellner, 'TV, Ideology and Emancipatory Popular Culture', *Socialist Review* 45 (1979): 13ff.
12. D. Kellner, 'Kulturindustrie und Massenkommunikation: Die kritische Theorie und ihre Folgen', in W. Bonss and A. Honneth, eds., *Sozialforschung als Kritik* (Frankfurt, 1982), pp. 482–515.
13. From Lazarfeld's early radio studies on the dual character of communication flows and the role of opinion leaders, the independent weight of everyday communication in relation to mass communication has been confirmed again and again: 'In the last analysis it is people talking with people more than people listening to, or reading, or looking at the mass media that really causes opinions to change.' Mills, *Power, Politics and People*, p. 590. See P. Lazarsfeld, B. Berelson, and H. Gaudet, *The People's Choice* (New York, 1948); P. Lazarsfeld and E. Katz, *Personal Influence* (New York, 1955). Compare O. Negt and A. Kluge, *Öffentlichkeit und Erfahrung* (Frankfurt, 1970), and, by the same authors, *Geschichte und Eigensinn* (Munich, 1981).
14. H. M. Enzenberger, 'Baukasten zu einer Theorie der Meiden', in *Palaver* (Frankfurt, 1974), pp. 91ff.
15. S. Benhabib, 'Modernity and the Aporias of Critical Theory', *Telos* 49 (1981): 38–60.
16. R. Inglehart, 'Wertwandel und politisches Verhalten', in J. Matthes, ed., *Sozialer Wandel in Westeuropa* (Frankfurt, 1979).
17. K. Hildebrandt and R. J. Dalton, 'Die neue Politik', *Politische Vierteljahresschrift* 18 (1977): 230ff.; S. H. Barnes, M. Kaase et al., *Political Action* (Beverly Hills/London, 1979).
18. J. Hirsch, 'Alternativbewegung: Eine politische Alternative', in R. Roth, ed., *Parlamentarisches Ritual und politische Alternativen* (Frankfurt, 1980).
19. On this point I found a manuscript by K. W. Brand very helpful: 'Zur Diskussion um Entstehung, Funktion und Perspektive der 'Ökologie- und Alternativbewegung', Munich, 1980.

Part 6

FOUCAULT: DISCOURSE, POWER AND REGULATION

INTRODUCTION

I. Knowledge and Discourse

Michel Foucault's work differs sharply from that of the other theorists covered here in that it opposes those models that place emphasis on the actions of the subject while also opposing those theories that look for underlying causes. While Foucault's work is greatly concerned with the exercise of power, he distances power relations from both the actions of subjects (the issue of who exerts power) and notions of underlying structures (such as mode of production) or centralised institutions like the state. He rejects top-down models of power as well as the model of legitimation and consensus that has been a major theme so far. This now shifts to a concern with organised practices, discourses, discipline and regulation.

Foucault's early works study social history according to changes in discourse, which is the overarching category that explains the cohesion and unity of social practices. His first book looks at the discourse of madness and reason. The foundation of the Hôpital Général in Paris is identified by Foucault as a decisive event. 'What, then, was the reality represented by this entire population which almost overnight found itself shut up, excluded more severely than the lepers?' (Foucault 1971: 45). Madness becomes an issue because it threatens the foundations of the new bourgeois order. The ambivalence towards madness in medieval society is transformed into a matter of great public concern during early bourgeois society:

> Madness was thus torn from that imaginary freedom which still allowed it to flourish on the Renaissance horizon. Not so long ago, it had

> floundered about in broad daylight: in *King Lear*, in *Don Quixote*. But in less than a half-century, it had been sequestered and, in the fortress of confinement, bound to Reason, to the rules of morality and to their monotonous nights. (Foucault 1971: 64)

But what was happening to the insane is really only part of a wider issue – the construction and maintenance of the discourse of reason. In a 'rational' social order, madness represents a kind of freedom, something that is outside that order, a radical other that is both in the social world and beyond it.

In the modern period there was a shift in emphasis from the body to the soul. The collapse of the classical discourse led to the emergence of new domains of psychology and morality and new ideas and practices concerned with diseases of the nerves. This shift is reflected in the birth of the asylum. This represents a deeper discursive shift in that the asylum is associated with a new science of mental disease based on a system of observation and classification, surveillance and judgment. Treatment of madness shifts away from physical constraint towards self-constraint. The new discourse places emphasis on the recognition of guilt and a new notion of responsibility. Self-awareness is now linked to shame, reinforced by perpetual judgement. The truth and cure of madness is located in the moral sphere and the asylum becomes 'a religious domain without religion, a domain of pure morality, of ethical uniformity' (Foucault 1971: 257).

In *The Birth of the Clinic* Foucault again shows how new social institutions and practices are bound up with the emergence of new social discourses. Medical discourse is transformed from the classical idea of a pathological essence independent of its manifestations, to the modern focus on the visible body. The appearance of the clinic is related to these reorganisations of discourse, from 'what is wrong with you?' to 'where does it hurt?' (Foucault 1976: xviii). This links to Foucault's notion of the gaze, which is that 'which establishes the individual in his irreducible quality'(Foucault 1976: xiv). The gaze determines the entire field of possible knowledge.

Eighteenth-century medicine was concerned much more with health whereas nineteenth-century medicine was regulated more in accordance with normality and in relation to a standard of functioning. The cohesion of these approaches is provided through discourse while the institution of the clinic is crucial to the maintenance of that discourse: 'The clinic figures, then, as a structure that is essential to the scientific coherence and also to the social utility and political purity of the new medical organisation' (Foucault 1976: 70).

In *The Order of Things* Foucault tries to show how 'rationality' is dependent on a discursive framework that determines what it is or is not possible to say, and what counts as truth or knowledge. This work is concerned with uncovering the laws, regulations and rules of formation of systems of thought. One discursive paradigm replaces another. The Renaissance, the classical age and the modern age are described as three distinct *epistemes*, or three distinct structures of representation, forming a cohesive unity:

> By *episteme*, we mean, in fact, the total set of relations that unite, at a given period, the discursive practices that give rise to epistemological figures, sciences, and possibly formalised systems... The episteme is not a form of knowledge (*connaissance*) or type of rationality... it is the totality of relations that can be discovered, for a given period, between the sciences when one analyses them at the level of discursive regularities. (Foucault 1989a: 191)

The episteme is a structure of knowledge which determines the way the world is experienced or seen. The classical episteme was organised such that representation was at its centre. This involves the idea of universal measurement and classification. Language is seen as transparent and unproblematic in the way it performs its function of representation. There is a coherence in the classical episteme between the theory of representation, the theory of language, the theory of a natural order and theories of wealth and value. In the classical age, the attempt at a universal method, the system of classification and the process of representation mirror the order of things in the world.

Whereas the classical episteme had no place for the human subject, the modern makes it central. In place of universal classification, certainty, and the infinity of God's cosmology, there emerges a new humanist paradigm, an anthropological episteme founded on human finitude through which history unfolds. The human subject is now trapped within language, life and labour and knowledge becomes finite. The new human sciences and disciplines such as political economy stress the importance of human labour. The nineteenth century brings with it a new kind of reasoning that throws into question the form of truth and the form of being and this is again related to the question of representation:

> The end of Classical thought – and of the *episteme* that made general grammar, natural history, and the science of wealth possible – will coincide with the decline of representation, or rather with the emancipation of language, of the living being, and of need, with regard to representation. (Foucault 1974: 209)

In *The Archaeology of Knowledge* Foucault develops the concept of the archive, which refers to the general conditions of possibility that makes knowledge possible in any given period. It is not so much a condition for the validity of statements but a condition for their reality. Discursive relations offer discourse objects of which it can speak; they determine what discourse must establish in order to speak of this or that object. Foucault calls this system a discursive formation:

> Whenever one can describe, between a number of statements, such a system of dispersion, whenever, between objects, types of statement, concepts, or thematic choices, one can define a regularity (an order, correlations, positions and functionings, transformations), we will say . . . we are dealing with a *discursive formation* . . . The rules of formation are conditions of existence (but also of coexistence, maintenance, modification, and disappearance) in a given discursive division. (Foucault 1989a: 38)

The social-institutional field only becomes meaningful once articulated within a discursive formation. In Foucault's early work the unity and cohesion of the social is provided, first by discourse, then by the episteme and now by the discursive formation. It is not the individual that gives discourse meaning but the discursive formation that provides an array of subject positions that individuals occupy. Foucault leaves very little room, therefore, for agency. So little room, in fact, that it is impossible to speak of social consent or consensus. Agents simply do not have this option; they are the more or less passive constructs of discourse. Their needs, wants, ideas, values and actions are entirely the product of the dominant discourse. This does not mean, however, that social cohesion is entirely guaranteed. Although discourses provide cohesion, the discursive system is always open to change. Foucault is willing to speak of discontinuities, ruptures and gaps and the replacement of one exhausted episteme or discursive formation by another. But these changes are the product of structural breakdowns and crises, not the result of human actions. It is only in Foucault's middle period that an extremely limited and one-sided account of human action emerges.

II. POWER AND DISCIPLINE

Foucault's work shifts emphasis from discourse to practice and then again to the effects of power. In the works on punishment and sexuality printed here there is an emphasis on the strategies, techniques and disciplines that power exercises on the body. *Discipline and Punish* examines the shift from centralised and overt repression and punishment to more covert and dispersed forms of authority, surveillance and judgment. The book opens with the spectacular execution of Damiens, highlighting the way in which public executions would serve to emphasise the power of the sovereign over wrongdoers. Public execution functions to visibly restore the power of sovereignty; it is a ritual showing 'the physical strength of the sovereign beating down upon the body of his adversary and mastering it' (Foucault 1979: 49).

Later there is a shift from the notion of revenge to the idea of appropriate punishment. Crime is no longer regarded as a direct attack on the sovereign, but is seen as a threat to wider society and to social norms. Foucault sees this process as one of training the body in that the body is caught up in a system of constraints, privations, obligations and prohibitions, getting the subject to conform to norms of social behaviour and thought, and a set of standards and values.

These changes, rather than representing a more humane approach, have more to do with the need for a more accurate, efficient, controllable, calculable system. Foucault sees the body as a political field invested with power relations and connected to a range of discourses, practices, institutions and social bodies. The agents of this society combine the functions of normality and surveillance: 'The judges of normality are present everywhere. We are in the society of the teacher-judge, the doctor-judge, the educator-judge, the 'social-worker'-judge; it is on them that the universal reign of the normative is based' (Foucault 1979: 304). Discipline is achieved through surveillance, delegation of supervision, hierarchic observation, normalising judgement and examination. Such processes of normalisation are related to social cohesion in the sense of imposing homogeneity and uniformity of thought, action and behaviour. Part of the disciplinary strategy involves techniques of segregation, the control of activities through careful scheduling and enforcement of regular behaviour. The prison controls the spatial-temporal body and represents an apparatus intended to render criminals docile and useful. The prison uses measures of repression and punishment, but it also sets itself the task of educating the prisoner in the interests of society. It uses a specialist staff that has the moral qualities and technical abilities appropriate to this educative function.

Foucault discusses the Panopticon, which subjects its inmates to the possibility of permanent surveillance and produces in the inmate a permanent, conscious visibility. This is important in 'normalising' the behaviour of the inmate, for it is not direct coercion, but rather the fear of observation, that forces the inmate to impose self-discipline and regulate their behaviour. Although such discussions are set within the context of the institution of prison, clearly such issues as disciplinary techniques and surveillance can be applied to social order in a wider sense.

III. Sexuality

In the first volume of *The History of Sexuality* Foucault shows how a discourse of sex develops and how this is linked to rationality and morality. Those who talked about sex wanted to analyse and classify it: 'Sex was not something one simply judged; it was a thing one administered. It was in the nature of a public potential; it called for management procedures; it had to be taken charge of by analytical discourses' (Foucault 1981: 24). The Victorians, rather than imposing a silence on sexual matters, develop new discourses and ways of talking about sex. Classification set standards by which deviations from the sexual norm could be judged. The issue of sexuality should be seen as related to wider consciousness of the body, political technologies of life, and the discipline and regulation, administration and government of people and populations. Foucault uses the term 'bio-power' to describe these issues that concern the wider social body – the questions concerning population, public health, birth control and marriage. These issues all relate to the development of a capitalist society and processes of industrialisation and urbanisation.

The discourse around sex makes it possible to group together in some sort of unity different anatomical elements, biological functions, sensations and pleasures, as well as social issues such as reproduction and birth control. The need to form a labour force demands a more open discussion of working-class sex. Sex emerges as a tool for disciplining the population, harnessing and intensifying the distribution of forces, establishing an economy of energies. Bio-power is subtle and all-encompassing with its strategies of control, routinisation of conduct, surveillance and normalising judgement.

The human body is at the centre of power struggles, and the way in which disciplinary techniques act upon the body indicates a micro-physics of power:

> The study of this micro-physics presupposes that the power exercised on the body is conceived not as a property, but as a strategy, that its effects of domination are attributed not to 'appropriation', but to dispositions, manoeuvres, tactics, techniques, functionings . . . In short this power is exercised rather than possessed; it is not the 'privilege', acquired or preserved, of the dominant class, but the overall effect of its strategic positions. (Foucault 1979: 26)

Again, it is stressed that this is a power that operates through bodies, not upon them. This is captured by the notion of capillary power that operates from below and runs through people rather than being imposed from above. Power is exercised rather than possessed. Domination is far-reaching but never fully stable. The social is a terrain of continual strategic interaction and struggle and it is argued that where there is power there is opposition.

Power and knowledge are bound together. It is not that one acts upon the other, but '[that] power and knowledge directly imply one another; that there is no power relation without the correlative constitution of a field of knowledge, nor any knowledge that does not presuppose and constitute at the same time power relations' (Foucault 1979: 27).

IV. Governmentality and the Self

The final extract, by Barry, Osborne and Rose, provides a summary of some of Foucault's ideas as well as introducing his theory of governmentality. The governmentality approach challenges the traditional model of sovereign authority and focuses instead on a network of different institutions and practices. Power operates not from a single source such as the state, but through a set of procedures and techniques. The governmentality approach starts from the micro level, where power is a part of our everyday routines and practices. These are appropriated by macro powers and interests such as the state or the ruling class, who utilise what already exists, adopting, adapting and developing them for their own purposes.

Foucault is opposed to the view that the state is a central institution that imposes its power from above. The state is not a single unified body but a composite reality connected to a wider and more dispersed range of powers that operate through networks rather than some centralised institution.

> The state is superstructural in relation to a whole series of power networks that invest the body, sexuality, the family, kinship, knowledge, technology, and so forth. . . . This metapower with its prohibitions can only take hold and secure its footing where it is rooted in a whole series of multiple and indefinite power relations that supply the necessary basis for the great negative forms of power. (Foucault 2001: 123)

Foucault rejects the traditional view that power is legitimate if it is based on consent. Disciplinary power is responsible for social cohesion without having to rely on achieving consent. Foucault's critique of the notion of consent is also bound up with his rejection of the sovereignty model, which focuses its attention on the role of the state. Sovereignty, for Foucault, is too narrow a concept and it is necessary to distinguish it from the mechanisms of governmentality, which are much wider. Governmentality is about the regulation of conduct using various technical means and encouraging individuals to regulate themselves. In presenting this alternative model, Foucault distinguishes between the practical rationality of government and the normative basis of sovereignty.

Rejection of the traditional model of state and sovereignty also implies rejection of the kind of domination/dominated schema that we have found in the writings of the other authors we have covered. Domination is the hegemonic effect of a multiplicity of micro powers. This allows for the possibility of multiple resistances. Foucault's late works start to move away from the more negative view of power with its one-sided focus on the institutional basis of power. There is a shift in focus towards power in relation to the subject. There is an interplay between power and freedom as individuals struggle against imposed identities:

> If power were never anything but repressive, if it never did anything but to say no, do you really think one would be brought to obey it? What makes power hold good, what makes it accepted, is simply the fact that it doesn't only weigh on us as a force that says no; it also traverses and produces things, it induces pleasure, forms knowledge, produces discourse. It needs to be considered as a productive network that runs through the instance whose function is repression. (Foucault 2001: 120)

This allows more space the self. Power may constrain individuals but it also constitutes the conditions of possibility for their freedom. Power is not just an objectifying force (producing docile bodies) but is also a source of subjectivity providing a basis on which opposition and resistance can develop. Politically this means an ethics of the self. Foucault makes a third shift in his final works in order to analyse the subject and 'the games of truth by which man proposes to think his own nature' (Foucault 1985: 7).

FROM 'THE CARCERAL'

Michel Foucault

We have seen that, in penal justice, the prison transformed the punitive procedure into a penitentiary technique; the carceral archipelago transported this technique from the penal institution to the entire social body. With several important results.

1. This vast mechanism established a slow, continuous, imperceptible gradation that made it possible to pass naturally from disorder to offence and back from a transgression of the law to a slight departure from a rule, an average, a demand, a norm. In the classical period, despite a certain common reference to offence in general,[1] the order of the crime, the order of sin and the order of bad conduct remained separate in so far as they related to separate criteria and authorities (court, penitence, confinement). Incarceration with its mechanisms of surveillance and punishment functioned, on the contrary, according to a principle of relative continuity. The continuity of the institutions themselves, which were linked to one another (public assistance with the orphanage, the reformitory, the penitentiary, the disciplinary battalion, the prison; the school with the charitable society, the workshop, the almshouse, the penitentiary convent; the workers' estate with the hospital and the prison). A continuity of the punitive criteria and mechanisms, which on the basis of a mere deviation gradually strengthened the rules and increased the punishment. A continuous gradation of the established, specialized and competent authorities (in the order of knowledge and in the

Michel Foucault (1979), 'The carceral', in *Discipline and Punish: The Birth of the Prison*, tr. Alan Sheridan, Harmondsworth: Penguin.

order of power) which, without resort to arbitrariness, but strictly according to the regulations, by means of observation and assessment hierarchized, differentiated, judged, punished and moved gradually from the correction of irregularities to the punishment of crime. The 'carceral' with its many diffuse or compact forms, its institutions of supervision or constraint, of discreet surveillance and insistent coercion, assured the communication of punishments according to quality and quantity; it connected in series or disposed according to subtle divisions the minor and the serious penalties, the mild and the strict forms of treatment, bad marks and light sentences. You will end up in the convict-ship, the slightest indiscipline seems to say; and the harshest of prisons says to the prisoners condemned to life: I shall note the slightest irregularity in your conduct. The generality of the punitive function that the eighteenth century sought in the 'ideological' technique of representations and signs now had as its support the extension, the material framework, complex, dispersed, but coherent, of the various carceral mechanisms. As a result, a certain significant generality moved between the least irregularity and the greatest crime; it was no longer the offence, the attack on the common interest, it was the departure from the norm, the anomaly; it was this that haunted the school, the court, the asylum or the prison. It generalized in the sphere of meaning the function that the carceral generalized in the sphere of tactics. Replacing the adversary of the sovereign, the social enemy was transformed into a deviant, who brought with him the multiple danger of disorder, crime and madness. The carceral network linked, through innumerable relations, the two long, multiple series of the punitive and the abnormal.

2. The carceral, with its far-reaching networks, allows the recruitment of major 'delinquents'. It organizes what might be called 'disciplinary careers' in which, through various exclusions and rejections, a whole process is set in motion. In the classical period, there opened up in the confines or interstices of society the confused, tolerant and dangerous domain of the 'outlaw' or at least of that which eluded the direct hold of power: an uncertain space that was for criminality a training ground and a region of refuge; there poverty, unemployment, pursued innocence, cunning, the struggle against the powerful, the refusal of obligations and laws, and organized crime all came together as chance and fortune would dictate; it was the domain of adventure that Gil Blas, Sheppard or Mandrin, each in his own way, inhabited. Through the play of disciplinary differentiations and divisions, the nineteenth century constructed rigorous channels which, within the system, inculcated docility and produced delinquency by the same mechanisms. There was a sort of disciplinary 'training', continuous and compelling, that had something of the pedagogical curriculum and something of the professional network. Careers emerged from it, as secure, as predictable, as those of public life: assistance associations, residential apprenticeships, penal colonies, disciplinary battalions, prisons, hospitals,

almshouses. These networks were already well mapped out at the beginning of the nineteenth century: 'Our benevolent establishments present an admirably coordinated whole by means of which the indigent does not remain a moment without help from the cradle to the grave. Follow the course of the unfortunate man: you will see him born among foundlings; from there he passes to the nursery, then to an orphanage; at the age of six he goes off to primary school and later to adult schools. If he cannot work, he is placed on the list of the charity offices of his district, and if he falls ill he may choose between twelve hospitals . . . Lastly, when the poor Parisian reaches the end of his career, seven almshouses await his age and often their salubrious régime has prolonged his useless days well beyond those of the rich man' (Moreau de Jonnès, quoted in Touquet).

The carceral network does not cast the unassimilable into a confused hell; there is no outside. It takes back with one hand what it seems to exclude with the other. It saves everything, including what it punishes. It is unwilling to waste even what it has decided to disqualify. In this panoptic society of which incarceration is the omnipresent armature, the delinquent is not outside the law; he is, from the very outset, in the law, at the very heart of the law, or at least in the midst of those mechanisms that transfer the individual imperceptibly from discipline to the law, from deviation to offence. Although it is true that prison punishes delinquency, delinquency is for the most part produced in and by an incarceration which, ultimately, prison perpetuates in its turn. The prison is merely the natural consequence, no more than a higher degree, of that hierarchy laid down step by step. The delinquent is an institutional product. It is no use being surprised, therefore, that in a considerable proportion of cases the biography of convicts passes through all these mechanisms and establishments, whose purpose, it is widely believed, is to lead away from prison. That one should find in them what one might call the index of an irrepressibly delinquent 'character': the prisoner condemned to hard labour was meticulously produced by a childhood spent in a reformatory, according to the lines of force of the generalized carceral system. Conversely, the lyricism of marginality may find inspiration in the image of the 'outlaw', the great social nomad, who prowls on the confines of a docile, frightened order. But it is not on the fringes of society and through successive exiles that criminality is born, but by means of ever more closely placed insertions, under ever more insistent surveillance, by an accumulation of disciplinary coercion. In short, the carceral archipelago assures, in the depths of the social body, the formation of delinquency on the basis of subtle illegalities, the overlapping of the latter by the former and the establishment of a specified criminality.

3. But perhaps the most important effect of the carceral system and of its extension well beyond legal imprisonment is that it succeeds in making the power to punish natural and legitimate, in lowering at least the threshold of tolerance to penality. It tends to efface what may be exorbitant in the

exercise of punishment. It does this by playing the two registers in which it is deployed – the legal register of justice and the extra-legal register of discipline – against one another. In effect, the great continuity of the carceral system throughout the law and its sentences gives a sort of legal sanction to the disciplinary mechanisms, to the decisions and judgements that they enforce. Throughout this network, which comprises so many 'regional' institutions, relatively autonomous and independent, is transmitted, with the 'prison-form', the model of justice itself. The regulations of the disciplinary establishments may reproduce the law, the punishments imitate the verdicts and penalties, the surveillance repeat the police model; and, above all these multiple establishments, the prison, which in relation to them is a pure form, unadulterated and unmitigated, gives them a sort of official sanction. The carceral, with its long gradation stretching from the convict-ship or imprisonment with hard labour to diffuse, slight limitations, communicates a type of power that the law validates and that justice uses as its favourite weapon. How could the disciplines and the power that functions in them appear arbitrary, when they merely operate the mechanisms of justice itself, even with a view to mitigating their intensity? When, by generalizing its effects and transmitting it to every level, it makes it possible to avoid its full rigour? Carceral continuity and the fusion of the prison-form make it possible to legalize, or in any case to legitimate disciplinary power, which thus avoids any element of excess or abuse it may entail.

But, conversely, the carceral pyramid gives to the power to inflict legal punishment a context in which it appears to be free of all excess and all violence. In the subtle gradation of the apparatuses of discipline and of the successive 'embeddings' that they involve, the prison does not at all represent the unleashing of a different kind of power, but simply an additional degree in the intensity of a mechanism that has continued to operate since the earliest forms of legal punishment. Between the latest institution of 'rehabilitation', where one is taken in order to avoid prison, and the prison where one is sent after a definable offence, the difference is (and must be) scarcely perceptible. There is a strict economy that has the effect of rendering as discreet as possible the singular power to punish. There is nothing in it now that recalls the former excess of sovereign power when it revenged its authority on the tortured body of those about to be executed. Prison continues, on those who are entrusted to it, a work begun elsewhere, which the whole of society pursues on each individual through innumerable mechanisms of discipline. By means of a carceral continuum, the authority that sentences infiltrates all those other authorities that supervise, transform, correct, improve. It might even be said that nothing really distinguishes them any more except the singularly 'dangerous' character of the delinquents, the gravity of their departures from normal behaviour and the necessary solemnity of the ritual. But, in its function, the power to punish is not essentially different from that of curing or educating. It receives from them, and from their lesser, smaller task, a sanction from below; but one that is no less important for that, since it is the sanction of technique and rationality. The carceral 'naturalizes' the legal power to punish, as it 'legalizes' the technical power to discipline. In thus homogenizing them, effacing what may be violent in one and arbitrary in the other, attenuating the effects of revolt that they may both arouse, thus depriving excess in either of any purpose, circulating the same calculated, mechanical and discreet methods from one to the other, the carceral makes it possible to carry out that great 'economy' of power whose formula the eighteenth century had sought, when the problem of the accumulation and useful administration of men first emerged.

By operating at every level of the social body and by mingling ceaselessly the art of rectifying and the right to punish, the universality of the carceral lowers the level from which it becomes natural and acceptable to be punished. The question is often posed as to how, before and after the Revolution, a new foundation was given to the right to punish. And no doubt the answer is to be found in the theory of the contract. But it is perhaps more important to ask the reverse question: how were people made to accept the power to punish, or quite simply, when punished, tolerate being so. The theory of the contract can only answer this question by the fiction of a juridical subject giving to others the power to exercise over him the right that he himself possesses over them. It is highly probable that the great carceral continuum, which provides a communication between the power of discipline and the power of the law, and extends without interruption from the smallest coercions to the longest penal detention, constituted the technical and real, immediately material counterpart of that chimerical granting of the right to punish.

4. With this new economy of power, the carceral system, which is its basic instrument, permitted the emergence of a new form of 'law': a mixture of legality and nature, prescription and constitution, the norm. This had a whole series of effects: the internal dislocation of the judicial power or at least of its functioning; an increasing difficulty in judging, as if one were ashamed to pass sentence; a furious desire on the part of the judges to judge, assess, diagnose, recognize the normal and abnormal and claim the honour of curing or rehabilitating. In view of this, it is useless to believe in the good or bad consciences of judges, or even of their unconscious. Their immense 'appetite for medicine' which is constantly manifested – from their appeal to psychiatric experts, to their attention to the chatter of criminology – expresses the major fact that the power they exercise has been 'denatured'; that it is at a certain level governed by laws; that at another, more fundamental level it functions as a normative power; it is the economy of power that they exercise, and not that of their scruples or their humanism, that makes them pass 'therapeutic' sentences and recommend 'rehabilitating' periods of imprisonment. But, conversely, if the judges accept ever more

reluctantly to condemn for the sake of condemning, the activity of judging has increased precisely to the extent that the normalizing power has spread. Borne along by the omnipresence of the mechanisms of discipline, basing itself on all the carceral apparatuses, it has become one of the major functions of our society. The judges of normality are present everywhere. We are in the society of the teacher-judge, the doctor-judge, the educator-judge, the 'social worker'-judge; it is on them that the universal reign of the normative is based; and each individual, wherever he may find himself, subjects to it his body, his gestures, his behaviour, his aptitudes, his achievements. The carceral network, in its compact or disseminated forms, with its systems of insertion, distribution, surveillance, observation, has been the greatest support, in modern society, of the normalizing power.

5. The carceral texture of society assures both the real capture of the body and its perpetual observation; it is, by its very nature, the apparatus of punishment that conforms most completely to the new economy of power and the instrument for the formation of knowledge that this very economy needs. Its panoptic functioning enables it to play this double role. By virtue of its methods of fixing, dividing, recording, it has been one of the simplest, crudest, also most concrete, but perhaps most indispensable conditions for the development of this immense activity of examination that has objectified human behaviour. If, after the age of 'inquisitorial' justice, we have entered the age of 'examinatory' justice, if, in an even more general way, the method of examination has been able to spread so widely throughout society, and to give rise in part to the sciences of man, one of the great instruments for this has been the multiplicity and close overlapping of the various mechanisms of incarceration. I am not saying that the human sciences emerged from the prison. But, if they have been able to be formed and to produce so many profound changes in the episteme, it is because they have been conveyed by a specific and new modality of power: a certain policy of the body, a certain way of rendering the group of men docile and useful. This policy required the involvement of definite relations of knowledge in relations of power; it called for a technique of overlapping subjection and objectification; it brought with it new procedures of individualization. The carceral network constituted one of the armatures of this power-knowledge that has made the human sciences historically possible. Knowable man (soul, individuality, consciousness, conduct, whatever it is called) is the object-effect of this analytical investment, of this domination-observation.

6. This no doubt explains the extreme solidity of the prison, that slight invention that was nevertheless decried from the outset. If it had been no more than an instrument of rejection or repression in the service of a state apparatus, it would have been easier to alter its more overt forms or to find a more acceptable substitute for it. But, rooted as it was in mechanisms and strategies of power, it could meet any attempt to transform it with a great force of inertia. One fact is characteristic: when it is a question of altering

the system of imprisonment, opposition does not come from the judicial institutions alone; resistance is to be found not in the prison as penal sanction, but in the prison with all its determinations, links and extra-judicial results; in the prison as the relay in a general network of disciplines and surveillances; in the prison as it functions in a panoptic régime. This does not mean that it cannot be altered, nor that it is once and for all indispensable to our kind of society. One may, on the contrary, site the two processes which, in the very continuity of the processes that make the prison function, are capable of exercising considerable restraint on its use and of transforming its internal functioning. And no doubt these processes have already begun to a large degree. The first is that which reduces the utility (or increases its inconveniences) of a delinquency accommodated as a specific illegality, locked up and supervised; thus the growth of great national or international illegalities directly linked to the political and economic apparatuses (financial illegalities, information services, arms and drugs trafficking, property speculation) makes it clear that the somewhat rustic and conspicuous work force of delinquency is proving ineffective; or again, on a smaller scale, as soon as the economic levy on sexual pleasure is carried out more efficiently by the sale of contraceptives, or obliquely through publications, films or shows, the archaic hierarchy of prostitution loses much of its former usefulness. The second process is the growth of the disciplinary networks, the multiplication of their exchanges with the penal apparatus, the ever more important powers that are given them, the ever more massive transference to them of judicial functions; now, as medicine, psychology, education, public assistance, 'social work' assume an ever greater share of the powers of supervision and assessment, the penal apparatus will be able, in turn, to become medicalized, psychologized, educationalized; and by the same token that turning-point represented by the prison becomes less useful when, through the gap between its penitentiary discourse and its effect of consolidating delinquency, it articulates the penal power and the disciplinary power. In the midst of all these mechanisms of normalization, which are becoming ever more rigorous in their application, the specificity of the prison and its role as link are losing something of their purpose.

If there is an overall political issue around the prison, it is not therefore whether it is to be corrective or not; whether the judges, the psychiatrists or the sociologists are to exercise more power in it than the administrators or supervisors; it is not even whether we should have prison or something other than prison. At present, the problem lies rather in the steep rise in the use of these mechanisms of normalization and the wide-ranging powers which, through the proliferation of new disciplines, they bring with them.

In 1836, a correspondent wrote to *La Phalange*: 'Moralists, philosophers, legislators, flatterers of civilization, this is the plan of your Paris, neatly ordered and arranged, here is the improved plan in which all like things are gathered together. At the centre, and within a first enclosure: hospitals for all diseases, almshouses for all types of poverty, madhouses, prisons, convict-prisons for men, women and children. Around the first enclosure, barracks, courtrooms, police stations, houses for prison warders, scaffolds, houses for the executioner and his assistants. At the four corners, the Chamber of Deputies, the Chamber of Peers, the Institute and the Royal Palace. Outside, there are the various services that supply the central enclosure, commerce, with its swindlers and its bankruptcies; industry and its furious struggles; the press, with its sophisms; the gambling dens; prostitution, the people dying of hunger or wallowing in debauchery, always ready to lend an ear to the voice of the Genius of Revolutions; the heartless rich . . . Lastly the ruthless war of all against all' (*La Phalange*, 10 August 1836).

I shall stop with this anonymous text. We are now far away from the country of tortures, dotted with wheels, gibbets, gallows, pillories; we are far, too, from that dream of the reformers, less than fifty years before: the city of punishments in which a thousand small theatres would have provided an endless multicoloured representation of justice in which the punishments, meticulously produced on decorative scaffolds, would have constituted the permanent festival of the penal code. The carceral city, with its imaginary 'geo-politics', is governed by quite different principles. The extract from *La Phalange* reminds us of some of the more important ones: that at the centre of this city, and as if to hold it in place, there is, not the 'centre of power', not a network of forces, but a multiple network of diverse elements – walls, space, institution, rules, discourse; that the model of the carceral city is not, therefore, the body of the king, with the powers that emanate from it, nor the contractual meeting of wills from which a body that was both individual and collective was born, but a strategic distribution of elements of different natures and levels.

METHOD

Michel Foucault

Hence the objective is to analyze a certain form of knowledge regarding sex, not in terms of repression or law, but in terms of power. But the word *power* is apt to lead to a number of misunderstandings – misunderstandings with respect to its nature, its form, and its unity. By power, I do not mean 'Power' as a group of institutions and mechanisms that ensure the subservience of the citizens of a given state. By power, I do not mean, either, a mode of subjugation which, in contrast to violence, has the form of the rule. Finally, I do not have in mind a general system of domination exerted by one group over another, a system whose effects, through successive derivations, pervade the entire social body. The analysis, made in terms of power, must not assume that the sovereignty of the state, the form of the law, or the over-all unity of a domination are given at the outset; rather, these are only the terminal forms power takes. It seems to me that power must be understood in the first instance as the multiplicity of force relations immanent in the sphere in which they operate and which constitute their own organization; as the process which, through ceaseless struggles and confrontations, transforms, strengthens, or reverses them; as the support which these force relations find in one another, thus forming a chain or a system, or on the contrary, the disjunctions and contradictions which isolate them from one another; and lastly, as the strategies in which they take effect, whose general design or institutional crystallization is embodied in the state apparatus, in the

Michel Foucault (1981), 'Method', in *A History of Sexuality, vol. 1: An Introduction*, tr. Robert Hurley, Harmondsworth: Penguin.

formulation of the law, in the various social hegemonies. Power's condition of possibility, or in any case the viewpoint which permits one to understand its exercise, even in its more 'peripheral' effects, and which also makes it possible to use its mechanisms as a grid of intelligibility of the social order, must not be sought in the primary existence of a central point, in a unique source of sovereignty from which secondary and descendent forms would emanate; it is the moving substrate of force relations which, by virtue of their inequality, constantly engender states of power, but the latter are always local and unstable. The omnipresence of power: not because it has the privilege of consolidating everything under its invincible unity, but because it is produced from one moment to the next, at every point, or rather in every relation from one point to another. Power is everywhere; not because it embraces everything, but because it comes from everywhere. And 'Power', insofar as it is permanent, repetitious, inert, and self-reproducing, is simply the over-all effect that emerges from all these mobilities, the concatenation that rests on each of them and seeks in turn to arrest their movement. One needs to be nominalistic, no doubt: power is not an institution, and not a structure; neither is it a certain strength we are endowed with; it is the name that one attributes to a complex strategical situation in a particular society.

Should we turn the expression around, then, and say that politics is war pursued by other means? If we still wish to maintain a separation between war and politics, perhaps we should postulate rather that this multiplicity of force relations can be coded – in part but never totally – either in the form of 'war', or in the form of 'politics'; this would imply two different strategies (but the one always liable to switch into the other) for integrating these unbalanced, heterogeneous, unstable, and tense force relations.

Continuing this line of discussion, we can advance a certain number of propositions:

- Power is not something that is acquired, seized, or shared, something that one holds on to or allows to slip away; power is exercised from innumerable points, in the interplay of nonegalitarian and mobile relations.
- Relations of power are not in a position of exteriority with respect to other types of relationships (economic processes, knowledge relationships, sexual relations), but are immanent in the latter; they are the immediate effects of the divisions, inequalities, and disequilibriums which occur in the latter, and conversely they are the internal conditions of these differentiations; relations of power are not in superstructural positions, with merely a role of prohibition or accompaniment; they have a directly productive role, wherever they come into play.
- Power comes from below; that is, there is no binary and all-encompassing opposition between rulers and ruled at the root of

power relations, and serving as a general matrix – no such duality extending from the top down and reacting on more and more limited groups to the very depths of the social body. One must suppose rather that the manifold relationships of force that take shape and come into play in the machinery of production, in families, limited groups, and institutions, are the basis for wide-ranging effects of cleavage that run through the social body as a whole. These then form a general line of force that traverses the local oppositions and links them together; to be sure, they also bring about redistributions, realignments, homogenizations, serial arrangements, and convergences of the force relations. Major dominations are the hegemonic effects that are sustained by all these confrontations.

- Power relations are both intentional and nonsubjective. If in fact they are intelligible, this is not because they are the effect of another instance that 'explains' them, but rather because they are imbued, through and through, with calculation: there is no power that is exercised without a series of aims and objectives. But this does not mean that it results from the choice or decision of an individual subject; let us not look for the headquarters that presides over its rationality; neither the caste which governs, nor the groups which control the state apparatus, nor those who make the most important economic decisions direct the entire network of power that functions in a society (and makes *it* function); the rationality of power is characterized by tactics that are often quite explicit at the restricted level where they are inscribed (the local cynicism of power), tactics which, becoming connected to one another, attracting and propagating one another, but finding their base of support and their condition elsewhere, end by forming comprehensive systems: the logic is perfectly clear, the aims decipherable, and yet it is often the case that no one is there to have invented them, and few who can be said to have formulated them: an implicit characteristic of the great anonymous, almost unspoken strategies which coordinate the loquacious tactics whose 'inventors' or decisionmakers are often without hypocrisy.
- Where there is power, there is resistance, and yet, or rather consequently, this resistance is never in a position of exteriority in relation to power. Should it be said that one is always 'inside' power, there is no 'escaping' it, there is no absolute outside where it is concerned, because one is subject to the law in any case? Or that, history being the ruse of reason, power is the ruse of history, always emerging the winner? This would be to misunderstand the strictly relational character of power relationships. Their existence depends on a multiplicity of points of resistance: these play the role of adversary, target, support, or handle in power relations. These points of resistance are present everywhere in the power network. Hence there is no single

> locus of great Refusal, no soul of revolt, source of all rebellions, or pure law of the revolutionary. Instead there is a plurality of resistances, each of them a special case: resistances that are possible, necessary, improbable; others that are spontaneous, savage, solitary, concerted, rampant, or violent; still others that are quick to compromise, interested, or sacrificial; by definition, they can only exist in the strategic field of power relations. But this does not mean that they are only a reaction or rebound, forming with respect to the basic domination an underside that is in the end always passive, doomed to perpetual defeat. Resistances do not derive from a few heterogeneous principles; but neither are they a lure or a promise that is of necessity betrayed. They are the odd term in relations of power; they are inscribed in the latter as an irreducible opposite. Hence they too are distributed in irregular fashion: the points, knots, or focuses of resistance are spread over time and space at varying densities, at times mobilizing groups or individuals in a definitive way, inflaming certain points of the body, certain moments in life, certain types of behavior. Are there no great radical ruptures, massive binary divisions, then? Occasionally, yes. But more often one is dealing with mobile and transitory points of resistance, producing cleavages in a society that shift about, fracturing unities and effecting regroupings, furrowing across individuals themselves, cutting them up and remolding them, marking off irreducible regions in them, in their bodies and minds. Just as the network of power relations ends by forming a dense web that passes through apparatuses and institutions, without being exactly localized in them, so too the swarm of points of resistance traverses social stratifications and individual unities. And it is doubtless the strategic codification of these points of resistance that makes a revolution possible, somewhat similar to the way in which the state relies on the institutional integration of power relationships.

It is in this sphere of force relations that we must try to analyze the mechanisms of power. In this way we will escape from the system of Law-and-Sovereign which has captivated political thought for such a long time. And if it is true that Machiavelli was among the few – and this no doubt was the scandal of his 'cynicism' – who conceived the power of the Prince in terms of force relationships, perhaps we need to go one step further, do without the persona of the Prince, and decipher power mechanisms on the basis of a strategy that is immanent in force relationships.

To return to sex and the discourses of truth that have taken charge of it, the question that we must address, then, is not: Given a specific state structure, how and why is it that power needs to establish a knowledge of sex? Neither is the question: What over-all domination was served by the concern, evidenced since the eighteenth century, to produce true discourses on sex? Nor is it: What law presided over both the regularity of sexual behavior and the conformity of what was said about it? It is rather: In a specific type of discourse on sex, in a specific form of extortion of truth, appearing historically and in specific places (around the child's body, apropos of women's sex, in connection with practices restricting births, and so on), what were the most immediate, the most local power relations at work? How did they make possible these kinds of discourses, and conversely, how were these discourses used to support power relations? How was the action of these power relations modified by their very exercise, entailing a strengthening of some terms and a weakening of others, with effects of resistance and counterinvestments, so that there has never existed one type of stable subjugation, given once and for all? How were these power relations linked to one another according to the logic of a great strategy, which in retrospect takes on the aspect of a unitary and voluntarist politics of sex? In general terms: rather than referring all the infinitesimal violences that are exerted on sex, all the anxious gazes that are directed at it, and all the hiding places whose discovery is made into an impossible task, to the unique form of a great Power, we must immerse the expanding production of discourses on sex in the field of multiple and mobile power relations.

Which leads us to advance, in a preliminary way, four rules to follow. But these are not intended as methodological imperatives; at most they are cautionary prescriptions.

I. Rule of Immanence

One must not suppose that there exists a certain sphere of sexuality that would be the legitimate concern of a free and disinterested scientific inquiry were it not the object of mechanisms of prohibition brought to bear by the economic or ideological requirements of power. If sexuality was constituted as an area of investigation, this was only because relations of power had established it as a possible object; and conversely, if power was able to take it as a target, this was because techniques of knowledge and procedures of discourse were capable of investing it. Between techniques of knowledge and strategies of power, there is no exteriority, even if they have specific roles and are linked together on the basis of their difference. We will start, therefore, from what might be called 'local centers' of power-knowledge: for example, the relations that obtain between penitents and confessors, or the faithful and their directors of conscience. Here, guided by the theme of the 'flesh' that must be mastered, different forms of discourse – self-examination, questionings, admissions, interpretations, interviews – were the vehicle of a kind of incessant back-and-forth movement of forms of subjugation and schemas of knowledge. Similarly, the body of the child, under surveillance, surrounded in his cradle, his bed, or his room by an entire watch-crew of parents, nurses, servants, educators, and doctors, all attentive to the least manifestations of his sex, has constituted, particularly since the eighteenth century, another 'local center' of power-knowledge.

II. Rules of Continual Variations

We must not look for who has the power in the order of sexuality (men, adults, parents, doctors) and who is deprived of it (women, adolescents, children, patients); nor for who has the right to know and who is forced to remain ignorant. We must seek rather the pattern of the modifications which the relationships of force imply by the very nature of their process. The 'distributions of power' and the 'appropriations of knowledge' never represent only instantaneous slices taken from processes involving, for example, a cumulative reinforcement of the strongest factor, or a reversal of relationship, or again, a simultaneous increase of two terms. Relations of power-knowledge are not static forms of distribution, they are 'matrices of transformations'. The nineteenth-century grouping made up of the father, the mother, the educator, and the doctor, around the child and his sex, was subjected to constant modifications, continual shifts. One of the more spectacular results of the latter was a strange reversal: whereas to begin with the child's sexuality had been problematized within the relationship established between doctor and parents (in the form of advice, or recommendations to keep the child under observation, or warnings of future dangers), ultimately it was in the relationship of the psychiatrist to the child that the sexuality of adults themselves was called into question.

III. Rule of Double Conditioning

No 'local center', no 'pattern of transformation' could function if, through a series of sequences, it did not eventually enter into an over-all strategy. And inversely, no strategy could achieve comprehensive effects if did not gain support from precise and tenuous relations serving, not as its point of application or final outcome, but as its prop and anchor point. There is no discontinuity between them, as if one were dealing with two different levels (one microscopic and the other macroscopic); but neither is there homogeneity (as if the one were only the enlarged projection or the miniaturization of the other); rather, one must conceive of the double conditioning of a strategy by the specificity of possible tactics, and of tactics by the strategic envelope that makes them work. Thus the father in the family is not the 'representative' of the sovereign or the state; and the latter are not projections of the father on a different scale. The family does not duplicate society, just as society does not imitate the family. But the family organization, precisely to the extent that it was insular and heteromorphous with respect to the other power mechanisms, was used to support the great 'maneuvers' employed for the Malthusian control of the birthrate, for the populationist incitements, for the medicalization of sex and the psychiatrization of its nongenital forms.

IV. RULE OF THE TACTICAL POLYVALENCE OF DISCOURSES

What is said about sex must not be analyzed simply as the surface of projection of these power mechanisms. Indeed, it is in discourse that power and knowledge are joined together. And for this very reason, we must conceive discourse as a series of discontinuous segments whose tactical function is neither uniform nor stable. To be more precise, we must not imagine a world of discourse divided between accepted discourse and excluded discourse, or between the dominant discourse and the dominated one; but as a multiplicity of discursive elements that can come into play in various strategies. It is this distribution that we must reconstruct, with the things said and those concealed, the enunciations required and those forbidden, that it comprises; with the variants and different effects – according to who is speaking, his position of power, the institutional context in which he happens to be situated – that it implies; and with the shifts and reutilizations of identical formulas for contrary objectives that it also includes. Discourses are not once and for all subservient to power or raised up against it, any more than silences are. We must make allowance for the complex and unstable process whereby discourse can be both an instrument and an effect of power, but also a hindrance, a stumbling-block, a point of resistance and a starting point for an opposing strategy. Discourse transmits and produces power; it reinforces it, but also undermines and exposes it, renders it fragile and makes it possible to thwart it. In like manner, silence and secrecy are a shelter for power, anchoring its prohibitions; but they also loosen its holds and provide for relatively obscure areas of tolerance. Consider for example the history of what was once 'the' great sin against nature. The extreme discretion of the texts dealing with sodomy – that utterly confused category – and the nearly universal reticence in talking about it made possible a twofold operation: on the one hand, there was an extreme severity (punishment by fire was meted out well into the eighteenth century, without there being any substantial protest expressed before the middle of the century), and on the other hand, a tolerance that must have been widespread (which one can deduce indirectly from the infrequency of judicial sentences, and which one glimpses more directly through certain statements concerning societies of men that were thought to exist in the army or in the courts). There is no question that the appearance in nineteenth-century psychiatry, jurisprudence, and literature of a whole series of discourses on the species and subspecies of homosexuality, inversion, pederasty, and 'psychic hermaphrodism' made possible a strong advance of social controls into this area of 'perversity'; but it also made possible the formation of a 'reverse' discourse: homosexuality began to speak in its own behalf, to demand that its legitimacy or 'naturality' be acknowledged, often in the same vocabulary, using the same categories by which it was medically disqualified. There is not, on the one side, a discourse of power, and opposite it, another discourse that runs counter to it. Discourses are tactical elements or blocks operating in the field of force relations; there can exist different and even contradictory discourses within the same strategy; they can, on the contrary, circulate without changing their form from one strategy to another, opposing strategy. We must not expect the discourses on sex to tell us, above all, what strategy they derive from, or what moral divisions they accompany, or what ideology – dominant or dominated – they represent; rather we must question them on the two levels of their tactical productivity (what reciprocal effects of power and knowledge they ensure) and their strategical integration (what conjunction and what force relationship make their utilization necessary in a given episode of the various confrontations that occur).

In short, it is a question of orienting ourselves to a conception of power which replaces the privilege of the law with the viewpoint of the objective, the privilege of prohibition with the viewpoint of tactical efficacy, the privilege of sovereignty with the analysis of a multiple and mobile field of force relations, wherein far-reaching, but never completely stable, effects of domination are produced. The strategical model, rather than the model based on law. And this, not out of a speculative choice or theoretical preference, but because in fact it is one of the essential traits of Western societies that the force relationships which for a long time had found expression in war, in every form of warfare, gradually became invested in the order of political power.

WRITING THE HISTORY OF THE PRESENT

Andrew Barry, Thomas Osborne and Nikolas Rose

Writing the History of the Present

How should one write the history of the present? The remarkable rebirth of so-called 'grand theory' in Britain and America in recent years has seen the formulation of numerous ambitious theses about our world, its nature, its pasts and its futures. In this style of work, the social theorist becomes a kind of philosopher *manqué*, retaining the armchair proclivities of the philosopher, yet adding a frisson of empirical observation, usually of a 'historical' order. Perhaps the key category has been that of *modernity*. Modernity takes on the status of a comprehensive periodization: an epoch, an attitude, a form of life, a mentality, an experience. The analysis of modernity is thus placed at the heart of the identity of social theory. And retrospective light is cast back upon the still-revered 'founding fathers' of the discipline of sociology in order to reveal that their concerns were also fundamentally with modernity, or rather with the difference made by modernity. In these terms, Weber's concern with rationalization, Marx's analysis of the internal contradictions of capitalism and Durkheim's notion of organic solidarity were all contributions to this consideration of modernity as difference. Modernity here, takes the form of a 300-year historical bloc, which is today, and has always been, the main object of a social theory that has thus always been inseparably bound up with a 'discontinuist' notion of history. Even historical

Andrew Barry, Thomas Osborne and Nikolas Rose (1995), 'Introduction', in Andrew Barry, Thomas Osborne and Nikolas Rose (eds), *Foucault and Political Reason: Liberalism, Neo-Liberalism and the Rationalitics of Government*, London: UCL Press.

analyses themselves, when undertaken from within the purview of particular sociological perspectives, are frequently concerned with constituting not novel theories of historical transformation, but the exact characteristics of the modern.

This concern with the present as modernity inevitably runs into certain problems as a result of an inherent impetus to totalization. Where are the limits – geographical, social, temporal – of modernity (Giddens 1990)? Is modernity a type of society, or an attitude or a mode of experience (Osborne 1992)? Is modernity a functionalist, a realist, or an idealist concept? Where is modernity heading? What comes after modernity? Or perhaps – the greatest iconoclasm – we have yet to reach modernity at all (Latour 1991)? In any case, the predictable consequence of these problems has been to formulate a repertoire of supplements to modernity to characterize *our* difference – postmodernity, late modernity, high modernity. These notions aspire to continuity with modernity at the level of the concept, whereas they are defined in opposition to it at the level of their object. Hence, as has often been observed, in spite of the obsession with difference so frequently displayed by the proponents of such supplementary notions – the postmodernists in particular – such concepts tend towards a reciprocal totalization; these too become concepts to grasp the essence of an epoch.

Now, it cannot be denied that the contributions in this value are also concerned with diagnosing the differences of the present. Indeed, they are instances of what has become known broadly, if a trifle grandly, as exercises in the 'history of the present'. But the contributors do not presume to have provided some general account of modernity or postmodernity; indeed they share a certain explicit or implicit scepticism about the will to know that animates such endeavours. Nor do they seek to package and market another brand of authority under whose auspices historical investigations are to take place. For if these essays have drawn upon the work of Michel Foucault in conducting their investigations, this has not been with an eye to setting up some rival new and improved theory of modernity and its fate. Instead, a range of more local conceptual devices have been utilized: strategies, technologies, programmes, techniques. These concepts do not serve to sum up the present historical 'conjuncture'; rather they are tools for understanding some of the contingencies of the systems of power that we inhabit – and which inhabit us – today. As such, perhaps the spirit of these contributions owes as much to an *empirical* as it does to any theoretical tendency in historical sociology. In place of the generalities of much grand theory, the contributions allocate theorizing a more modest role; concepts are deployed to demonstrate the negotiations, tensions and accidents that have contributed to the fashioning of various aspects of our present.

The conception of the present at stake in this work thus does not relate to some mythical Foucauldian 'worldview'. The 'Foucault effect' can more accurately be characterized in terms of two kinds of rather local influence.

In the first place, there is at work here a general *ethos* with which the study of the present is approached. In the second place, there is a concern with the vicissitudes of *liberalism* in the shaping of the political contours of this present. It is here that the analytic grid deployed by Foucault, and centred on the concept of governmentality is of some importance.

Foucault might be said to approach the question of the present with a particular *ethos* but not with any substantive or *a priori* understanding of its status. His concern is not to identify some current, perhaps definitive, 'crisis' in the present. Foucault makes no reference to concepts such as post-fordism, postmodernity, 'McDonaldization' or late capitalism that have often been used to characterize a certain kind of break with the past. Nor is he concerned simply with a blanket denunciation of the present. No political programmatics follow automatically from his work in this field. Foucault once argued in an interview, that one of the 'most destructive habits of modern thought . . . is that the moment of the present is considered in history as the break, the climax, the fulfilment, the return of youth, etc'. – confessing that he had himself found himself at times drawn into the orbit of such a temptation (Foucault 1989d: 251). But if it is the case that, for example, the closing pages of *Madness and Civilization* are unquestionably apocalyptic in their pronouncements on the present, and that Foucault himself was to regret the adoption of such apocalyptic tones, in a sense, the conception of the present does retain a certain stability across his work. Above all, one might say, Foucault was concerned to introduce an 'untimely' attitude in our relation towards the present. Untimely in the Nietzschean sense: acting counter to our time, introducing a new sense of the fragility of our time, and thus acting on our time for the benefit, one hopes, of a time to come (Nietzsche 1983: 60, cf. Rose 1993a: 1, Bell 1994: 155).

Our time, that is to say, is not presumed to be the bearer or culmination of some grand historical process, it has no inevitability, no spirit, essence or underlying cause. The 'present', in Foucault's work, is less an epoch than an array of questions; and the coherence with which the present presents itself to us – and in which guise it is re-imagined by so much social theory – is something to be *acted upon* by historical investigation, to be cut up and decomposed so that it can be seen as put together contingently out of heterogeneous elements each having their own conditions of possibility.

Such a fragmentation of the present is not undertaken in a spirit of post-structuralist playfulness. It is undertaken with a more serious, if hopefully modest, ambition – to allow a space for the work of freedom. Here, indeed, the place of ethics is marked in Foucault's thought. Analyses of the present are concerned with opening up 'a virtual break which opens a room, understood as a room of concrete freedom, that is possible transformation'; the received fixedness and inevitability of the present is destabilized, shown as just sufficiently fragile as to let in a little glimpse of freedom – as a practice of difference – through its fractures.

These concerns with the present and its contingency do not partake in the relativism that has become so fashionable; their approach is not so much 'relativist' as 'perspectivist'. The angle they seek does not attempt to show that our ways of thinking and doing are only the habits of a particular time and place. Rather than relativize the present, these perspectival studies hope to 'destabilize' it. Destabilizing the present is 'perspectival' in that it does not seek to define the geographical and temporal limits of a culture, but to bring into view the historically sedimented underpinnings of particular 'problematizations' that have a salience for our contemporary experience. Hence the nonsensical nature of those claims – in praise or condemnation – that Foucault's work seeks to found a new global 'approach' on a par with, for example, historical materialism; or that it can be 'applied' to any issue from advertising to nuclear physics. Foucault's work always fails these tests of its universal 'applicability', but such failure is not necessarily a *failing*. Further, Foucault's emphases are best put to use, not in those areas where we are so clearly the inheritor of a history, but in those domains where an untimely analysis seems *least* possible; above all, in those domains that emphasize psychological and anthropological constants or the immutability of nature.

The effect of such perspectival analysis is not intended to be solely an 'intellectual' one. Rather what is at stake is the production of a certain kind of experience, a refiguring of experience itself. At their best, what is produced in such investigations is a shattering of conventional thought that strikes at the heart of our most taken-for-granted motivations. Here, the sense of an assault upon our ethical certainties, of coming up against obstacles that prevent one knowing immediately 'what is to be done', has a positive function. What occurs is a potentially productive uncoupling of experience from its conditions. In an interview, Foucault talks of bringing about a kind of paralysis in his readers; 'But paralysis isn't the same thing as anaesthesia – on the contrary. It's in so far as there's been an awakening to a whole series of problems that the difficulty of doing anything comes to be felt' (Foucault in Burchell et al. 1991: 84, Burchell in Burchell et al. 1991: 119–20 and 146, cf. Osborne 1994: 496).

Although these 'histories of the present' address themselves to our political reason, then, this is not in the sense that any specific political prescriptions or proscriptions flow. This does not condemn historians of the present themselves in any way to be without politics or 'beyond politics'. For there is certainly an ethos of engagement tied to this way of conceiving of the present, one that may itself be historical but should not be despised for that. In his essay on Kant and the Enlightenment, Foucault insists that if modernity connotes anything it is not a period or a mode of experience but an 'ethos', a way of orientating oneself to history. Kant's distinction was hardly to have inaugurated this modernity itself, so much as to have posed the question of the present as an issue. Here we find some hints as to

Foucault's own understanding of the necessary ethos of the intellectual in the present. Foucault highlights Kant's 'pragmatic anthropology', so different from the medium of the three Critiques, which opened up a space for Enlightenment not as certainty but as a kind of permanent questioning of the present, indeed a 'commitment to uncertainty' (Gordon 1986: 74). As Colin Gordon emphasizes, for Foucault this commitment entailed a novel version of critique itself: not so much to establish the limits of thought, but to locate the possible places of transgression (Gordon 1986: 75). This understanding of the present does not take the anti-Enlightenment stance of other grand genealogies of the present moment. Gordon cites the work of Cassirer, Hayek, Adorno and Horkheimer as instances of genealogical thought linked to a 'semiology of catastrophe'. But as Foucault himself notes, one 'does not [have] to be "for" or "against" the Enlightenment' (Foucault 1986: 43). Rather, the style of Foucault's histories of the present owes something to the classical orientation of Tocqueville or Weber, where 'the analysis addresses the hazards and necessities of a system, not the unrecognized invasions of an alien, pathological mutation' (Foucault 1986: 78, see also Owen 1994).

LIBERALISM AND NEO-LIBERALISM

The names of Weber and Tocqueville lead us felicitously to the second domain in which Foucault's influence has been influential on the analyses in this volume: the analytics of liberal political reason. In the late 1970s Foucault initiated a range of researches on what he termed arts of government or political rationality. This work was never brought together in a single volume and Foucault's remarks on it are scattered across a number of interviews and essays, as well as his lectures at the Collège de France (Foucault 1989b, see Gordon 1991 for a lucid introduction to this work). For Foucault, political rationalities are more than just ideologies; they constitute a part of the fabric of our ways of thinking about and acting upon one another and ourselves. Foucault's concern with the history of political rationality also raises, as does Weber's work in a different register, the question of the relation between the mutations of politics and the history of systems of expertise. Indeed what it throws into question is precisely the nature and limits of 'the political', the political as itself a transactional space, a historically variable zone of rationalization and division. But why this concern with government, and with liberalism in particular? Does a focus on liberalism, coupled with the focus on ethics and freedom in Foucault's later work, represent a retreat into the categories and dreams of political philosophy, when set against the images conjured up by the themes of surveillance, discipline and normalization that marked the analyses of power in *Discipline and Punish* and the first volume of the *History of Sexuality*?

It would be a mistake to think that Foucault exchanged a vision of a society dominated by discipline with a vision of a society dominated by a form of government based around the exercise of freedom. In Foucault's account, disciplinary power and government have historically co-existed. 'We need to see things not in terms of the replacement of a society of sovereignty by a disciplinary society by a society of government; in reality one has a triangle, sovereignty-discipline-government' (Foucault 1991: 102). Indeed, part of the attractiveness of the idea of government is that it makes it difficult to sustain the common perception – derived from Weber, the Frankfurt school as well as from Foucault – that society has become dominated by routine, discipline and rationalization (Burchell, this volume). On the contrary. The possibilities for liberal forms of freedom may historically depend upon the exercise of discipline. Freedom, in a liberal sense, should thus not be equated with anarchy, but with a kind of well-regulated and 'responsibilized' liberty. The task, according to Foucault, was not to denounce the idea of liberty as a fiction, but to analyze the conditions within which the practice of freedom has been possible. Freedom is thus neither an ideological fiction of modern societies nor an existential feature of existence within them; it must be understood also and necessarily as a formula of rule. Foucault's concern here might be characterized as an attempt to link the analysis of the constitution of freedom with that of the exercise of rule; that is, with the extent to which freedom has become, in our so-called 'free societies', a resource for, and not merely a hindrance to, government.

It is clear that Foucault means something rather different by liberalism than do political philosophers. He does not speak of a liberal 'period', nor is he concerned principally with writing the history of the philosophical ideas of liberty or of rights. From Foucault's perspective, liberalism is more like an *ethos* of government. Liberalism is understood not so much as a substantive doctrine or practice of government in itself, but as a restless and dissatisfied ethos of recurrent critique of State reason and politics. Hence, the advent of liberalism coincides with the discovery that political government could be its own undoing, that by governing over-much, rulers thwarted the very ends of government. Hence liberalism is not about governing less but about the continual injunction that politicians and rulers should govern cautiously, delicately, economically, modestly (Rose 1993b, Osborne 1994). Thus, liberalism represents, in a certain sense, a cautious and self-critical – if not necessarily enlightened – approach to the problem of government.

The emergence of liberal mentalities of government in the early nineteenth century was, according to Foucault, of critical historical significance. In brief, it was only with the emergence of liberalism that it was possible for a domain of 'society' to emerge (Foucault 1989b: 112). In effect, society was the product of a mutation in the demands of governmental rationalities. Why is this so? One way of understanding the connection between liberalism and the historical emergence of society is to contrast liberalism with the political rationality of police; a form of rationality that sought to govern, so to speak, *in toto*, down to the minutiae of existence.

Liberalism emerges where this question of totalized government becomes turned around:

> It seems to me that at that very moment it became apparent that if one governed too much, one did not govern at all – that one provoked results contrary to those one desired. What was discovered at that time – and this was one of the great discoveries of political thought at the end of the eighteenth century – was the idea of *society*. That is to say, that government not only has to deal with a territory, with a domain, and with its subjects, but that it also has to deal with a complex and independent reality that has its own laws and mechanisms of disturbance. This new reality is society. From the moment that one is to manipulate a society, one cannot consider it completely penetrable by police. One must take into account what it is. It becomes necessary to reflect upon it, upon its specific characteristics, its constants and variables. (Foucault 1989c: 261)

Liberalism is thus delivered to the social sciences in a double way. On the one hand, liberal political reason is the historical condition of the very object of their disciplines – 'society'. On the other hand, liberal political reason establishes a field of concerns that are as much *technical* as they are political or ideological. The social sciences provide a way of representing the autonomous dynamics of society and assessing whether they should or should not be an object of regulation. In effect, the social sciences can act as a kind of technical solution to all the anxiety that, for liberalism, marks the relations between society and the public authorities. Far from seeing liberalism as an absence of government, or of a lessening of political concern with the conduct of conduct, histories of the present draw attention to the intellectual and practical techniques and inventions via which civil society is brought into being as both distinct from political intervention and yet potentially alignable with political aspirations. The supposed separation of State and civil society is the consequence of a particular problematization of government, not of a withdrawal of government as such.

Inscribed within the very logic of liberal forms of government is a certain naturalism: the social domain to be governed is a natural one, sensitive to excessive intervention (Osborne 1995). As government cannot override the natural dynamics of the economy without destroying the basis on which liberal government is possible, it must preserve the autonomy of society from State intervention. At the same time, it must ensure the existence of political spaces within which critical reflections on the actions of the State are possible, thus ensuring that such actions are themselves subject to critical observation. In brief, the activity of rule must take care to observe and maintain the autonomy of the professions and the freedom of the public sphere from political interference. Thus, in the process in which intellectuals and scientists act as critics of the State, they can none the less serve to act in the interests of good government.

Foucault's account of liberalism thus directs our attention to the technical means with which the aspirations and ideals of liberal political rationalities might have been put into practice. This is not a matter of deconstructing the internal logic or contradictions within liberal political philosophy; rather it is to attend to the relations of the *ethos* of liberalism and its *techne*: its organization as a practical rationality directed towards certain ends. This emphasis upon *techne* gains further significance when one comes to consider the way in which liberalism has been refigured in its neo-liberal incarnation. As Graham Burchell argues, neo-liberalism replaces the naturalism of liberalism with a certain kind of constructivism (Burchell 1995). In the styles of neo-liberal political reason that began to be formulated after the Second World War, it was the responsibility of political government to *actively* create the conditions within which entrepreneurial and competitive conduct is possible. Paradoxically, neo-liberalism, alongside its critique of the deadening consequences of the intrusion of the State into the life of the individual, has none the less provoked the invention and/or deployment of a whole array of organizational forms and technical methods in order to extend the field within which a certain kind of economic freedom might be practised in the form of personal autonomy, enterprise and choice (Rose 1995).

There have been, of course, other sociologies of neo-liberalism; most particularly those addressed to the rise to political power of the New Right in the 1980s. In Britain it is the work of Stuart Hall and his colleagues that immediately springs to mind in this context. This neo-Gramscian perspective sought to show how an ideological bloc – prototyped by the Thatcherite phenomenon in Britain – sought more or less successfully to gain a hegemonic position within the political conjuncture of the late 1970s. For Hall, there was a crucial structural ambiguity about Thatcherism, evidenced in its mixture of authoritarianism and populism. Thatcherism embodied a 'highly contradictory strategy'; 'simultaneously dismantling the Welfare State, "anti-statist" in its ideological representation, *and* highly State-centralist and dirigiste in many of its strategic operations' (Hall 1988: 152). There were many merits to this position – not least the empirical sensitivity that it espoused, and the refusal simply to treat the Thatcher phenomenon as a monolithic bloc of class-derived 'interests'. Nevertheless it will serve briefly to mark some differences from the style of the analyses that follow. Although Hall's analysis certainly does not reduce Thatcherism to the realm of ideology, the insistence that part of its function was to permeate 'common sense' within civil society made its ideological impulse of considerable importance. But what Hall misses by way of this ideological perspective is any sense of Thatcherism as a positive – in the technical not the ethical sense – art of government; that is, of an inventive and constructive alignment of interests, powers, objects, institutions and persons (cf. Laclau & Mouffe 1985, Barrett 1992: 64–8). Hall's analysis of the New Right in terms of the constitution of hegemony and the specificity of national context remains instructive, if not entirely borne out by subsequent events. None the less, the focus of the essays collected here is on the 'ethical' and 'technical' character of neo-liberalism as an art of government, not upon the 'ideological' conditions under which it may or may not be able to operate. In a certain sense, then, we return to something of enduring value in the work of Max Weber. The material conditions of particular regimes of authority, of economic action, of social regulation, are to be located, at least in part, through an analysis of their technical methods such as accounting and auditing: and this is equally, indeed particularly, true of government in its 'neo-liberal' form (Miller 1992, Power 1994).

Above all, it is a mistake to see neo-liberalism as simply a negative political response to the welfarism or corporatism of previous decades. Hall retains this emphasis in his contention that Thatcherism embodies a fiscal retreat by the State, even if this is countermanded by an enhancement of repressive powers. This is to impose too reductive, reactive and univocal an interpretation upon the variety of phenomena embraced under the designation of Thatcherism; a consequence, no doubt, of the obsession with the question of the State that has dominated so much recent thinking in this area. This 'retreat from the State' is also itself a positive technique of government; we are perhaps witnessing a 'degovernmentalization of the State' but surely not 'degovernmentalization' *per se*. Rather, these studies suggest, that what has been at issue has been the fabrication of techniques that can produce a degree of 'autonomization' of entities of government from the State: here the State, allying itself with a range of other groups and forces, has sought to set up – in Latourian language – chains of enrolment, 'responsibilization' and 'empowerment' to sectors and agencies distant from the centre, yet tied to it through a complex of alignments and translations.

The Technical and the Political

The theme of expertise and the relation between expertise and politics has been an important one in social theory. It was central to the work of Weber, and to the development of Weber's analysis in the critical theory of the Frankfurt school and in the work of Jürgen Habermas. More recently, many sociologists of science have become increasingly concerned, both at a theoretical and political level, with the relation between expertise and politics, and expertise and law. What connections are there between the approach to the study of expertise developed from the work of Foucault and these other related traditions in sociology?

In common with Weber and Habermas, Foucault emphasized the historical relation between the technical and the political; however, the nature and consequences of this connection were thematized very differently. For

Habermas, this relation has taken a particular form. On the one hand, science and technology have become increasingly divorced from politics. They have been constituted as a domain autonomous from and impervious to the critical gaze of the public sphere and, even, to the control of the State itself. On the other hand, according to Habermas, political decisions themselves have increasingly been transformed into technical ones. In short, argues Habermas, there has been a 'scientization of politics' (Habermas 1971). Crucially, Habermas, like so many other social theorists, poses a certain antinomy between aspirations to the full realization of human potential and the rise and domination of the technological, with its instrumental reasoning, its rationalizations and 'objectifications', its specialists and its bureaucrats, its dreams of order, predictability and control.

This opposition hampers thought about our present and its ethical character – it must be refused: this is one of the most distinctive features of the histories of the present represented here. To speak of the conduct of conduct as being made thinkable under certain rationalizations and practicable through the assembling of technologies is not, thereby, to subject these endeavours to a critique. The introduction of the theme of technology here thus does not encourage one to dream of an alternative – an anti-technological future of the full realization of humanity – any more than it licenses one to participate in the dream of those who see technology as leading to human emancipation from the demands of toil, the constraints of time and space and even of human finitude. Further, to recognize that subjectivity is itself a matter of the technologizing of humans is not to regard this process as amounting to some kind of crushing of the human spirit under the pressure of a corset of habits, restrictions and injunctions. Human capacities are, from the perspective of these investigations, inevitably and inescapably technologized. An analytics of technology has, therefore, to devote itself to the sober and painstaking task of describing the consequences, the possibilities invented as much as the limits imposed, of particular ways of subjectifying humans.

Rather than conceiving of the relation between the technical and the political as an opposition, the authors of these studies highlight the variable ways in which expertise plays a part in translating society into an object of government. One implication of this is that instead of viewing technology or expertise as distinct from politics, 'technical' terms themselves – such as apparatus, machine or network – best convey a sense of the complex relays and linkages that tie techniques of conduct into specific relations with the concerns of government. These notions of technology, in the sense of complex and heterogenous relations amongst disparate elements, stabilized in particular ways, enables us to reconnect, in a productive way, studies of the exercise of power at the 'molecular' level – in schools, prison cells, hospital wards, psychiatric diagnoses, conjugal relations and so forth – with strategies to programme power at a molar level in such 'centres of calculation' as the Cabinet Office, the War Office, the Department of State, the party manifesto, the Government White Paper or the enactment of legislation (Latour 1987: 232–57, Rose and Miller 1992: 185).

These investigations of the relations of the political and the technical, like those conducted under the auspices of the Frankfurt school and its successors, come to bear upon the question of politics itself. Here, the limits of the political are not defined in terms of the boundaries of an apparatus – the State – or in terms of the fulfilment of certain necessary functions – repressive and ideological State apparatuses – but as themselves discursive. Rather, politics has itself to be investigated genealogically, in terms of the ways of coding and defining or delimiting the possible scope of action and components of an apparatus of rule, the strategies and limits proper for rulers, and the relations between political rule and that exercised by other authorities. Such a perspective is useful, for it enables us to analyze, without prior commitments, what is entailed in the shifting boundaries of the political and the technical. This is required not only to give intelligibility to the implications of, for example, the introduction of budgetary disciplines into domains previously directed by decisions of elected politicians, but also to understand what is at stake in the deployment of such slogans as 'the personal is political' or in current demands within political discourse itself for an end to 'big government' in order to give back 'liberty to the people'. Here we see different variations on the theme that politics should or should not be conceived of as a particular sort of endeavour conducted by specific persons and institutions and under particular mandates, distinct from the exercise of authority by priests over parishioners, teachers over pupils, parents over children, men over women and so forth. In denaturalizing politics and making it a possible object for genealogy, this approach therefore establishes the conditions for investigating what is at stake in the contemporary rise of anti-political themes at the heart of controversies about the exercise of power (cf. Hindess 1996).

These essays address the problem of expertise in a further sense, through their concern with the role of expertise in what has been termed, following Bruno Latour's use of this phrase, 'action-at-a-distance' (Latour 1986). As Nikolas Rose argues, public authorities seek to employ forms of expertise in order to govern society at a distance, without recourse to any direct forms of repression or intervention (Rose, this volume). Of key importance to neo-liberalism, for example, is the development of techniques of auditing, accounting and management that enable a 'market' for public services to be established autonomous from central control. Neo-liberalism, in these terms, involves less a retreat from governmental 'intervention' than a re-inscription of the techniques and forms of expertise required for the exercise of government. The 'distance' over which liberal government is exercised is, however, real as well as metaphorical. As Andrew Barry argues, liberalism has had particular use for electrical communication technologies in increasing the quantity and rapidity of the flow of information between spatially dispersed points without the need for the development of an extensive system of surveillance controlled by the State (Barry, this volume). Indeed, although the focus of the majority of genealogies of expertise has been on the social and human sciences, and of the 'human technologies' made possible by such mathematical inventions as statistics and calculation, Barry's study shows us the productivity of this approach when directed towards the rise of those forms of knowledge and intervention with a 'higher epistemological profile' such as physics and chemistry.

But this stress on the relations between expertise and politics does not imply that it is one of functionality or of co-optation. Rather, the relations established, although 'functionalizable', are contingent. As Foucault himself argued, the discipline of architecture acquired particular political significance in relation to the political rationality of police as it did for Jeremy Bentham in proposing a practice of reformatory incarceration. This does not mean either that architecture is inevitably to be understood, let alone explained, in terms of its functioning within modern forms of political power, or that 'similar' styles and forms of architecture might not be articulated with quite different political projects. Likewise, if particular technologies such as auditing and accountancy have a particular utility to neo-liberalism, this does not mean that there is an intrinsic relation between the techniques and the politics, such that they must be discarded by those who seek an alternative art of government. In any case, it is never in these analyses merely a question of being either for or against the technological. Humans' relations to technology are not merely those of a passive 'reduction'; rather, technology is an aspect of what it is to be human (Canguilhem 1994). And if technology is political, it is because technology always carries with it a certain 'telos' of operations, a certain directive capacity. In other words, technology – both in terms of the human side of technology and of the technology of what it is to be human – is integral to those relations of authority and subjectivity that insert our selves into the space of the present, giving us the status of living beings capable of having 'experience' of the present. In short, technology neither is, nor could be either, 'outside' politics or corrosive of politics; it is tied irrevocably to our political self-understanding and our understanding of the political.

BIBLIOGRAPHY

Adorno, T. and Horkheimer, M. (1986), *Dialectic of Enlightenment*, London: Verso.

Althusser, L. (1969), *For Marx*, Harmondsworth: Penguin.

Althusser, L. (1976), *Essays in Self-Criticism*, London: New Left.

Ariès, P. (1962), *Centuries of Childhood*, New York: Vintage.

Barrett, M. (1992), *The Politics of Truth: From Marx to Foucault*, Cambridge: Polity.

Bell, V. (1994), 'Dreaming and time in Foucault's philosophy', *Theory, Culture and Society*, 11.

Boddy, R. and Crotty, J. (1974), 'Class conflict, Keynesian policy and the business cycle', *Monthly Review*, October.

Boddy, R. and Crotty, J. (1975), 'Class conflict and macro-policy: the political business cycle', *Review of Radical Political Economy*, 7.

Bukharin, N. (1969), *Historical Materialism*, Ann Arbor: University of Michigan Press.

Burchell, G. (1995), 'Liberal government and techniques of the self', in A. Barry, T. Osborne and N. Rose (eds), *Foucault and Political Reason: Liberalism, Neo-Liberalism and the Rationalities of Government*, London: UCL Press.

Burchell, G., Gordon, C. and Miller, P. (eds) (1991), *The Foucault Effect: Studies in Governmentality*, Hemel Hempstead: Harvester Wheatsheaf.

Canguilhem, G. (1994), *A Vital Rationalist*, New York: Zone.

Cutler, A. (1971), 'Fascism and political theory', *Theoretical Practice*, 2.

Durkheim, E. (1951), *Suicide*, New York: Free Press.

Durkheim, E. (1964), *The Division of Labor in Society*, New York: Free Press.

Durkheim, E. (1982), *The Rules of Sociological Method*, New York: Free Press.

Durkheim, E. (1995), *The Elementary Forms of the Religious Life*, New York: Free Press.

Engels, F. (1942), *The Origin of the Family, Private Property and the State*, New York: International.

Engels, F. (1954), *Anti-Dühring*, London: Lawrence and Wishart.

Engels, F. (1978), *The Origin of the Family, Private Property and the State*, Peking: Foreign Languages Press.

Foucault, M. (1971), *Madness and Civilisation*, London: Routledge and Kegan Paul.

Foucault, M. (1974), *The Order of Things*, London: Routledge and Kegan Paul.
Foucault, M. (1976), *The Birth of the Clinic*, London: Routledge and Kegan Paul.
Foucault, M. (1979), *Discipline and Punish*, Harmondsworth: Penguin.
Foucault, M. (1981), *The History of Sexuality, vol. 1: An Introduction*, Harmondsworth: Penguin.
Foucault, M. (1985), *The History of Sexuality, vol. 2: The Use of Pleasure*, Harmondsworth: Penguin.
Foucault, M. (1986), 'What is enlightenment?', in P. Rabinow (ed.), *The Foucault Reader*, London: Penguin.
Foucault, M. (1989a), *The Archaeology of Knowledge*, London: Routledge and Kegan Paul.
Foucault, M. (1989b), *Résumé des cours*, Paris: Juillard.
Foucault, M. (1989c), 'An ethics of pleasure', in S. Lotringer (ed.), *Foucault Live*, New York: Semiotext(e).
Foucault, M. (1989d), 'How much does it cost for reason to tell the truth?', in S. Lotringer (ed.), *Foucault Live*, New York: Semiotext(e).
Foucault, M. (1991), 'Governmentality', in G. Burchell, C. Gordon and P. Miller (eds), *The Foucault Effect: Studies in Governmentality*, Hemel Hempstead: Harvester Wheatsheaf.
Foucault, M. (2001), *The Essential Works of Foucault 1954–1984, vol. 3: Power*, Harmondsworth: Penguin.
Frisby, D. (1985), *Fragments of Modernity*, Cambridge: Polity.
Giddens, A. (1990), *The Consequences of Modernity*, Cambridge: Polity.
Glyn, J. and Sutcliffe, B. (1972), *British Capitalism, Workers and the Profits Squeeze*, Harmondsworth: Penguin.
Gordon, C. (1986), 'Question, ethos, event: Foucault on Kant and Enlightenment', *Economy and Society*, 15:1.
Gordon, C. (1991), 'Governmental rationality: an introduction', in G. Burchell, C. Gordon and P. Miller (eds), *The Foucault Effect: Studies in Governmentality*, Hemel Hempstead: Harvester Wheatsheaf.
Gough, I. (1975), 'State expenditure in advanced capitalism', *New Left Review*, 92.
Gramsci, A. (1971), *Selections from the Prison Notebooks*, London: Lawrence and Wishart.
Gramsci, A. (1977), *Selections from the Political Writings 1910–1920*, London: Lawrence and Wishart.
Gramsci, A. (1995), *Further Selections from the Prison Notebooks*, London: Lawrence and Wishart.
Habermas, J. (1971), *Towards a Rational Society*, London: Heinemann.
Habermas, J. (1987a), *The Theory of Communicative Action, vol. 2: Lifeworld and System: A Critique of Functionalist Reason*, Cambridge: Polity.
Habermas, J. (1987b), *The Philosophical Discourse of Modernity*, Cambridge: Polity.
Habermas, J. (1988), *Legitimation Crisis*, Cambridge: Polity.
Habermas, J. (1989), *The Structural Transformation of the Public Sphere*, Cambridge: Polity.
Habermas, J. (1991), 'Legitimation problems in the modern state', in *Communication and the Evolution of Society*, Cambridge: Polity.
Hall, S. (1988), *The Hard Road to Renewal*, London: Verso.
Hindess, B. (1996), *Discourses of Power: From Hobbes to Foucault*, Oxford: Blackwell.
Horkheimer, M. (1987), *Eclipse of Reason*, New York: Continuum.
Hunt, R. (1975), *The Political Ideas of Marx and Engels, vol. 1: Marxism and Totalitarian Democracy 1818–1850*, London: Macmillan.
Kent, S. (1983), 'Weber, Goethe, and the Nietzschean allusion: capturing the source of the "iron cage" metaphor', *Sociological Analysis*, 44:4.
Laclau, E. and Mouffe, C. (1985), *Hegemony and Socialist Strategy*, London: Verso.

Latour, B. (1987), *Science in Action*, Milton Keynes: Open University Press.

Latour, B. (1991), *We Have Never Been Modern*, Hemel Hempstead: Harvester Wheatsheaf.

Lenin, V. (1970), 'State and revolution', in *Selected Works, vol. 2*, Moscow: Progress.

Mandel, E. (1971), *The Formation of the Economic Thought of Karl Marx*, London: New Left.

Marcuse, H. (1964), *One-Dimensional Man*, Boston: Beacon Press.

Marcuse, H. (1969), *Eros and Civilisation*, London: Sphere.

Marx, K. (1970), *Critique of Hegel's* Philosophy of Right, Cambridge: Cambridge University Press.

Marx, K. (1971), *Capital*, Moscow: Progress, vol. 3.

Marx, K. (1973a), *The Eighteenth Brumaire of Louis Bonaparte*, in *Political Writings, vol. 2: Surveys from Exile*, Harmondsworth: Penguin.

Marx, K. (1973b), *Grundrisse: Foundations of the Critique of Political Economy (Rough Draft)*, Harmondsworth: Penguin.

Marx, K. (1974), *The Civil War in France*, in *Political Writings, vol. 3: The First International and After*, Harmondsworth: Penguin.

Marx, K. (1975a), Preface (to *A Contribution to the Critique of Political Economy*), in *Early Writings*, Harmondsworth: Penguin.

Marx, K. (1975b), *Critique of Hegel's Doctrine of the State*, in *Early Writings*, Harmondsworth: Penguin.

Marx, K. (1975c), *Excerpts from James Mill's* Elements of Political Economy, in *Early Writings*, Harmondsworth: Penguin.

Marx, K. (1975d), *Economic and Philosophical Manuscripts*, in *Early Writings*, Harmondsworth: Penguin.

Marx, K. (1975e), *A Contribution to the Critique of Hegel's Philosophy of Right*, in *Early Writings*, Harmondsworth: Penguin.

Marx, K. (1975f), *Contribution to the Critique of Hegel's Philosophy of Law: Introduction*, in K. Marx and F. Engels, *Collected Works, vol. 3*, London: Lawrence and Wishart.

Marx, K. (1981), *Capital*, Harmondsworth: Penguin, vol. 3.

Marx, K. (1987), *The Civil War in France*, in K. Marx and F. Engels, *Collected Works, vol. 22*, London: Lawrence and Wishart.

Marx, K. and Engels, F. (1965), *The German Ideology*, London: Lawrence and Wishart.

Marx, K. and Engels, F. (1967), 'Preface to 1872 German edition of the Communist Manifesto', in *The Communist Manifesto*, ed. A. J. P. Taylor, Harmondsworth: Penguin.

Marx, K. and Engels, F. (1973), *The Communist Manifesto*, in *Political Writings, vol. 1: The Revolutions of 1848*, Harmondsworth: Penguin.

Marx, K. and Engels, F. (1975), *Selected Correspondence*, Moscow: Progress.

Marx, K. and Engels, F. (1976), *The German Ideology*, in *Collected Works, vol. 5*, London: Lawrence and Wishart.

Merton, R. K. (1957), 'Social structure and anomie', in *Social Theory and Social Structure*, New York: Free Press.

Miliband, R. (1969), *The State in Capitalist Society*, London: Weidenfeld and Nicolson.

Miller, P. (1992), 'Accounting and objectivity; the invention of calculating selves and calculable spaces', in A. Megill (ed.), *Rethinking objectivity*, special edition of *Annals of Scholarship*, 9:1–2.

Nietzsche, F. (1983), *Human, All Too Human: A Book for Free Spirits*, tr. R. Hollingdale, Cambridge: Cambridge University Press.

Offe, C. (1974), 'Structural problems of the capitalist state', in K. von Beyme (ed.), *German Political Studies*, London: Russell Sage.

Osborne, P. (1992), 'Modernity is a qualitative, not a quantitative concept', *New Left Review*, 192.

Osborne, T. (1994), 'Sociology, liberalism and the historicity of conduct', *Economy and Society*, 23:4.
Osborne, T. (1995), 'Security and vitality: drains, liberalism and power in the 19th century', in A. Barry, T. Osborne and N. Rose (eds), *Foucault and Political Reason: Liberalism, Neo-Liberalism and the Rationalities of Government*, London: UCL Press.
Owen, D. (1994), *Maturity and Modernity: Nietzsche, Weber, Foucault and the Ambivalence of Reason*, London: Routledge.
Parsons, T. (1954), *Essays in Sociological Theory*, New York: Free Press.
Parsons, T. (1964), 'Youth in the context of American society', in *Social Structure and Personality*, New York: Free Press of Glencoe.
Poulantzas, N. (1969), 'The problem of the capitalist state', *New Left Review*, 58.
Poulantzas, N. (1973), *Political Power and Social Classes*, London: New Left.
Poulantzas, N. (1974), *Fascism and Dictatorship*, London: New Left.
Poulantzas, N. (1975), *Classes in Contemporary Capitalism*, London: New Left.
Poulantzas, N. (1976), 'The capitalist state', *New Left Review*, 95.
Power, M. (1994), *The Audit Society*, London: Demos.
Rocher, G. (1974), *Talcott Parsons and American Sociology*, London: Nelson.
Rose, N. (1993a), 'Towards a critical sociology of freedom', inaugural lecture, Goldsmiths College, London, 5 May 1992, London: Goldsmiths College.
Rose, N. (1993b), 'Government, authority and expertise in advanced liberalism', *Economy and Society*, 22:3.
Rose, N. (1995), 'Governing "advanced" liberal democracies', in A. Barry, T. Osborne and N. Rose (eds), *Foucault and Political Reason: Liberalism, Neo-Liberalism and the Rationalities of Government*, London: UCL Press.
Rose, N. and Miller, P. (1992), 'Political power beyond the state: problematics of government', *British Journal of Sociology*, 43:2.
Weber, M. (1949), *The Methodology of the Social Sciences*, New York: Free Press.
Weber, M. (1964), *The Theory of Social and Economic Organization*, New York: Free Press.
Weber, M. (1968), *On Charisma and Institution Building*, ed. S. Eisenstadt, Chicago: Chicago University Press.
Weber, M. (1970), *From Max Weber: Essays in Sociology*, tr. and ed. H. H. Gerth and C. Wright Mills, London: Routledge and Kegan Paul.
Weber, M. (1974), *The Protestant Ethic and the Spirit of Capitalism*, London: Allen and Unwin.
Weber, M. (1978), *Economy and Society*, ed. G. Roth and C. Wittich, 2 vols, Berkeley: University of California Press.
Weber, M. (1991), *From Max Weber: Essays in Sociology*, rev. ed., tr. and ed. H. H. Gerth and C. Wright Mills, London and New York: Routledge.
Weber, M. (1992), *The Protestant Ethic and the Spirit of Capitalism*, London and New York: Routledge.
Weber, M. (1993), *Basic Concepts in Sociology*, New York: Citadel Press.

FURTHER READING

Adorno, T. (1987), 'Late capitalism or industrial society?', in V. Meja, D. Misgeld and N. Stehr (eds), *Modern German Sociology*, New York: Columbia University Press.
Adorno, T. (1991), *The Culture Industry*, tr. and ed. J. M. Bernstein, London: Routledge.
Alcoff, L. (1990), 'Feminist politics and Foucault: the limits to a collaboration', in A. Dallery and C. Scott (eds), *Crises in Continental Philosophy*, Albany: State University of New York Press.
Alway, J. (1995), *Critical Theory and Political Possibilities*, Westport, CT: Greenwood Press.
Anderson, P. (1976), 'The Antinomies of Antonio Gramsci', *New Left Review*, 100.
Anderson, P. (1979), *Considerations on Western Marxism*, London: Verso.
Anderson, P. (1992), *English Questions*, London: Verso.
Beetham, D. (1985), *Max Weber and the Theory of Modern Politics*, Cambridge: Polity.
Beetham, D. (1987), *Bureaucracy*, Buckingham: Open University Press.
Bendix, R. (1966), *Max Weber: An Intellectual Portrait*, London: Methuen.
Benjamin, W. (1973), 'The work of art in the age of mechanical reproduction', in *Illuminations*, Glasgow: Fontana.
Calhoun, C. (ed.) (1992), *Habermas and the Public Sphere*, Cambridge, MA: MIT Press.
Cook, D. (1996), *The Culture Industry Revisited: Theodor W. Adorno on Mass Culture*, Lanham, MD: Rowman and Littlefield.
Craib, I. (1984), *Modern Social Theory: From Parsons to Habermas*, Hemel Hempstead: Harvester Wheatsheaf.
Fenton, S. (1984), *Durkheim and Modern Sociology*, Cambridge: Cambridge University Press.
Fontana, B. (1993), *Hegemony and Power: On the Relation between Gramsci and Machiavelli*, Minneapolis: University of Minnesota Press.
Habermas, J. (1978), *Knowledge and Human Interests*, London: Heinemann.
Habermas, J. (1984), *The Theory of Communicative Action, vol.1*, Cambridge: Polity.
Held, D. (1980), *Introduction to Critical Theory*, Berkeley: University of California Press.
Horkheimer, M. (1972), *Critical Theory: Selected Essays*, New York: Seabury Press.

Horkheimer, M. (1974), *Critique of Instrumental Reason*, New York: Seabury Press.
Jameson, F. (1990), *Late Marxism*, London: Verso.
Jessop, B. (1982), *The Capitalist State*, Oxford: Martin Robinson.
Löwith, K. (1982), *Max Weber and Karl Marx*, London: Allen and Unwin.
Lukes, S. (1973), *Émile Durkheim: His Life and Work*, Harmondsworth: Penguin.
McCarthy, J. (1984), 'The critique of impure reason: Foucault and the Frankfurt school', in M. Kelly (ed.), *Critique and Power: Recasting the Foucault/Habermas Debate*, Cambridge, MA and London: MIT Press.
Machiavelli, N. (1988), *The Prince*, Cambridge: Cambridge University Press.
McNay, L. (1992), *Foucault and Feminism*, Cambridge: Polity.
McNay, L. (1994), *Foucault: A Critical Introduction*, New York: Continuum.
Marx, K. (1952), *Wage Labour and Capital*, Moscow: Progress.
Marx, K. (1963), *The Poverty of Philosophy*, New York: International.
Miliband, R. (1977), *Marxism and Politics*, Oxford: Oxford University Press.
Parsons, T. (1977), *Social Systems and the Evolution of Action Theory*, New York: Free Press.
Parsons, T. (1991), *The Social System*, London and New York: Routledge.
Poulantzas, N. (1978), *State, Power, Socialism*, London: New Left.
Smart, B. (1983), *Foucault, Marxism and Critique*, London: Routledge and Kegan Paul.
Smart, B. (1986), 'The politics of truth and the problem of hegemony', in D. Couzens Hoy (ed.), *Foucault: A Critical Reader*, Oxford: Blackwell.

COPYRIGHT ACKNOWLEDGEMENTS

Grateful acknowledgement is made to the following sources for permission to reproduce material in this book previously published elsewhere. Every effort has been made to trace copyright holders, but if any have been inadvertently overlooked the publisher will be pleased to make the necessary acknowledgement at the first opportunity.

PART 1: MARX AND ENGELS

'Preface (to *A Contribution to the Critique of Political Economy*)', from Karl Marx, *Early Writings*, Penguin Books. Selection and Notes copyright © New Left Review, 1974. Translation copyright © Lawrence and Wishart, 1973, 1971. Reprinted with permission of *New Left Review*.

'The Fetishism of the Commodity', from Karl Marx *Capital: Volume 1*, introduced by Ernest Mandel, translated by Ben Fowkes, Penguin Books. Edition and notes copyright © New Left Review 1976, translation copyright © Ben Fowkes, 1976. Reprinted with permission of *New Left Review*.

'The Communist Manifesto', from Karl Marx *The Revolutions of 1848: Political Writings Volume 1*, edited by David Fernbach, Penguin Books. Selection and Notes copyright © New Left Review, 1973. Reprinted with permission of *New Left Review*.

'The Eighteenth Brumaire', from Karl Marx *Surveys From Exile* edited and introduced by David Fernbach, Penguin Books. Selection and Notes copyright © New Left Review, 1973. Translation copyright © Ben Fowkes, 1973. Reprinted with permission of *New Left Review*.

'Economic and Political Manuscripts', from Karl Marx, *Early Writings*, Penguin Books. Selection and Notes copyright © New Left Review, 1974. Translation copyright © Gregor Benton, 1974. Reprinted with permission of *New Left Review*.

'Recent Theories of the Capitalist State', by Bob Jessop. Reprinted from *Cambridge Journal of Economics*, 1977, 1, (4), 353–73. Copyright © 1977 by Bob Jessop.

PART 2: GRAMSCI

'The Modern Prince', from *Selections from the Prison Notebooks of Antonio Gramsci* by Antonio Gramsci, edited and translated by Quintin Hoare and Geoffrey Nowell Smith. Reprinted with the permission of Lawrence and Wishart. Copyright © 1971 by Geoffrey Nowell Smith and Quintin Hoare.

'State and Civil Society', from *Selections from the Prison Notebooks of Antonio Gramsci* by Antonio Gramsci, edited and translated by Quintin Hoare and Geoffrey Nowell Smith. Reprinted with the permission of Lawrence and Wishart. Copyright © 1971 by Geoffrey Nowell Smith and Quintin Hoare.

'The Intellectuals', from *Selections from the Prison Notebooks of Antonio Gramsci* by Antonio Gramsci, edited and translated by Quintin Hoare and Geoffrey Nowell Smith. Reprinted with the permission of Lawrence and Wishart. Copyright © 1971 by Geoffrey Nowell Smith and Quintin Hoare.

'Americanism and Fordism', from *Selections from the Prison Notebooks of Antonio Gramsci* by Antonio Gramsci, edited and translated by Quintin Hoare and Geoffrey Nowell Smith. Reprinted with the permission of Lawrence and Wishart. Copyright © 1971 by Geoffrey Nowell Smith and Quintin Hoare.

PART 3: DURKHEIM AND FUNCTIONALISM

'Introduction', from *The Elementary Forms of the Religious Life*. Reprinted with the permission of Routledge and The Free Press, a division of Simon and Schuster Adult Publishing Group, from *The Elementary Forms of the Religious Life* by Emile Durkheim, translated by Joseph Ward Swain. Copyright © 1965 by The Free Press. All rights reserved.

From *Division of Labour in Society*. Reprinted with the permission of Palgrave Macmillan and The Free Press, a division of Simon and Schuster Adult Publishing Group, from *The Division of Labour in Society* by Emile

Durkheim, translated by W. D. Halls. Introduced by Lewis A. Coser. Translation, Copyright © 1984 by Higher and Further Education Division, Macmillan Publishers, Ltd. All rights reserved

'Egoistic Suicide' from *Suicide: A Study in Sociology*. Reprinted with the permission of The Free Press, a division of Simon and Schuster Adult Publishing Group, from *Suicide: A Study in Sociology* by Emile Durkheim, translated by John A. Spaulding and George Simpson. Edited by George Simpson. Copyright © 1951, copyright renewed 1979 by The Free Press. All rights reserved

PART 4: WEBER AND RATIONALISM

'Politics as a Vocation', from *From Max Weber: Essays in Sociology* by Max Weber, edited by H. H. Gerth and C. Wright Mills, translated by H. H. Gerth and C. Wright Mills, Routledge 1991, copyright © 1946, 1958, 1973 by H. H. Gerth and C. Wright Mills. Used by Permission of Oxford University Press, Inc.

'Bureaucracy', from *From Max Weber: Essays in Sociology* by Max Weber, edited by H. H. Gerth and C. Wright Mills, translated by H. H. Gerth and C. Wright Mills, Routledge 1991, copyright © 1946, 1958, 1973 by H. H. Gerth and C. Wright Mills. Used by Permission of Oxford University Press, Inc.

'Class, Status, Party', from *From Max Weber: Essays in Sociology* by Max Weber, edited by H. H. Gerth and C. Wright Mills, translated by H. H. Gerth and C. Wright Mills, Routledge 1991, copyright © 1946, 1958, 1973 by H. H. Gerth and C. Wright Mills. Used by Permission of Oxford University Press, Inc.

'Without Regard for Persons', from *Capitalism and Modernity: An Excursus on Marx and Weber* by Derek Sayer. Published by Routledge. Copyright © 1990 Derek Sayer.

PART 5: CULTURE AND COMMUNICATION IN THE FRANKFURT SCHOOL

'The Concept of Enlightenment', from *The Dialectic of Enlightenment* by Theodor W. Adorno and Max Horkheimer, translated by John Cumming. Reprinted with the permission of Verso Books, Copyright © 1979 by NLB.

'The Culture Industry', from *The Dialectic of Enlightenment* by Theodor W. Adorno and Max Horkheimer, translated by John Cumming. Reprinted with the permission of Verso Books, Copyright © 1979 by NLB.

'The New Forms of Control', from *One-Dimensional Man* by Herbert Marcuse. Copyright © 1964 by Herbert Marcuse. Reprinted by Permission of Beacon Press, Boston and Routledge.

Habermas from *The Theory of Communicative Action Volume 2: Lifeworld and System: A Critique of Functionalist Reason* by Jürgen Habermas. Translator's preface and translation Copyright © 1987 by Beacon Press. Originally published as *Theorie des Kommunikativen Handelns, Band 2: Zur Kritik der Funktionalistischen* Vernunft, Copyright © 1981 by Suhrkamp Verlag, Frankfurt am Main. Reprinted by permission of Suhrkamp Verlag and Beacon Press, Boston.

PART 6: FOUCAULT

'The Carceral', from *Discipline and Punish: The Birth of the Prison* by Michel Foucault. English Translation Copyright © 1977 by Alan Sheridan (New York: Pantheon). Originally published in French as Surveiller et Punir Copyright © 1975 by Editions Gallimard. Reprinted by permission of Georges Borchardt, Inc., for Editions Gallimard and Penguin Books.

'The Deployment of Sexuality', from *The History of Sexuality: Volume 1, An Introduction* by Michel Foucault, translated by Robert Hurley (Alan Lane 1979). First Copyright © 1978 by Random House, Inc., New York. Originally published in French as *La Volonté du Savoir* Copyright © 1976 by Editions Gallimard. Reprinted by permission of Georges Borchardt, Inc., for Editions Gallimard and Penguin Books.

'Introduction', from *Foucault and Political Reason* edited by Andrew Barry, Thomas Osborne and Nikolas Rose. Published by Taylor and Francis Books Ltd (UCL Press) 1996. Used by Permission of Andrew Barry, Thomas Osborne and Nikolas Rose.

INDEX